D0201029

Theories of Poverty and Underemployment

Theories of Poverty and Underemployment

Orthodox, Radical, and Dual Labor Market Perspectives

David M. Gordon
National Bureau of Economic
Research

Lexington Books
D.C. Heath and Company
Lexington, Massachusetts
Toronto   London

HD
5724
.G635

Work on this book was supported by funds granted by the U.S. Office of Economic Opportunity, Washington, D.C. 20506, pursuant to the provisions of the Economic Opportunity Act of 1964. The views expressed here are those of the author and do not necessarily reflect those of the Office of Economic Opportunity.

Copyright © 1972 by D.C. Heath and Company.

All rights reserved. No part of this publication may be reproduced or transmitted in any form or by any means, electronic or mechanical, including photocopy, recording, or any information storage or retrieval system, without permission in writing from the publisher.

Published simultaneously in Canada.

Printed in the United States of America.

International Standard Book Number: 0-669-81604-3

Library of Congress Catalog Card Number: 72-179328

Table of Contents

54852

Preface

The United States uncovered an "urban crisis" during the 1960s. With domestic blindfolds finally removed, eyes blinking uncertainly in the glare of exploding discontent, the public focused dazedly on the urban ghetto. Americans became transfixed by the squalor, poverty, violence, and crime of large, primarily black central city slums. Partly moved by compassion, largely stirred by fear, many began looking for the first time at the diseases infecting our inner cities.

A recurrent theme began to dominate every image of tragedy in those inner city slums. Ghetto residents were poor and underemployed. The twin problems of poverty and underemployment cried out for our most urgent attention. Until the country could solve those two problems, the urban crisis would apparently persist. By 1967, the late Senator Robert F. Kennedy was ready to conclude [1969, p. 154] : "This nation faces many problems. . . . But of all our problems, none is more immediate—none is more pressing—none is more omnipresent—than the crisis of unemployment in every major city in the Nation."

To most observers, the symptoms of ghetto employment problems eventually became apparent. Many of the urban poor and underemployed were black or members of other minority groups, concentrated in clearly segregated communities. Residents of the ghetto seemed somehow "trapped" in poverty, tied to a separate labor market. Many of the workers appeared to have few skills. Most of them worked in menial, low-wage jobs. They often relied on public assistance or "hustled" for extra cash. Some shuttled in and out of the labor force; others seemed "poorly motivated" on the job. And their attitudes toward their work were often matched by their employers' attitudes toward them. As Elliot Liebow has written [1967, pp. 58, 212] :

With few exceptions, jobs filled by the streetcorner men are at the bottom of the employment ladder in every respect, from wage level to prestige. Typically, they are hard, dirty, uninteresting and underpaid. . . . [The worker] has little vested interest in such a job and learns to treat it with the same contempt held for it by the employer and society at large. From his point of view, the job is expendable; from the employer's point of view, he is.

While the symptoms of ghetto employment problems may finally have seemed self-evident, the causes of those problems did not. Although most social scientists could agree that the roots of poverty and underemployment were economic, economists could not themselves agree on specific causal explanations for those problems. Early in the decade economists had rushed to analyze poverty and underemployment, but by its end they were proposing ultimately diverging explanations. Many economic studies of the problems had produced mountains of information, but economists were probably farther from uncontroverted theories of poverty and underemployment—from a real consensus about their causes—than they had been when they began.

By 1970, three principal economic perspectives were evolving to "explain" ghetto employment problems: *orthodox economic theory, dual labor market theory*, and *radical economic theory*. Orthodox theory already existed; orthodox economists proposed some extensions and revisions of conventional theory to explain some of the puzzling features of these newly-perceived problems. Dual labor market theory emerged during the decade to interpret the results of some individual studies of ghetto labor markets. Radical economic theory, resurging during the sixties in response to many concerns, began to develop its own interpretation of ghetto employment problems in the United States. Although the three analytic explanations of urban poverty and underemployment described and sought to explain the same reality, they drew from and implied fundamentally different theories of income determination and distribution. In view of the differences among those underlying theories, it had become necessary by the end of the decade to resolve some basic questions about income determination and distribution in order properly to understand the more specific causes of a much narrower range of economic problems. One could no longer ignore those fundamental issues.

This book attempts to review and to clarify the emerging competition among these three alternative economic explanations of ghetto employment problems in the United States. It intends not so much to resolve the fundamental differences among them—for that task is too immense—but rather to propose some standards by which to pursue the debate. The book has three parts. The first part introduces the competition, describing the context in which it emerged. The second provides a summary of the three competing theories. The final part compares the three theories with each other and with information about the real world.

This book is a review of ideas in progress. Nearly everything discussed in these pages has been proposed and written within the past five years. All of the debate is so fresh that the ink has barely dried. The immediacy of the discussion carries some serious disadvantages. As an interpreter of the debates described in these pages, I do not have the perspective that I may well have five or ten years from now. And it has been literally impossible to report on everything that has been written in the course of the recent competition, for the time has been impossibly short.

Why have I rushed ahead with the publication of this book, then, when further reflection and study would have helped solidify its argument and flesh out its empirical surveys? I answer that question very simply and tentatively. It has seemed to me that this kind of book would help clarify the terms of the debate before it gets sidetracked or mired in useless diversions. Some issues seem to me critical to pursue while others seem entirely superfluous. I hope to separate the two.

Another reason for immediate publication is probably even more important. During the past three or four years, I have spent a great deal of time plunging down blind alleys, reading volumes of material which ultimately obfuscated the debate in my own mind more than they clarified it. Many other students will undoubtedly be asking the same questions I posed for myself at the beginning of that process. I hope that the surveys in this book can save them some of the wasted time and intellectual confusion which I endured.

This book was originally intended as a set of introductory chapters for my doctoral dissertation [D.M. Gordon, 1971b]. For a variety of reasons, they were not included in the final version of the dissertation. A summary of some of this discussion is contained in those final pages, however, and some passages have been used verbatim.

Although I have cast this book in relatively objective terms, it seems important to warn the reader that I cannot possibly attain a truly objective perspective on the debate. I am incontestably a partisan in the debate although I have tried to keep my partisanship on the sidelines here. Having begun graduate school as a budding orthodox economist and then having helped formulate the dual labor market models, I have come out of my several years' reflection on these problems as a radical economist. The reader should keep that evolution in mind as he digests my ostensibly objective comparisons of these paradigms throughout the book.

Acknowledgments

Two institutions provided generous support during the preparation of this book. The U.S. Office of Economic Opportunity financed the year in which it was written, through a research grant awarded to the National Bureau of Economic Research, while the National Bureau provided many support facilities during that period. I want to thank Michael C. Barth of OEO for his encouragement from the federal side, and John Meyer of the National Bureau for his tolerance and stimulation through some difficult times. This book has been neither reviewed nor approved by the Directors of the National Bureau.

I have received stimulation and advice from many friends and colleagues during the long gestation of this book. My most important contacts have been with my friends in the Harvard collective of the Union for Radical Political Economics. For both their specific advice and their invaluable moral support, I want especially to thank Sam Bowles, Rick Edwards, Herb Gintis, Steve Marglin, and Mike Reich. Albeit at a distance, I have felt part of an exciting intellectual community with whose members I have shared strong personal and political objectives. Without that trust I would not have been able to complete this project.

I have also been helped by the criticism and comment of many others. Some of my colleagues at the National Bureau, though rarely sympathetic to my approach, have helped clarify some issues in the argument. My two thesis readers, John Meyer and Peter Doeringer, made many useful comments through several different versions of these chapters. My wife Dinni gave me some valuable editorial suggestions. Joe Persky helped sort through several of the critical points of the book, and Barry Bluestone, Ben Harrison, and Howard Wachtel gave me some useful advice. I have had the inestimable advantage, finally, of being able to rely on a family consortium of critics. My parents and my brother, all of them slightly puzzled by my ideas, were nonetheless unfailing in their detailed, constructive, and extremely useful comments. Frances Selhorst of the National Bureau provided some tolerant, bemused and invaluable help with the editorial tasks of the earlier drafts. John Beck of Lexington Books has been a gracious editor.

Part 1: Anomaly and Crisis

1

Poverty and Underemployment: Problems and Puzzles

Economists discovered their disagreements about poverty and underemployment very slowly and tortuously. Like most Americans, they had overlooked the problems for many years. Flushed with the guilt of neglect, many raced to explain the phenomena before they had been properly defined. Analysis and definition proceeded simultaneously, as a result, stumbling through a confusing array of analytic, statistical, and political concerns. And as the confusions about method and measure began to resolve themselves, some more basic uncertainties emerged. The real world sometimes seemed inconsistent with theoretical expectations, generating what Thomas Kuhn [1962] calls "empirical puzzles." Confronting those puzzles, struggling to unravel the mysteries, many economists began to develop competitive, mutually inconsistent ideas. A competition among paradigms, in Kuhn's terms, began to unfold.

This introductory chapter provides some of the initial setting for that process. In order to understand the eventual terms of the competition among theoretical paradigms, one must begin by exploring the definitional dialectics and empirical puzzles through which that competition evolved.

Some New Concerns

Both academics and the American public responded quickly to the discovery of an "urban crisis" during the 1960s. Many forces prompted and framed the learning process: the inescapable political pressures of ghetto riots and demonstrations, the shifting social images reflected in the media, the new information developed through more careful study of domestic problems, and the experience acquired in the course of public policy experimentation. Through that confusing experience, two dominant domestic preoccupations emerged—our concerns with poverty and underemployment. Although concern with these two problems had developed independently during the decade from slightly separate origins, the problems seemed by 1970 to overlap in the public mind, fused in a single, slightly fuzzy impression of poverty and the labor market. One must trace the independent evolution of perspectives on poverty and underemployment from their rather different beginnings in order to understand the terms in which ghetto employment problems were finally defined.[1]

At the beginning of the past decade, both experts and the government almost completely ignored the poor. After the insistent prodding of several journalists,

3

the government began slowly to appreciate the severity of poverty, moving gradually both to define it and to fight it.[2] As economists also began to focus some attention on the problem, two important changes in economic definitions of poverty seemed to evolve during the decade. These changes influenced both expert and government perspectives and helped effect an eventual intersection with concern about underemployment.

First, many experts eventually urged a shift from initial "absolute" definitions of poverty to a "relative" definition. The original absolute definitions focused on budgets. Those whose incomes fell below some absolute dollar amount judged necessary to sustain a minimally acceptable standard of living were considered poor. Relative definitions compare the incomes of the poor to those of the nonpoor; they focus on the income gap separating those two groups. Those who earn incomes too far below those of most Americans are considered poor.[3]

Several factors prompted the gradual shift from absolute to relative definitions. Some experts thought that although absolute poverty might eventually disappear as a result of accelerated economic growth and more munificent income maintenance policies, many attendant social problems would remain—problems like economic isolation and inequality. Relative poverty definitions encompassed many of those problems. (See Tobin [1967] for a dramatic statement of this argument.) Absolute standards of poverty also ignored the increasingly expensive requisites for daily "subsistence" in urbanizing, technologically more complicated societies. Telephones and automobiles become more and more indispensable in the United States, for instance, even for the poor. (See Ornati [1966] and President's Commission on Income Maintenance Programs [1969].) Finally, analysts began to suspect that a sense of "relative deprivation"—or relative poverty—helped *explain* both the absolute and relative poverty of many Americans. Some of the poor seemed to feel permanently trapped in relative poverty. Burdened with a growing sense of fatalism about their lives, they often seemed to overlook remedies which might conceivably have increased their incomes. To measure the conditions upon which these citizens based their despair, many analysts found measures of inequality most appealing.

In general, many seemed to agree with the arguments marshalled by Victor Fuchs in his advocacy of a relative definition [1969, pp. 198, 199, emphasis in the original] :

'Low' income or 'poverty' in the United States in the 1960's is largely a matter of economic *distance*. When most Americans have a great deal, those who have *much* less are poor regardless of their absolute level of income. . . . [A relative poverty standard] explicitly recognizes that all so-called 'minimum' or 'subsistence' budgets are based on contemporary standards and political realities and have no intrinsic or scientific basis. Secondly, it focuses attention on what seems to underly the present concern with poverty, namely, the first tentative gropings toward a national policy with respect to the distribution of income at the lower end of the scale. Finally, it provides a more realistic basis for appraising the success or failure of antipoverty programs.

The government had not yet officially installed the reduction of relative poverty as a policy objective, to be sure, but a concern with inequality had crept into its pronouncements and programs nonetheless. "Nearly every report on poverty issued by the Federal Government," as Herman Miller has noted [quoted in S.M. Miller and Roby, 1970, p. 42], "contains the direct or implicit caveat that poverty is relative and that any absolute standard loses its meaning and validity over time." Martin Rein notes a similar accent in recent programs [1968, p. 117]: "Paradoxically, we measure poverty in subsistence terms, but the programs and policies we have evolved to reduce poverty in America are based on a broader definition of the dimensions of well-being."

The second change in perceptions about poverty seems equally important. Many economists began to revise the analytic categories among which they tentatively perceived, distributed, and counted the poor. Initially, many pictured the poor in either of two groups: those steadily working poor, thoroughly attached to the labor market; and those incapable of work for reasons of health or family. Fiscal policies promoting higher rates of growth would lift the former group out of poverty, while traditional categories of public assistance and social security would provide for the latter, an increasingly small residual.[4] Gradually, the utility of those categorical sets seemed to diminish. Many began to distinguish between the "permanent" and the "temporary" poor. Some Americans seemed trapped in permanent poverty—an "underclass" as Sundquist put it [1968]—whether they were employed, unemployed, or out of the labor force, whether they were healthy and capable of work or not. In contrast, the "temporary" poor included those whose incomes fell below the poverty line for cyclical or random reasons and could be expected to rise back above that line soon.[5]

The growth of attention to the underemployed reflected many of the same kinds of changes in expert and government perceptions.[6] The decade began with some narrow definitions of labor market problems. At both the macro- and the micro-economic levels, those problems were defined and measured by the unemployment rate. With an analytic underpinning at both the macro- and the micro-economic levels, manpower policy was intended to help those who remained unemployed after a relatively low aggregate unemployment rate had been achieved.[7] Focusing especially on the problems of workers in "depressed areas," manpower policy effectively sought to help white, blue-collar, semi-skilled workers by training them for new kinds of jobs. The black urban underemployed were still essentially invisible.[8]

These quite narrow definitions of public concern about employment problems began steadily to broaden. As many have noted, several factors explained the origins of these new concerns. Greater prosperity, first of all, seemed to have fulfilled initial employment objectives. With or without the help of manpower training programs and the Vietnam War, many of the workers at whom manpower policy had primarily been aimed were now steadily employed.[9] The civil rights movement and ghetto riots had also forced attention on the employment difficulties of blacks, especially those in the middle of central cities. (See National Advisory Commission on Civil Disorders [1968].) And the continuing evolution and frequent failure of manpower programs produced new impressions of problems which affected objectives and priorities.[a]

As both experts and the government became increasingly concerned with those central city areas in which unemployment rates remained especially high in the midst of general prosperity, employment concepts changed. A variety of additional labor market characteristics joined "unemployment" as symptoms of labor market disadvantage. For many workers in the ghetto, unemployment seemed a small component of a much broader syndrome of connected labor market difficulties. Problems like low wages, job instability, menial work, low skills, poor worker motivation, discrimination, poor job information, and inadequate job access seemed equally to demand attention. Each problem seemed somehow causally related to the others. If you had one problem, you were likely to suffer from some of the others as well. Some of these perceptions were especially fueled by the results of government programs, according to which it appeared that efforts to remedy one disadvantage required simultaneous and complementary efforts to cure some others. (See Thurow [1968b] for some useful comments.)

Increasingly, a concept of underemployment replaced unemployment at the core of manpower policy formulation, encompassing most of these new symptoms. In 1966, the emergent concept was formalized by a conglomerate statistical measure of "subemployment," applied briefly to some national and local surveys. In its local applications, the percentage of workers who were "subemployed" usually exceeded the unemployment rate in the ghetto by a factor of roughly three to four. The subemployed included the unemployed (according to traditional definitions); those working part time who wanted full-time work; household heads under 65 working full time and earning less than $65 a week; half the number of "nonparticipants" among men between 20 and 64 (a reflection of presumably "disguised unemployment"); and half the estimated "missing males" or "census undercount."[10]

A continuous revision of manpower programs flowed from these trends. Building on to and moving away from the original concepts of the 1962 Manpower Development and Training Act (MDTA), government policy sought to attack many additional dimensions of employment problems. It tried to change the attitudes of many workers, inducing more positive attitudes toward work and greater potential job stability.[11] It hoped not only to provide specific skills through institutional training but also to increase opportunities for prevocational

---

[a]Although they could not yet prove it very rigorously, most observers of traditional manpower training programs began to regard them as failures at improving the employment opportunities of disadvantaged workers. Thurow concluded quite simply [1968b, p. 92] that ". . . they did not prove to be very successful. . . ."

remedial training and for on-the-job training.[12] It experimented to encourage
the private development of new jobs, principally in order to accommodate the
special needs of underemployed workers for gradual on-the-job training and experience.[13] In scattered efforts, it sought to correct some of the labor market
imperfections which analysts presumed were having especially strong effects on
ghetto employment problems: for instance, employer and union discrimination;
poor labor market information; and the movement of primary employment to
the increasingly inaccessible suburbs.[14] Finally, hoping to embrace many objectives, it began to encourage the idea of black capitalism and ghetto economic
development. Thrusts in this direction would help provide jobs, train workers,
improve motivation, and return resources to the ghetto all at once.[15]

As a result of these changes in perceptions, the separate concerns for poverty
and underemployment effectively merged—despite the distance separating initial
concerns about absolute poverty and unemployment. At the simplest level, jobs
paying poverty wages now constituted part of the definition of each problem.
More fundamentally, the sources of each problem were increasingly thought to
rest in the basic operation of the labor market and the process of income determination. The growing attention to relative poverty focused attention on the
determinants of income not only among the poor but among all workers, while
the concern with underemployment emphasized the interconnections among a
wide variety of labor market mechanisms. More and more, it became necessary
to understand the causes of both problems in order to discuss solutions to
either.[16]

Some New Questions

These emerging definitions of ghetto employment problems—the effective con-
junction of concerns about poverty and underemployment—began to reveal several extremely important uncertainties in economic understanding of those problems. This short section tries to outline briefly the questions and uncertainties
about the labor market which seemed to develop most insistently. Not everyone
perceived or was troubled by these questions, of course, and some tried desperately to avoid them. But many did probe these puzzles, and most of them arose
logically from trends in perceptions about ghetto employment problems.

At the beginning of the decade, analysis of income and employment had
relied on three relatively unquestioned assumptions about the labor market.

First, most analyses assumed that those with employment problems were too
unskilled to qualify for existing job vacancies. "The underlying assumption was
that jobs existed in the private economy or could be brought into existence
through economic expansion if only the unemployed and underemployed could
be qualified to fill them." [Sundquist, 1968, p. 53] Reflecting conventional economic assumptions about the dimensions of productivity manifest in the labor

market, "education and training programs were to be the principal means for raising marginal products." [Thurow, 1968b, p. 92]

Second, analysts presumed a certain stability within the three standard labor force categories: employed, unemployed, and not in the labor force. The unemployed remained unemployed rather than dropping out of the labor force. Workers not in the labor force were generally assumed to be unable to work for health or family reasons.

Third, underpinning the second assumption, nearly everyone assumed that those in the labor force rarely lost their motivation to work, whatever their employment problems. They were determined, able-bodied workers who believed in the importance of employment. In their study of labor force participation rates among "prime-age males," for instance, Bowen and Finegan note the conventional expectations: ". . . the inclinations toward labor force participation on the part of this group are so uniformly strong," they wrote [1965, p. 126], "that it might be thought surprising if the (small) intercity differences in participation rates were systematically related to anything."

By the end of the decade, the continuing concentration on ghetto employment problems had raised a host of new analytic questions about poverty and the labor market. In a few cases, experience simply suggested the insufficiency of earlier presumptions. In other cases the character of the problems seemed to dispute more directly the validity of initial views about income and employment.

First, fundamental questions arose about the functions and importance of job stability. Varieties of evidence suggested that one of the dominant differences between the poor and the nonpoor centered around the randomness and instability of work histories among the poor.[17] Their indifferent and capricious work habits seemed often to pose more serious barriers to decent employment than their relative lack of skills. And yet, few analysts felt that they adequately understood why job stability played such an important role. Hall wrote rather dramatically at the end of the decade [1970a, pp. 389, 392] :

Some groups exhibit what seems to be pathological instability in holding jobs. . . . The true problem of hard-core unemployment is that certain members of the labor force account for a disproportionate share of unemployment because they drift from one unsatisfactory job to another, spending the time between jobs either unemployed or out of the labor force. . . . [This phenomenon of instability] remains an urgent unsolved problem of modern economic research.

Second and concomitantly, many began to lose interest in the statistical categories by which the labor force had traditionally been defined. Rapid and rather unpredictable movement by the poor among all three labor force categories seemed to require some new analytic categories. The concept of underemployment, measured by a subemployment rate, encompassed some of this need. Attention was focused on a generic class of "secondary" workers, variably and almost randomly distributed among the three traditional labor force categories, sharing a syndrome of labor market problems.[b]

Third, many students of the problems began to suspect that one could easily misstate the disadvantages of the "underclass" by speaking simplistically of their low "skills" or "productivities"—as if skill or productivity constituted a uniform, one-dimensional vector of characteristics. One increasingly found that labor force and on-the-job experience dominated many of the income inequalities among workers, for instance, but the connections between productivity and experience were often the most difficult relationships to divine and understand.[18] Above all, many found it progressively more important to specify exactly what kinds of "skills" led to what kinds of stable employment. Citing a number of different explanations of the skill disadvantages of the poor, for instance, Anthony Pascal concluded [1968, p. 68], "We know exceedingly little about their relative importance. . . ."

Fourth, basic assumptions about worker motivation seemed to crumble, and one waited uncertainly for new ideas to replace the old. One could no longer presume that all "prime-age" male workers inevitably preferred work under almost any conditions to all other activities. This growing suspicion about worker motivation was responding to two separate trends. First, some important historical shifts in the motivations of disadvantaged workers seemed to have emerged. I have called this the "promised land" effect (in D.M. Gordon, ed. [1971, Chapter Two]), after Claude Brown's book, *Manchild in the Promised Land* [1965]. Brown draws an important distinction between older generations of black workers and the youngest, post-World War II generation of blacks. The former had all migrated from somewhere (principally the South) and the hopefulness of their migration had usually induced them to tolerate menial jobs. The latter had often been born and raised in northern ghettos, entering the labor force at the bottom but without the hopefulness of recent migrations. They were less likely to endure the frustration of the bottom rungs. Brown put it succinctly [1965, pp. 7-8]:

The children of these disillusioned colored pioneers inherited the total lot of their parents—the disappointments, the anger. To add to their misery, they had little hope of deliverance. For where does one run to when he's already in the promised land?

Second, extra-employment income sources had probably become more attractive and more plausible for many ghetto workers over time. One understands little

---

[b]It should be noted that, although many shared this new perception about the inadequacy of traditional labor force categories, this new awareness had not been translated into changes in conventional macro-economic analyses of the labor market. Analytic discussion of unemployment and labor force participation rates (and econometric use of those variables) continued to assume that the categories were completely separable. For a useful discussion of this problem, see Hall [1970a].

about the history of ghetto crime—of "hustling" as it's often called—but it seems likely that "illegitimate" opportunities for young blacks increased dramatically with the rapid growth and expansion of dense northern ghettos.[19] And in many states, income available from public assistance rose rapidly too, sometimes exceeding income available from many low-wage jobs.[20] Unfortunately, however, one realized that an identification of those two sources of change did not suffice to establish some new certainties about motivation and behavior among these groups.

Fifth, it became apparent that researchers should investigate the structure of demand for labor more thoroughly. As many have attributed greater importance to on-the-job experience as a determinant of relative skill levels, for instance, the structure of jobs and of job ladders has been viewed as an increasingly important factor in the labor market. It has been nearly impossible to retain the simpler vision of earlier perceptions—that manpower policy needed merely to "qualify" the disadvantaged to fill existing jobs. At the least, policies ought to respond to and affect the structure of jobs as well.[21] But no one seemed very certain about the determinants or characteristics of job structures and ladders. Writing of the "demand determinants of wage differentials," for instance, Arrow notes [1971, p. 5]: "The relevant theoretical literature is surprisingly small in view of the importance of the subject and the great attention it has received by the public."

Sixth, analysts began to pay more attention to many additional causes of ghetto employment problems, exploring factors related less to the demand for and supply of skills than to the operations of the labor market and the dynamics of community economic development. Some studied the effects of employment suburbanization, housing segregation, and transportation systems on the distribution of employment opportunities and workers, arguing in some cases that those geographic factors combined to limit opportunities for black ghetto workers. (See Kain [1968], Mooney [1969], Kain and Meyer [1970], and Ornati [1970].) Others, sensing the importance of job information, began to construct and apply relatively formal analyses of informational imperfections. (See Phelps et al. [1970], McCall [1970a], and Holt et al. [1971].) Most notably, many began to apply the frameworks of economic development analysis to their studies of the ghetto, proposing strategies often similar to those suggested for speeding the development of poorer nations. (See Vietorisz and Harrison [1970], and Tabb [1970].)

Finally and perhaps most important, many questions necessarily focused on the problems of racial inequality and discrimination. This new emphasis arose not simply because many of the poor and underemployed were blacks or other minority group workers. Beyond those simple demographic facts, the concern with discrimination grew from new assumptions about the central role of skin color in the formation of both workers' and employers' perceptions of the problem. In addition, the increasing proportions of minority workers, women, and teens both in the labor force and among the "underemployed" raised important questions about similarities and differences among the three kinds of discrimination—by race, sex, and age. Finally, given the apparent rigidity of racial barriers, one began to wonder about the analytic similarities and functional interconnections between these and other "imperfections" dividing groups—imperfections like minimum wage legislation and unionization.

2 Competition Among Paradigms

In a period of "normal research," as Thomas Kuhn calls it [1962], the myriad empirical puzzles described in chapter 1 would have generated even more specific questions, embellishing and tightening the application of the reigning theoretical paradigm. They would have suggested, as one colleague put it in this context, "enough for twenty good doctoral dissertations."

It appears, however, that economics has moved beyond "normal research" and has entered a period of scientific "anomaly" and "crisis," to use Kuhn's terms again. Many economists, watching the emergence of these specific and largely unanswered questions, have responded by moving temporarily away from specific research, by raising even more general questions about poverty and the labor market, by probing the very core of conventional income distribution theory. Some seem to have reached that critical awareness of empirical anomaly which leads to breakdowns in normal scientific research—in Kuhn's words [1962, p. 52], "the recognition that nature has somehow violated the paradigm-induced expectations that govern normal science." With that awareness, some have begun to construct new paradigms to explain the basic processes of income determination in advanced capitalist economies. And the crisis can be neither ignored nor resolved, one gathers from Kuhn [1962, p. 53], until the "anomalous has become the expected" once again.

By now, with the benefit of hindsight, it seems clear whence the impressions of anomaly arose. In several different ways, all the changing concerns and questions about ghetto employment problems during the past decade focused increasing attention on the process of income distribution in the United States. Relative definitions of poverty gained attention, to begin with, and these definitions almost tautologically raised questions about the determinants of the distribution of income. In much the same way, an inclination to posit a "class" of the "permanently poor" led to questions about the sources of discontinuity and the definition of class in the income determination process. And all the emergent questions about underemployment involved income distribution questions: Why is employment stability so important in the determination of income? How important are different kinds of skills? What is the role of discrimination? Should we expect labor market "imperfections" to continue, or will the forces of competition erode them over time?

Orthodox economic theory provided some models of the determination and distribution of income, of course, which suggested approaches to resolving these questions. The models specified some questions and implied some probable an-

13

swers. But to a growing number of economists, observations about reality seemed to confound the expectations of the orthodox models. To a certain extent, at one level, a set of specific facts apparently contradicted some specific orthodox hypotheses. More important and more generally, a wide variety of phenomena suggested that the orthodox model generated the wrong questions, that one ought to approach the facts of poverty and underemployment from a different perspective.

In particular, recent experience with ghetto employment problems raised for many economists some critical questions about the role of *labor market stratification* in determining and distributing incomes. One observed an enticing continuity in the market distribution of income, to be sure, but many felt that this statistical continuity disguised some basic *discontinuities* in the labor market. Those who earn low incomes may be poor, it appeared, because they earn relatively little in lucrative labor markets, or because they earn average amounts in low-income labor markets, or some combination of both. In trying to understand poverty in the labor market, this suggested, we must pay careful attention both to the distribution of income *within* any given market and to the distribution of workers *among* a series of relatively distinct markets. In trying to develop solutions to ghetto employment problems, equally, we must analyze the determinants not only of individual characteristics but also of market structures.

Orthodox analysis could be manipulated to explore these kinds of questions, one guessed, and some orthodox economists began trying to apply orthodox theory to explain them. But orthodox theory did not consider these questions as a matter of course. It tended to take market structures for granted and to probe the determinants of behavior within those given structures. Some economists sought to develop economic models which dealt directly with these basic concerns about the relationship between labor market structure and income. Having first tinkered with emendations to orthodox theory and then having expressed their dissatisfaction with that theory, these economists began to form their own ideas, drawing on a wide variety of intellectual and empirical sources. Their ideas gradually evolved as formal theories, or "paradigms," to explain the distribution of income. By the end of the decade, diverging theories of income and employment had begun to spar, providing alternative explanations of poverty and underemployment in the United States. A competition among paradigms, in Kuhn's terms, had begun.

At a superficial and subjective level, after all the hesitant beginnings, one can easily identify the competitors for they have quite clearly identified themselves. Three have stepped forward to proclaim themselves in the ring. Whether or not they are indeed competitive, they believe that they are.

In one corner stands the reigning combatant, orthodox economic theory. Most economists in America continue to apply the basic orthodox model of income distribution and most have responded to new questions about poverty and underemployment by developing the orthodox model to answer them. Richard

Leftwich, for one, argues that the continued hegemony of orthodox theory is fully justified [1966, pp. 307-308] :

Some maintain that marginal productivity is not an adequate basis for income determination and distribution—that there is no close correlation between the remunerations received by resource owners and the values of marginal product or the marginal revenue products of the resources which they own. If these critics are correct, and can produce the evidence substantiating their criticisms, then marginal productivity must go by the board—as must most of the rest of the marginal analysis of economic activity. To date the necessary evidence has not been forthcoming and marginal productivity continues to occupy the center of distribution theory.

However much the orthodox model has been molded and revised to explain the recent ghetto phenomena, the basic structure of marginal productivity theory has been retained intact.

In the opposite corner stands radical economic theory. Radicals have regained energy and impact in the economics profession, and they have begun reformulating a radical paradigm which derives from but does not depend exclusively on the work of Karl Marx. Ghetto economic problems in the United States have clearly helped stimulate the radical resurgence (see Edwards, MacEwan et al. [1970], Bronfenbrenner [1970], and Gurley [1971]), and the emerging radical paradigm is being applied to reinterpret the sources of those problems. Without question, the radicals view their theories as direct competitors with those of orthodox analysis; they often refer to Kuhn's work to illustrate the sense in which they feel that they are competing. (See Sweezy [1970], and *Review of Radical Political Economics* [1971].) Edwards, MacEwan et al. [1970, p. 352] have clearly portrayed the terms of combat:

Orthodox economic analysis . . . is based upon an acceptance of the *status quo* in social relations. . . . The marginalist approach is useful only if, accepting the basic institutions of capitalism, one is primarily concerned with its administration. If one questions the virtue of capitalism as a system, then the basic social relations and the institutions of the system must themselves be subjected to analysis. A new approach is necessary.

Still developing, still embryonic, radical theory has not yet produced a rigorous and complete analysis of ghetto employment problems in this country. In this book, I have tried to provide as formal a development and application of the radical model as possible in order to permit a useful comparison with its two competitors.

In a relatively neutral corner, finally, we find dual labor market theory. This third paradigm has emerged through direct experience with several different analyses of ghetto employment problems. It has been formulated by several different groups of analysts in slightly different ways. It differs somewhat from the other two theories in its relative specificity and ideological neutrality. In its most precise formulation, it intersects with a theory of "internal labor markets" developed by Doeringer and Piore [1971]. Especially in that version, its proponents emphasize its inconsistencies with orthodox analysis. Doeringer and Piore write [1971, pp. 1, 5]:

These problems were initially approached with the traditional analytic tools of economic theory. But, in one way or another, each of the issues strained the conventional framework and required introduction of a number of institutional or *ad hoc* explanations. Reliance upon market imperfections or non-market institutions to explain deviations from the results predicted by conventional economic theory can be, at best, intellectually unappealing. At worst, it neglects, or even masks, variables which are significant for policy. In this volume, a number of these variables are identified and incorporated into a more comprehensive approach to labor market analysis than that provided by the competitive labor market model. . . .

To the extent that there is a coherent labor market theory against which an internal market theory must be tested, it is derived from neoclassical theory.

Each of these three paradigms has developed in very different ways, at quite different levels of generality and abstraction. One has trouble anticipating the precise terms on which the competition can most fruitfully proceed. Each paradigm speaks a different language, in effect, and some standards for translation seem necessary. Even in the natural sciences, as Kuhn [1970b] argues extensively, those standards seem almost beyond our reach. Scientists are able to communicate across paradigms, he writes [1970b, p. 277], only "if they have sufficient will, patience, and tolerance of threatening ambiguity, characteristics which . . . cannot be taken for granted." One treads on unfamiliar methodological turf, in particular, because experience with this kind of competition in the social sciences has been chaotic and confusing.

Two important procedural questions must be addressed. First, one needs some methodological standards by which to decide whether the respective theoretical perspectives can legitimately be called "competing paradigms." The participants' protestations notwithstanding, one cannot blithely assume that a paradigm is a paradigm simply because its adherents proclaim that identity. Second, one must be able to agree, however informally, on a set of rules by which to arbitrate the competition. How does one choose sides, weigh predictions, or even compare assumptions?

Neither of these sets of standards flows easily from the literature. I have chosen an eclectic approach to these questions in this book. Some review of my methodological choices seems necessary as a prelude to the substantive theoretical summaries of Part 2.

Kuhn's seminal discussion of paradigms and scientific revolutions has attracted considerable attention in the social sciences. Although Kuhn himself expresses doubts about the transferability of his analysis to the social sciences [1962, p. 15, and 1970c, pp. 208-210], many dissident social scientists have found striking parallels between his view of the natural scientific community and their own of the social scientific world. Not only in economics but also in disciplines like sociology, political science, and psychology, Kuhn's essential framework is being applied more and more frequently to the history of paradigms and revolutions in the study of society.[1]

The discussion of paradigms in economics is barely beginning. As Kuhn might have predicted, those in opposing camps have been talking through each other, rarely engaging in constructive communication. Radical economists have been developing the analysis of paradigms very tentatively, trying to find concrete ways of expressing some common ideas and feelings.[2] Orthodox economists, although they have usually acknowledged that orthodox theory constitutes a "paradigm" in Kuhn's sense, have frequently chaffed at the discussion of paradigm competition because they do not feel that other theoretical perspectives, and particularly radical theory, warrant such scientific legitimation or respect.[3] Robert Solow's recent comments seem typical of the orthodox response [1971, pp. 63, 64]:

In short, we neglected radical economics because it is negligible. . . . I think radical economists have corrupted Thomas Kuhn's notion of a scientific paradigm, which they treat as a mere license for loose thinking. . . . As far as I can see, radical political economics . . . is more a matter of posture and rhetoric than of scientific framework. . . .

In what senses, then, has a paradigm competition been emerging in economics? Kuhn's original book [1962] caused some confusion about the nature of paradigms and their competition. (Margaret Masterman [1970], in a sympathetic review, counts twenty-one different senses in which Kuhn deploys the concept of a "paradigm.") From Masterman's essay [1970] and from Kuhn's later explanations of his ideas [1970a, 1970b, 1970c], one can isolate two principal uses of the paradigm concept. In its broader sociological sense [Kuhn, 1970c, p. 175], a paradigm comprises "the entire constellation of beliefs, values, [and] techniques" shared by the members of a particular scientific community. The components of this shared group commitment include "symbolic generalizations," "belief in particular models," "values" covering a broad philosophic and methodological spectrum, and what Kuhn calls [1970c, p. 187] "exemplars." In his later essays, Kuhn suggests that we use the phrase "disciplinary matrix" to replace "paradigm" in this broader sense. The matrix has functional importance, for it provides cohesion to the scientific community.

In a much narrower sense, Kuhn suggests that a "paradigm" constitutes a set of "exemplars" or "analogies" which scientists apply in the "puzzle-solving" research characteristic of normal science. These paradigms are usually crude perceptual devices suggesting ways of relating one set of phenomena to another.

Striving to avoid some of the jargon which misled many readers about his first exposition, Kuhn later expands on this theme [1970c, pp. 193-194, 195-196]:

One of the fundamental techniques by which the members of a group, whether an entire culture or a specialists' sub-community within it, learn to see the same things when confronted with the same stimuli is by being shown examples of situations that their predecessors in the group have already learned to see as like each other and as different from other sorts of situations. . . .

An appropriately programmed perceptual mechanism has survival value. To say that the members of different groups may have different perceptions when confronted with the same stimuli is not to imply that they may have just any perceptions at all. In many environments a group that could not tell wolves from dogs could not endure. Nor would a group of nuclear physicists today survive as scientists if unable to recognize the tracks of alpha particles and electrons. It is just because so very few ways of seeing will do that the ones that have withstood the tests of group use are worth transmitting from generation to generation.

Given these two meanings of "paradigms," do the three theoretical perspectives discussed in these pages conform to either or both?

Orthodox economic theory seems clearly to constitute a paradigm on both epistemological levels. More generally, orthodox economists share a wide variety of beliefs, models, values and methodological inclinations, as both orthodox and radical economists have repeatedly agreed. (From the orthodox side, see especially Stigler [1959], D.F. Gordon [1965], Coats [1969], and Solow [1971]. From the radical side, see Gurley [1971], and *Review of Radical Political Economics* [1971].) Donald Gordon echoes the general consensus [1965, p. 122]: ". . . we have in economic theory a degree of consensus around a basic model, which makes us closer to the natural sciences than to some other fields." And at the more specific level, orthodox economists obviously share a set of "exemplars" which guide their pursuit of normal scientific research. Confronted with real world phenomena, orthodox economists view them uniformly through the perceptual lenses of demand and supply, equilibrium, or maximization under constraint. These analogical tools are learned through apprenticeship to the field, transmitted, as Kuhn prescribes, from generation to generation.

Despite the protestations of many orthodox economists, radical economic theory seems also to constitute a paradigm in both of Kuhn's senses of the concept. As even a few orthodox economists have acknowledged, radical economists have become a socially identifiable group of scholars with many shared commitments. They share many symbolic generalizations, like the Marxian generalizations about strata and class. They believe in some particular models, like the Baran-Sweezy analysis of the development of monopoly capital. And they share a wide variety of values, ranging from the highly political—that the radical political economist, as Gurley puts it [1971, p. 55], "actively takes the side of the poor and the powerless"—to the explicitly methodological, insisting, for example, on the importance of dialectical analysis. Much more narrowly, radical economists approach their study of real phenomena with some uniform perceptual tools. Given a specific problem or puzzle, they will almost always tend to ask a fairly consistent set of questions about it: Who has what kind of power in this situation? How have individual choices been channeled by the institutional setting in which people act? Can we identify the dialectical contradictions inherent in these events which seem likely to produce qualitative changes in their character? However foreign these questions may seem to orthodox economists, a group of political economists is learning to see the relevance of these questions to a broadening range of situations. They do not work from a text encoding the rules of radical research, but they are developing a set of "exemplars," in precisely Kuhn's sense, through which they are beginning to view the world.[a]

The dual labor market theory does not present such complete paradigm credentials. A community of scholars sharing a wide variety of values and models has not emerged around the dual labor market theory. Indeed, some of those who are applying and extending the theory seem to disagree about a few fundamental issues inherent in the dual labor market view. (See chapter 4.) In this sense, the theory cannot be ranked beside the orthodox and radical views as a fully developed "disciplinary matrix." But the dual labor market theory is clearly providing a set of exemplars or analogies by which some economists are beginning to perceive economic phenomena in the United States. Models of "dualism" have been spurred by the dual labor market theory, and the dual market model is providing several different groups of economists with a specific way of seeing the world.

Relying on the extent to which the dual labor market theory conforms to this narrower definition of a paradigm, I have quite purposefully chosen to include the theory as a fully competing paradigm in this book. It may indeed turn out that the dual labor market theory is eventually subsumed under either of the other two views, or that it expands into a more fully developed disciplinary matrix on its own. It seems much too early to tell whether and how a real "revolution" in economic theories of poverty and underemployment may occur. But at the moment, the dual labor market theory is playing an important role as a kind of halfway house between orthodox and radical theory, providing a tangible perceptual image which does not depend on the full commitments implicit in the other two perspectives. As both Kuhn and Masterman point out, moreover, there is nothing intrinsic about the paradigm concept which precludes what

---

[a]Some orthodox economists have argued that radical economics does not constitute a scientific paradigm because it has not been specified with sufficient rigor to permit verification of its hypotheses. As Solow puts it [1971, p. 64], "The function of a scientific paradigm is to provide a framework for 'normal science.' But there is little evidence that radical political economics is capable of generating a line of normal science, or even that it wants to." In fact, it appears that the radical perspective has recently been generating a wide variety of specific research foci of precisely this normal scientific sort. Several examples are provided in Parts 2 and 3 below.

Masterman calls [1970, p. 74] "multi-paradigm science."[b] Nor does Kuhn's analysis focus solely on earth-shaking revolutions, the sort that happen once or twice a century. He makes it quite clear [1970b, pp. 249ff] that he intends his analysis of paradigms and revolutions to extend to small but qualitative changes in theoretical perspectives—to "micro-revolutions," as he originally called them, a "little studied type of conceptual change which occurs frequently in science and is fundamental to its advance" [1970b, p. 250]. I would argue that the dual labor market theory represents a small but qualitative perceptual change in this exact micro-revolutionary sense. I have included it as a paradigm in this book because I think the essence of that revolutionary change in perception helps crystallize a great many issues around which the emerging paradigm competition will revolve.

If one therefore accepts these three theoretical perspectives as competing paradigms, how should one arbitrate their competition?

At the most superficial level, an appropriate methodological approach seems obvious. As Paul Sweezy has put it [1970, p. 2], "It seems to me that from a scientific point of view the question of choosing between . . . approaches can be answered quite simply. Which more accurately reflects the fundamental characteristics of social reality which is under analysis?" Unfortunately, at least in the social sciences, one can rarely agree on such an assessment. Social reality moves through such rapid and complicated change that one can rarely stop the world long enough to conduct controlled experiments. Theories of society must often abstract from that dynamic complexity, working with relatively simple models of reality. Many such models may seem simultaneously "consistent" with observed phenomena, frustrating tests designed to reveal the relative accuracy of the theoretical predictions. In the case of ghetto employment problems, as the later chapters will suggest, this situation of comparable explanatory power seems prevalent.

In these instances, other criteria must provide avenues for choice. Kuhn argues strongly [1970b, p. 186] that "what scientists share is not sufficient to command uniform assent about such matters as the choice between competing theories." Milton Friedman, in his classic essay on "positive economics" [1953, p. 10], essentially agrees: "The choice among alternative hypotheses equally consistent with the available evidence must to some extent be arbitrary."

Friedman recommends two auxiliary criteria by which to judge competing theories: simplicity and fruitfulness. Although economists often rely on these two criteria as important justifications for their own views, neither criterion seems axiomatically supreme or scientifically predestined. "Judgments of accu-

---

[b]Masterman does argue [loc.cit.] that periods of multi-paradigm science are likely to evolve into periods of "dual-paradigm" science, as "deeper, though cruder" paradigms develop which may often subsume the smaller theories "by attaching them somehow or other" to themselves. I suspect that this is beginning to happen in this competition, and that the dual labor market theory will eventually be subsumed. See some further discussion in Parts 2 and 3 below.

racy are relatively . . . stable," Kuhn writes [1970b, p. 185], but "judgments of simplicity, consistency, plausibility and so on often vary greatly from individual to individual." Different scientists may place varying weights on criteria like consistency and simplicity, on the one hand, or they may judge the relative consistency of a given theory in different ways. And some scientists may even propose new or different values to adjudicate the choice among theories. Radicals might argue, for instance, that a "positive" theory should build from a normative view of human beings which lends dignity to individuals and helps suggest a humane and decent society. (See Gintis [1969, 1970b] for a discussion of some of these themes.)

The end result of these kinds of disagreements about values, Kuhn suggests, is that theories may sometimes be "incommensurable." As a result of differences in language, perceptions, and values, in Kuhn's words [1970c, p. 198], "the superiority of one theory to another is something that cannot be proved in the debate." Kuhn extends the argument [1970b, pp. 266, 268] :

The point-by-point comparison of two successive theories demands a language into which at least the empirical consequences of both can be translated without loss or change. That such a language lies ready to hand has been widely assumed since at least the seventeenth century when philosophers took the neutrality of pure sensation-reports for granted and sought a 'universal character' which would display all languages [by] expressing them as one. . . . I have argued at length that no such vocabulary is available. In the transition from one theory to the next words change their meanings or conditions of applicability in subtle ways. . . .

Why is translation, whether between theories or languages, so difficult? Because, as has often been remarked, languages cut up the world in different ways, and we have no access to a neutral sub-linguistic means of reporting.

However frustrating these situations of incommensurability may be, Kuhn argues that scientists have some recourse. They must begin to acknowledge their membership in different language communities and work at cross-translation. Each scientist may, as he puts it [1970c, p. 202], "try to discover what the other would see and say when presented with a stimulus to which his own verbal response would be different. If they can sufficiently refrain from explaining anomalous behavior as the consequence of mere error or madness, they may in time become very good predictors of each others' behavior."

Eventually, Kuhn suggests, translation may lead to persuasion or conversion. Whether persuasion or conversion occurs cannot easily be predicted, but the importance of the translational effort seems incontestable. This essay is intended as an aid in that task. I have tried to develop, articulate, and formalize the three competing paradigms in sufficiently general and comparable terms to permit translation. I cannot myself provide a perfect translation for anyone, for I am personally immersed in one of the paradigms; I am, as Kuhn notes of his relation to the debate about his own views [1970b, p. 232] , "too much a participant, too deeply involved, to provide the analysis which the breakdown of communication warrants." Nor can I easily foresee the outcome of the competition. I believe that it has begun and I have tried to help in cross-paradigm communication, but the reader should approach my comparative conclusions with suspicion. This essay must work with what Kuhn calls [1962, p. 90] the "symptoms of a transition from normal to extraordinary research"—the "proliferation of competing articulations, the willingness to try anything, the expression of explicit discontent, the recourse to philosophy and to debate over fundamentals. . . ." As the description of those symptoms implies and the very nature of the transition portends, those caught in the passage will eventually seem the most unreliable guides.

Part 2: Theories of Poverty and Underemployment

3

Orthodox Economic Theory

Orthodox economic theory constitutes a fairly consistent corpus of economic theory and analysis, dominant in the Western world and particularly in English and American universities. Although many differences exist within the orthodox perspective, it can unquestionably be considered as a single scientific paradigm, for orthodox theory's differences with competing paradigms outweigh its internal differences. The phrase "orthodox economic theory" has been used in this precise comparative sense by many economists, within and outside the orthodox perspective.[1] As Mark Blaug writes in his review of the history of economic thought [1962, p. ix], "This book is a study of the logical coherence and explanatory value of what has come to be known as orthodox economic theory. The history of this body of received doctrine goes back at least as far as Adam Smith."

Many orthodox economists began during the 1960s to apply orthodox theory to the problems of urban poverty and underemployment. These applications depended on orthodox theories of income determination and distribution, but it has been surprisingly difficult to identify, specify and articulate the general theories in any rigorous way.[a] This has been true at least partly because applications

[a]Although they are conventionally separated in the orthodox literature, I am linking theories of income "determination" and income "distribution" in this discussion. A note of explanation seems appropriate. Theories of income *distribution* have traditionally sought to explain observed patterns in the market distribution of income—to explain, for instance, the positive skewness of the distribution in many advanced capitalist countries. (See any of the recent surveys of the literature for an amplification of this problem: Lydall [1968], Reder [1969], Mincer [1970], and Bjerke [1970].) Theories of income *determination* have attempted to explain the processes through which income is generated—to isolate and examine the key parameters affecting the determination of wages and other income. (See Dunlop [1957], Hicks [1963], and Fleisher [1970] for three discussions of the determination of labor incomes.) The two traditions are obviously related, although their connections are rarely discussed. Most theories of income determination carry some implications for the shape of the final market distribution of income (through their specification of a process of income generation), although a variety of assumptions must usually be made to produce a unique set of predictions. And most theories of income distribution contain some presumptions about the process of income determination—about the presence or absence of competition, for instance. With one exception, I have tried to incorporate both traditions into this discussion. I have ignored those theories of income distribution which do not seem to depend on or imply any assumptions about the process of income determination—which tinker, for instance, with the applicability of Pareto and log-normal distributions. This "theoretic-statistical" school of income distribution theories, as Bjerke calls them [1970], does not depend on any assumptions about human behavior. The theories start and finish with "observations about the nature of the distribution" [Lydall, 1968, p. 13], but "they cannot, as yet, be related to the main body of economic theory" [Reder, 1969, p. 206].

of orthodox theory have proceeded at two very different levels. It sometimes seemed doubtful that work at those two levels could be integrated very clearly.

At one level, some economists worked at fairly eclectic empirical research, probing some of the puzzles about ghetto employment problems which seemed most fascinating and anomalous. In their work, they rarely specified the precise connections between their empirical research and the broader theoretical hypotheses upon which that work was based. Their failure to specify those connections had two explanations. They were working at "normal research," first of all, and were unlikely to raise questions about the basic structure of their underlying paradigmatic assumptions. Second, and perhaps more important, orthodox theory did not readily provide a unified, coherent, easily articulated theory of income determination and distribution to which analysts could refer. Every recent survey of orthodox income distribution theory has emphasized this lack of consensus and coherence. (See Becker [1967], Lydall [1968], Reder [1969], Mincer [1970], and Bjerke [1970].) Reder describes orthodox income distribution theory [1969, p. 229] as a "mosaic," a "cluster of imperfectly joined, ill-fitting pieces." Becker makes the same point [1967, p. 39]: "The body of economic analysis rather desperately needs a reliable theory of the distribution of income."

In the absence of explicit exegesis of the links between general income theory and specific studies of poverty and underemployment, it becomes necessary to *infer* those connections by isolating the critical assumptions underlying the empirical work. Several distinct areas of research seem to me most important in providing the arenas for this inferential examination:

1. studies of the effects on poverty and underemployment over time of economic growth, technological change, changing industrial structure, and, derivatively, changing occupational demand;
2. cross-sectional analysis across regional or industrial units of poverty, wages, and employment, incorporating measures of exogenous variation in industrial structure and labor force composition;
3. cross-sectional analysis of income generation functions among individuals, with special emphasis on the income effects of education, age, and experience;
4. studies of the effects on poverty and underemployment of various labor market "imperfections," like industrial concentration, unionization, minimum wage legislation, imperfect market information, residential segregation, and racial discrimination;
5. efforts to understand the characteristics and functional importance of job stability and labor market mobility;
6. examinations of the determinants of labor force participation rates and the structure of labor supply incentives; and
7. some relatively qualitative, impressionistic studies of local labor markets; in-

dustry and firm behavior (particularly in the hiring and training of disadvantaged workers); and public programs (especially those designed to provide institutional or on-the-job training).

In interpreting these studies of poverty and underemployment, one must essentially engage in an exercise of "revealed theoretical preference." Some manifest "bundles" of empirical analysis help "reveal" the application of a set of theoretical assumptions and hypotheses, just as consumer choice helps reveal an underlying structure of consumer preference. These revealed theoretical preferences help define the "disciplinary matrix" and "exemplars" within which orthodox economists explain urban poverty and underemployment.

At quite a different level, some other economists began to apply a new tool of economic theory—the concept of "human capital"—to explain the phenomena of poverty and underemployment. Although human capital analysis arose from a concern with different problems than these, it eventually implied a unified theory of the distribution of income which itself prompted an application to the puzzles of ghetto employment problems. Because human capital analysis—unlike the more eclectic analyses—does flow from a few critical and clearly formulated theoretical assumptions, one can approach it more deductively, first examining its central assumptions and then weighing their relative importance in its application.[b] The core of human capital theory has been recently formulated and surveyed (see Becker [1964, 1967], Mincer [1970], and Schultz [1971]), and there is little need to review it comprehensively here. Its applications to the problems of poverty and underemployment were just beginning to be stated by the end of the decade, however, and it does seem necessary to consider some of these explorations. The ways in which human capital analysts began to apply their theory to ghetto employment problems bear some important lessons about the general orthodox paradigm, lessons which perfectly complement those of the more eclectic empirical studies.

The Disciplinary Matrix

Taking these two levels of orthodox analysis together, one can formalize some of the features of the orthodox paradigm and begin to frame that paradigm in ways permitting its translation into and comparison with the two competing theories of poverty and underemployment. Despite some differences in conventions of "language," in other words, the two levels of orthodox analysis agree on "sub-

[b]Indeed, many human capital analysts were emphasizing that their theories may help fill the vacuum in orthodox theory which persists in the absence of some other coherent, unified theory of income distribution. Gary Becker writes [1967, p. 39]: "... this approach ... should demonstrate that such a theory need not be a patchwork of Pareto distributions, ability vectors and ad hoc probability mechanisms, but can rely on the basic economic principles that have proven their worth elsewhere."

stance." (See Friedman [1953] for a clear explanation of this important epistemological distinction.) I would argue that six principal clusters of assumptions and hypotheses comprise this common "substantive" core, constituting the most important elements of the "disciplinary matrix" underlying each of the two strands of analysis.[c] In the following pages I have tried to survey these six clusters as briefly as possible.

Income and Marginal Productivity

Orthodox economists almost always try to explain as much as possible about poverty and underemployment in terms of a single parameter—*marginal productivity*. Their effort derives from a single fundamental theoretical hypothesis: in the short run, given assumptions of perfect competition and market equilibrium, workers' wages equal their marginal productivities, or, as Thurow puts it somewhat more precisely [1969, p. 20], "the distribution of marginal products is identical with the distribution of earned income." Given a concern with income and employment status, one must try to translate that concern into an analysis of marginal product.

The analysis involves some important assumptions. The real world admittedly violates some of the conditions underlying the perfect identity of wage and marginal product, since economists are more than prepared to admit that a dynamic economy is always out of equilibrium (but adjusting toward it) and that the market displays various departures from conditions of perfect competition. But orthodox economists still assume that the market processes of advanced capitalist economies resemble the postulated model closely enough—that competitive forces are sufficiently prevalent and that equilibrating adjustments have effect— to justify a basic reliance on the income/marginal productivity hypothesis. In Friedman's terms [1953], orthodox economists continue to view the world "as if" wage equals marginal product, whether they can prove that it does or not. Thurow emphasizes the attendant elements of faith [1970a, pp. 20-21]:

There is practically no direct information on whether or not labor is paid its marginal product. Economists take it as an article of faith or else claim that it is the best null hypothesis, and economic theory is based on the assumption that labor is indeed paid its marginal product. Without this assumption, much of economic analysis falls apart.[2]

This central hypothesis is revealed in the analysis of poverty and underemployment in many ways. In order to analyze the effects of economic growth and the relationship between skill and unemployment, the hypothesis has been ap-

---

[c]The order, structure and emphasis in this outline of the orthodox "disciplinary matrix" is dependent on my concern here with theories of poverty and underemployment. Were I focusing on another kind of subject, I might have designed the summary another way.

plied quite literally as the "queue theory" of labor economics, according to which employers rank present and potential employees along a single ordinal vector by the workers' respective marginal productivities.[3] It also underlies the neoclassical theories of factor shares [Solow, 1968; Harcourt, 1969], and through those theories the analyses of production functions, technological change and industrial structure which are critical to analyses of variations in workers' productivities.[4] The hypothesis also provides the basic theoretical foundation for discussions of the Phillips Curve and its widespread employment policy applications.[5] Human capital analysis itself depends on the assumption, as Thurow [1970a] most clearly states.

In its more simplistic formulations, the hypothesis involves some assumptions about the homogeneity of labor supplied by workers. This assumption about labor unit homogeneity can be dropped, it appears, without disturbing its basic application of the income/marginal productivity hypothesis. Labor can be assumed to consist of different vectors of productivity, for instance, like physical dexterity and mental aptitude. The demand for labor then varies as a function of a weighted factor of those separate components. Given the same assumptions about competition and market equilibrium, wages will vary with a weighted combination of those separate productivity components. This approach seems in particular to provide the primary (implicit) theoretical justification for conventional empirical analyses of wage and income variations in terms of variations of (hypothesized) productivity components like education, ability, and experience; those analyses, in turn, dominate nearly every analytic discussion of the characteristics of the poor and underemployed.[6]

This fundamental hypothesis about marginal productivity therefore informs orthodox discussion of poverty and the labor market with a uniform initial perspective, however subtly it may later be qualified. Thurow puts it simply [1969, p. 26]: "If an individual's income is too low, his productivity is too low. His income can be increased only if his productivity can be raised." At least in the long run, the converse is also presumed to be true—that an individual whose productivity increases, *ceteris paribus*, will automatically increase his wages.[d]

Orthodox economists rely on the income/productivity hypothesis so heavily that some of them sometimes teeter on the brink of tautological argument. Thurow warns against this occasional carelessness on the part of his colleagues [1970a, p. 20, emphasis in the original]:

... there is a limit beyond which earnings and labor's marginal product become tautologically equivalent. At one extreme, everyone is by definition paid his marginal product. If he earns a different amount, then he must have a different marginal product. Any useful definition of a man's marginal product, however, must conceptually include situations where it is possible for a man to be paid *other* than his marginal product.

---

[d]In the short run, the structure of organization and technology, expectations and uncertainty may all combine to prevent a translation of changes in individual characteristics into wage changes. See Reder [1962].

This tendency, against which Thurow warns, seems most pronounced in some of the human capital analysis. Technically, in the human capital literature, earnings are not a function of returns to human capital investments alone, for the analysis presumes that there are monetary returns to something called natural ability and that, concomitantly, workers with no human capital might still earn something. (See Becker [1967, p. 2, eq. 1].) Despite that technical qualification, however, many human capital analysts seem increasingly inclined to assume that *all* income is exclusively a return to human capital investment through the equilibrating identity of income and marginal product. Even preschool differences in ability are seen as functions of market decisions about human capital investment. "Indeed," Becker writes [1967, p. 3], "in the developmental approaches to child rearing, all the earnings of a person are ultimately attributed to different kinds of investments made in him." What we normally call "ability," in other words, can actually be viewed as an endogenously determined component of human capital, attributable to parental investment in love and nutrition. Because it is always difficult to measure these kinds of human differences quantitatively, human capital analysts seem more and more inclined to assume that the marginal productivity hypothesis can explain every difference in income simply because they can hypothesize ways in which every difference in individual capacity may flow from different investments and rates of return.

Demand and Supply

Based on its orientation toward analyses within the market/exchange framework, orthodox theory molds ideas about income determination and distribution directly into hypotheses about demand and supply. The distribution of labor earnings, as Reder says [1969, p. 214], "ultimately depends upon the interaction of supply and demand forces." As Friedman points out, the hypotheses about demand and supply constitute elements of the "language" of economic theory [1953, p. 8]:

[Demand and supply] are the two major categories into which the factors affecting the relative prices of products or factors of production are classified. The usefulness of the dichotomy depends on the 'empirical generalization that an enumeration of the forces affecting demand in any problem and of the forces affecting supply will yield two lists that contain few items in common.'

Given the attempt to place all hypotheses within the framework of those two categories, orthodox economists must be able to formulate all their supply and demand hypotheses as functions of the same parameter since the curves must "intersect" to produce an equilibrium. This creates the critical necessity, in theories of income and employment, of distinguishing between (monetary equivalents of) the characteristics of jobs and the characteristics of people. Do employers demand productivity characteristics in people, or do they simply require that job capacities be filled, whether by people, machines, or by accident? Do they seek to mold men to jobs, or jobs to men, in light of demand and supply considerations?

This highly abstract problem has in fact created a certain amount of difficulty on the demand side, as Reder especially notes [1968, 1969]. Short-run variations in demand for labor should reflect variations in the marginal physical productivities of workers, but marginal physical products cannot often be measured or specified in homogeneous units. Since the theory of demand "is, after all, a matter of the interrelation of prices and quantities of homogeneous goods," as Reder points out [1969, p. 219], it is therefore natural "for economists concerned with this problem to seek parameters which reflect differences in demand intensity in situations where differences in marginal products are not conducive to quantification." In one way or another, two demand parameters have been suggested by orthodox economists: the "scale of operations" affected by a given worker in a given job [Mayer, 1960; Lydall, 1968; Reder, 1969], and the "sensitivity" of a job's product to superior performance in that job [Reder, 1969]. These two parameters correspond, very roughly, to the average *magnitude* and potential *variation* of a workers' impact in a given job, but it seems unclear from the theory, a priori, whether variations in job specifications or variations in individual characteristics are more closely associated with variation in either of the two parameters.

Human capital analysts solve this problem of specification with a single semantic stroke. Employers demand what workers supply—stocks of "human capital" embodied in individuals. In this particular respect, human capital analysis provides some hypotheses about the parameters of demand for labor which fill holes in the precedent orthodox analysis.

Hypotheses about the supply of labor productivities come much more easily in orthodox analysis. Individuals are presumed to have varying talents, skills, and capacities which become manifest as varying productivities in given job situations. In the short run, these skills remain unequally distributed. Economists seem to agree on five principal sources of these capacities: native ability, formal education, vocational education, on-the-job training, and on-the-job experience. Natural abilities remain relatively unspecified, although analysts sometimes regard them as residual productivities once the other components have been held constant. (See Griliches [1970, Section V].) General education is presumed primarily to affect an individual's ability to read and reason, and these abilities are presumed to influence an individual's marginal productivity. (See Vaizey and Robinson, eds. [1966], Blaug, ed. [1968], and Halsey, Floud, and Anderson, eds. [1965].) Vocational education teaches individuals a narrower set of productive abilities which increases their productivities in some jobs. (See "Vocational Education" [1968].) On-the-job training and experience provide overlapping kinds of productivities, but one can distinguish them heuristically; on-the-job training provides skills applicable only to the present job (or to a particular occupational category, narrowly defined), while on-the-job experience develops a set of productive abilities a worker can apply to any job.[7] Whatever the distinctions, the two kinds of productivity acquired on the job range from specific skills like machine operation and repair to more general skills like understanding instructions and working well with fellow employees.

Human capital analysis takes this one step further. These five sources of labor productivity generate skills which fall along a single spectrum, ranging from the most "general" skills like native ability to the most "specific" skills like machine operation. Becker [1964] develops the distinction between "general" and "specific" skills into some hypotheses about the allocation of the costs of training between employer and employee. Operationally, it becomes relatively difficult to distinguish between "general" and "specific" skills acquired through on-the-job training and experience, and later analyses by Mincer [1970, 1971], for instance, do not try to develop empirical measures which separate the two.

This analysis of the "supply" of labor productivity has been applied particularly to the analysis of poverty and underemployment. Those who are poor are presumed to have relatively small amounts of these various kinds of productivity, and evidence is adduced for these assumptions by examining the educational attainments of the poor (Morgan et al. [1962], and Thurow [1969]), the effects of vocational training (Mangum [1967], and Solie [1968]), and the effects of age on income in general and at different occupational levels (Morgan [1962], Brady [1965], Fuchs [1967], and Lydall [1968]). In policy terms, in order to improve opportunities for the poor and underemployed, one ought variously to increase their store of general educational skills, provide them with more vocational training, and provide them with more on-the-job experience and training.[e]

Equilibrium and Harmony

The demand for and the supply of labor productivity are supposed to intersect, of course, to create a point of market equilibrium. Unfortunately, orthodox productivity theories have trouble in precisely specifying the process of this intersection, trouble which flows from the uncertainty of the analysis of demand parameters. As Reder has put it most carefully [1969, p. 227]:

A theory of income size distribution consistent with (general equilibrium) theory requires that a set of transformations be established between the units of "talent" that measure supply and the units of "capacity" that measure demand. Needless to say, I cannot specify such a set of transformations nor so far as I am aware can anyone else at this time. . . .

[e]Most analyses continue, of course, by arguing with Tobin [1968, p. 91] that "adult education, training and retraining are difficult, slow and costly processes . . ." and that "our main hope must be in the education of our children."

As Reder continues [1969, p. 228, emphasis in the original] :

Personal attributes such as intelligence and physical strength are better suited for measuring supply than demand. What employers seek is 'productive capacity' which is separated from 'personal attributes' by a thick curtain of sociopsychological variables conveniently labeled incentive, attitude and experience. It is safe to say the role of these variables in the theory of wages is not well understood. Scale of operations and sensitivity are interesting correlates of labor demand; they are important indicators of the demand prices for (successful) applicants for particular *jobs* but they are not useful indicators for analyzing the demands for the services of *individuals*. [8]

The importance of this problem appears at two different levels of orthodox analysis. At the conceptual level, it sometimes seems to lead analysts to skirt the problem by formulating hypotheses solely in terms of individual capacities, taking job characteristics as given—to try to measure productivity variations, that is, solely in terms of variations in individual characteristics.[f] At the policy level, the inability precisely to formulate the parameters of equilibrium seems to create a generalized, rather imprecise faith in the equilibrium process through which some marginal changes bring about marginal effects. If additional vocational training increases the supply of workers with a particular skill, for instance, one automatically assumes that employers using that skill will respond by adjustments in their elasticities of substitution among capital and labor of various skills [Thurow, 1969], even though their demand for labor may be mediated through some totally unidentified transformation variables—by a poorly perceived "curtain" which may or may not operate as it is supposed to. The problem, in other words, is that orthodox economists assume responses in variables which they have not yet specified very rigorously. This makes it difficult to compare their arguments with those from other perspectives which may postulate no response at all or response in more fundamental, or different kinds of variables.

The continuing movement of the economy toward points of equilibria gains force from another kind of underlying assumption, one which orthodox economists rarely state very explicitly. Orthodox economists seem to presume a basically recurring *harmony* of interests among all economic actors, whether employers or employees. Building from the Paretian analyses of perfectly competitive systems, economists often suggest that present outcomes represent optimal situations. Were we to move from the present equilibrium, there would be a net loss in social welfare. Everyone has a stake in maintaining the present arrangements, as a result, because everyone is ultimately better off. As Zweig explains [1971, p. 44], ". . . in market exchanges, both parties gain from trade, establishing a supposed harmony of interest among all in the perpetuation of exchange

---

[f]Even when industry is a unit of observation, industrial characteristics are standardized by the "skill mix" of the industry to escape the necessity of explaining variations among industries in occupational structures. For one example of this kind of procedure, quite common in cross-sectional analysis, see Stoikov and Raimon [1968] .

through markets organized on a private, capitalist basis. Each economic actor, whatever his position, is a cooperative and committed member of capitalist society, in which he does the best he can."

This presumption of ultimately harmonious relations among economic actors plays an important role in orthodox approaches to poverty and underemployment. Although the poor and the underemployed may not fare so well under current arrangements—although they may indeed be dissatisfied with present outcomes—many orthodox economists imagine that public or private policies can be designed which will benefit everyone involved. It should be possible, they expect, that current dissatisfactions can be worked out in such a way that the economy returns to its natural state of equilibrium and harmony.

Simplicity and Universality

Orthodox theory begins with an interest, as Maurice Dobb puts it [1963, p. 27], in "those properties that are common to any type of exchange society." It seeks universally applicable hypotheses which transcend institutional and historical variations within or among societies. Dobb continues [1963, p. 27-28]:

Institutional, or historico-relative, material, while it has not been excluded entirely, has only been introduced into the second story of the building, being treated in the main as changes in 'data' which may influence the value of the relevant variables, but do not alter the main equations by which the governing relationships are defined.

Orthodox models also begin with assumptions of perfect competition, or, to put it in other terms, with theories which are formulated "as if" markets were perfectly competitive. These assumptions, although they are usually relaxed, help provide a kind of substantive justification for the search for universally applicable hypotheses. If a relationship between two variables can be postulated for one sector of the economy, then the forces of competition will spread that relationship to other sectors (at least in the long run). Through the forces of competition, for instance, the influence of changes in labor quality on wages in one industry will eventually be spread to all other industries, and will tend to preserve the universal applicability of the income/marginal productivity hypothesis.[g] Without the competitive assumption, the orthodox search for universal hypotheses would seem that much less natural a predilection.

---

[g]It seems useful to cite a clear example of this disposition in the literature. In his seminal study of *The Service Economy*, Fuchs [1968] discusses the probability that the forces of competition effect a clear and direct relationship between changes in labor quality and wage changes among industries over time. He notes approvingly [p. 60] "The high correlation between productivity and compensation per man across major groups . . . suggests that differential trends in productivity have been associated with differential trends in labor quality."—a conclusion which relies on the competitive mechanism. He then comments in a footnote about the same correlation, "An alternative inference—that the differential trends in compensation are a result of the weakness of competitive forces and are unrelated to labor quality—seems less plausible but cannot be rejected a priori."

Orthodox analysis, finally, seeks theoretical simplicity for its own sake. Friedman in particular has propounded this principle [1953, pp. 10, 14] :

The choice among alternative hypotheses equally consistent with the available evidence must to some extent be arbitrary, though there is general agreement that relevant considerations are suggested by . . . criteria [like] 'simplicity'. . . . A theory is 'simpler' the less the initial knowledge needed to make a prediction within a given field of phenomena; . . . A hypothesis is important if it 'explains' much by little. . . .

Together, these three inclinations infuse orthodox analysis with a preference for *continuity*—for hypotheses which apply in continuous fashion throughout an economy, for tests of functionally similar relationships among all economic groups and sectors, for the replication of universal relationships over time.

This disposition can be seen throughout the orthodox literature on poverty and underemployment. The "queue" theory presumes, for instance, a universality in the criteria for employer rankings of workers across industries and labor markets. One could imagine, in contrast, a theory which hypothesized quite different criteria among different kinds of employers. The search for universal relationships also informs the estimation of uniformly-specified income generation functions for all groups in the labor force (as, for instance, in Morgan, et al. [1962], Hanoch [1967], and Thurow [1969]). One could suggest, instead, a quite different specification for different groups.[h] In much the same way, to pick one more example, the structure of economic aspirations and motivations is presumed to remain constant over time, despite important historical or institutional changes. If it was true historically that European immigrants to the United States sought to achieve economic mobility by "investing" in themselves and their children, so shall we assume that young blacks born in northern ghettos will be motivated to act in similar ways.[i]

---

[h]Without entering into the other paradigms at this stage of the essay, some examples of alternative suggestions might be noted. One could suggest, on employer preferences, that employers might use potential exploitability as a criterion in certain un-unionized competitive industries. And Michelson [1969] has suggested an alternative and quite plausible hypothesis about black decisions to invest in education—alternative to and different from, that is, the conventional analysis of lifetime income maximization.

[i]These assumptions about universality, simplicity, competition, and continuity inform the ways in which orthodox economists approach the analysis of market "imperfections." In general, market imperfections are presumed simply to limit the extent of the market within which the general analytic axioms apply. They are presumed *not* to affect, in contrast, the functional form of the presumably universal structural relationships which apply in every sector. This is classically true, of course, of the traditional hypotheses about "noncompeting groups," between which exogenous factors throw up a barrier but among which conventional relationships hold true. It applies equally to more recent analyses of market imperfections like the minimum wage, labor unions, monopolistic competition, and discrimination. The analysis of discrimination provides one of the clearest examples. In its original formulation by Becker [1957] and in its extensions by Krueger [1963], Welch [1967], Thurow [1969], McCall [1970c], Arrow [1971], and Bergmann [1971], the orthodox analysis of discrimination views it as an exogenously determined psychological fact which serves to divide the market into racially homogeneous sectors. Within those sectors, one analyzes the determination and distribution of incomes in exactly similar ways. For further comments, see M. Reich [1971].

Institutional Constants and Marginal Change

Orthodox analyses usually involve hypotheses about marginal changes from a fixed institutional structure. Given a state of the world, individuals make choices within a constant, unyielding environment. This methodological approach flows, at least partly, from orthodox attempts to develop *determinant* models; if some elements of the environment are not fixed for the purposes of analysis, then partial hypotheses become too conditional. Sraffa [1960] has most clearly identified the technical importance of this approach, and many other orthodox economists have emphasized its importance.

Although orthodox economists appreciate the importance of this methodological predisposition in the abstract, however, its importance in application is noted less frequently. Several examples can help illustrate the ways in which assumptions about fixed institutional structures permeate the orthodox perspective on poverty and underemployment.

One important example concerns the relationship between jobs and people, or, more precisely, between job and individual characteristics. "Job characteristics should be endogenous in a general equilibrium model," as Reder points out [1969, p. 228], but they are in fact assumed to be constant by orthodox analysts for reasons of convenience. Scoville [1969, pp. 36-37] emphasizes this difference between classical economics, in which job structure and design were endogenous, and neoclassical economics, "in which the emphasis shifts to the question of choice by individuals among pre-existing occupations." This neoclassical assumption about the fixity of job characteristics involves several closely related hypotheses. It depends, first of all, on the hypothesis that if job characteristics are not totally fixed but do indeed change, their changes are not sufficiently important to undercut the validity of hypotheses about individual behavior. It assumes, equally, that changes in individual behavior, which economists presume have been made in response to a given occupational structure, are not in fact indirectly caused by changes in job structure, design, and characteristics. Or, to turn the arguments around in one more direction, the assumptions about constant job characteristics presume that, if job characteristics do in fact change, individuals act *as if* job characteristics are constant; as Mandelbrot has put it [1962, p. 59], "we shall assume that each individual must choose *one* of the N possible 'occupations.' Naturally, two occupations, that make the same offers to every income-earner, may be considered as being identical." One could hypothesize, in contrast, that if job structures do indeed change very significantly, individuals might seek, for psychological reasons, to minimize the extent to which they must endure occupational change during their lifetimes (instead of switching from occupation to occupation in order to continue maximizing lifetime incomes).

Orthodox economists make some of the same kinds of working assumptions about extra-labor market institutions as well, especially about the schools. Individuals are presumed to make optimizing decisions with respect to fixed educational elements. If educational institutions have in fact been changing, economists choose to ignore those changes, or, for longer-term purposes, to regard them as exogenous. This involves, most clearly, the working hypothesis that changes in educational institutions are not, in contrast, endogenous to the process of economic growth and development.

Two features of these assumptions about institutions seem most important. First, they involve some important guesses about the aggregate impact of marginal individual choices. As long as orthodox economists continue to analyze choice within a constant institutional structure, they presume that individual choices will not add up to a *qualitative* change in the institutional structure to which individuals respond. Second, the assumptions involve some sort of faith that the impact of a given institutional structure will remain constant long enough to warrant focus on actions made in response to that initial structure. Leontief worries about the empirical implications of this kind of expectation [1971, p. 4]: "On the relatively shallow level where empirically implemented economic analysis now operates even the more invariant of the structural relationships, in terms of which the system is described, change rapidly."

These inclinations have been reproduced in human capital analysis, as Reder argues at some length [1969, pp. 231ff]. Commenting on the importance, stability, and uniqueness of relations between income and human capital, Reder writes [1969, p. 231]:

This is not to argue that the distribution of human capital is unrelated to the distribution of earnings. Rather it is to say that both distributions are determined simultaneously by an underlying set of consumer tastes, productive techniques, and wealth ownership. The distribution of wealth greatly influences the shapes and positions of the S curves. These underlying variables determine the positions and interrelations of the D and S curves through relative prices. They also determine the size and distribution of the stock of capital (human and otherwise) and the distribution of earnings. Any particular relationship between the size distributions of human capital and of earnings is conditional upon the interrelation of these underlying exogenous variables.

Maximization and Choice

Orthodox economists usually structure their analyses by assuming that individuals and firms try to maximize their objective functions (subject to constraint). In theories of income determination and distribution, this amounts to a kind of assumption about "worker sovereignty." The theories imply, in effect, that workers have had a variety of choices (about hours, schooling and training, and job quality) and that their present situations, *ceteris paribus*, can be viewed as *optima* freely chosen. In emphasis if not in precise substantive hypothesis, the theories seem to suggest that individuals have a nearly unlimited range of opportunities in the course of their lifetimes. This implication seems to play the same role in theories of income as the notion of "consumer sovereignty" plays in theories of consumption and demand. In consumer theory, that is, orthodox economists concentrate on the results of free consumer choice among a given bundle of commodities with different prices; they rarely focus on the ways in which institutions tend to define or limit the bundles available for choice. In the same way, theories of income concentrate on the ways in which workers make education, training, mobility, and experience decisions among a given bundle of opportunities, rather than focusing on the ways in which institutions tend to define and limit the bundles of opportunities available to them.

This inclination to view income and employment in terms of maximization and choice has two principal applications in the analysis of poverty and the labor market. First, it leads to some imputations about rationality and irrationality. In recent analyses of the (measured) returns to education, for instance, some economists have tended to ascribe rationality to those who invested in educational increments with high rates of return, and irrationality to those who invested in educational increments with no rates of return or who did not invest in educational levels with high rates of return. (See the literature revolving around Hanoch [1967], and leading to Michelson [1969].) The readiness to impute rationality and irrationality implies that one's model can adequately encompass, identify, measure, and analyze those features of the institutional environment which affect individual calculations—which constitute the constraints of individual maximization calculus—and that the results have not in fact been biased by mis-specification.

Second, this perspective on the labor market has led economists to apply the maximization/choice model to varieties of behavior which they had previously dismissed as irrational or imponderable. This has been increasingly true of the analysis of worker stability (particularly in Phelps et al. [1970], and McCall [1970a]); of crime (Becker [1967], Stigler [1969], Tullock [1969], and Thurow [1970b]); and of employer incentives to provide on-the-job training (Thurow [1968b, 1969]).

The Response to Anomaly

As orthodox economists applied these central elements of their paradigm toward the resolution of the most important puzzles about urban poverty and underemployment, two principal problems became increasingly apparent. First, orthodox analysts confronted the persistence and apparent inexplicability of wage, income, or employment differentials between various groups, as between whites and blacks or men and women. Over time, as a result of the competitive mechanisms postulated by orthodox theory, one might have expected these differentials to erode, but they did not seem to have diminished appreciably for years. Cross-sectionally, one would expect to be able to "explain" the differentials by controls for obvious productivity components like education and age. At best, it usually turned out, one could only explain about half of the differentials with these kinds of controls in the comparisons between whites and blacks. With comparisons between sexes, the controls were much less effective.[9]

Second, orthodox economists could not immediately agree on appropriate ways of explaining the critical importance of job stability and instability within the framework of the orthodox perspective. Many different kinds of analyses were developed, but they had not yet been integrated very coherently within the general framework. (See Hall [1970a] for a clear discussion of some of the problems.)

In facing these problems, orthodox economists essentially chose either of two principal responses. On the one hand, they kept extending and expanding the concept of productivity, incorporating a wide variety of essentially neglected phenomena within the framework of productivity analysis. On-the-job experience, for instance, was now seen to provide many kinds of often immeasurable, largely intangible productivities like reliability and capacity to follow instructions, as I noted above. If one could not always measure these characteristics for statistical analysis, one had to admit that their variations *might* indeed explain a large share of some unexplained residuals. The concept of human capital seemed especially absorptive, for one could quite easily argue within the human capital framework that variations in nearly any relevant labor market characteristic could reflect variations in either human capital investment stocks or in the rate of return to those investments; Mincer [1970] in particular expresses the hope that the continued application of human capital analysis will illuminate elements of job stability as well as the distribution of income.

The second and essentially reverse inclination was to argue that economic analysis could only explain a limited set of phenomena. Some of the puzzles emerging in the study of ghetto employment problems, according to this view, reflect the consequences of changing tastes or other exogenous factors for whose presence, structure, or changes economic analysis does not intend to try to provide an explanation.

One particularly interesting application of the orthodox perspective to the puzzles of poverty and underemployment provides some clear illustrations of nearly all the general features of the orthodox paradigm and reflects very sharply these trends in the orthodox response to these particular anomalies. In his analysis of "Learning and Experience in the Labor Market," Sherwin Rosen [1971] tries to incorporate many recent perceptions about job stability and on-the-job training and experience into a relatively general model of individual income and occupational mobility. Rosen begins by acknowledging the increasing importance of highly specific on-the-job training and experience. Many employers tend increasingly to prefer workers not only with considerable manifest human capital but also with the potential and reliability to learn specific skills on the job. Further, these on-the-job learning opportunities, given the state of production techniques and the organization of job structures, are fairly fixed in the short run. The distribution of (relatively fixed) production functions and job structures determines the distribution of available opportunities for investment in this particular kind of human capital. Through the competitive process and variations in the distribution of returns to investment opportunities, a price structure is attached to the supply of on-the-job learning opportunities. Because these opportunities are tied to specific firms and specific job structures, there can be discontinuities in the price structure attached to the supply of those opportunities. At the same time, workers have a set of demand prices for different learning opportunities, based on the distribution of potential returns available to them. If a given job's learning price—reflected in the difference between income in a "learning" job and a non-learning job for which he could qualify—exceeds the worker's demand price for that job, then the worker will simply not apply for that job and will not seek to invest in additional human capital. Those workers with relatively higher abilities and relatively more advantageous financing opportunities will tend more intensively to demand jobs with greater learning opportunities because their returns will be higher and/or their costs lower. Those workers who have less ability, who face disadvantageous investment-financing opportunities, or who suffer some kind of labor market discrimination may be priced out of the learning market altogether. Rosen writes [1971, pp. 27-28, emphasis in the original] :

Anything producing differences among individuals in ability or financing cost can result in cases where *some classes of workers do not participate at all* in certain job markets. In terms of our [assumed] elementary two-job world, the market can very well establish an equilibrium price on the total opportunity package of job [one] that is high enough to literally price lesser able or poorer workers out of the market. . . .

Some workers, priced completely out of the learning market, may not acquire any additional human capital after their formal education ends. These workers are likely to spend less time on any given job (because they lose nothing in quitting), are much more likely to have low incomes (because they have less human capital), and are especially likely to have flat "age-income" profiles.

Apart from the unequalizing influence of factors like ability, capital market imperfections, and discrimination (all of which also affect investments in formal education), the most important unequalizing feature of the market for on-the-job investments is the *fixity* of on-the-job learning and investment opportunities. The price structure of learning opportunities cannot easily be equalized through competition because of the specificity of the job situations. Rosen writes [1971, pp. 16, 29, emphasis in the original] :

The nature of the market is such that workers have their choice among all-or-nothing bargains or "package deals" in which they sell their services and purchase *fixed* quantities of knowledge. Thus, though investment is assumed infinitely elastic, fixed quantity-price contracts are what limit the amounts of investment at any age. In a sense, there is a supply limitation. Individuals purchase different amounts of investment by *switching* work activities and in fact can allocate lifetime work activity to maximize lifetime income or human wealth in this way. . . .

That distinct unit prices for the same "good" can exist in the market is a result of the all-or-nothing nature of labor contracts. Tie-in contracts imply that different learning possibilities are in a sense different "commodities." A worker must devote *all* his efforts to one job or another and arbitrage is not possible, since knowledge is embodied in him and not freely transferrable to others.

Further, the range of job opportunities to which workers can (most profitably) switch is substantially influenced by prior learning opportunities, no doubt, so that the effects of the all-or-nothing learning contracts are multiplied throughout labor market careers. Given initial discontinuities, the gap between workers with no on-the-job skills and those with some could continue to spread.

Rosen's analysis provides some explanations of many of the observed symptoms of urban poverty and underemployment in the United States. It helps illuminate the interconnections between income and stability, incorporates hypotheses about the segregation of workers in different kinds of markets, and provides some clear expectations about the impact of employer preferences about worker reliability. At the same time, Rosen's model reflects both the general orthodox paradigm and some of the specific orthodox responses to recent anomalies. The model directly builds from the assumption that income adjusts to variations in marginal productivities. It incorporates new perceptions about important factors in the labor market and on the job into the framework of demand and supply. It presumes the central importance of equilibria and speculates that some specific policies can correct current situations in the interests of all. It also illustrates with exceptional clarity some of the orthodox inclination toward universally applicable analyses. Rosen acknowledges this preference quite explicitly [1971, p. 3]:

The reader will note that the discussions of the model, though weighted toward poor minority groups, are not wholly confined to them. This is based on an implicit assumption that a useful and general theory should be capable of explaining a wide variety of results from a single unified structure. I for one will not be content with a separate theory of the labor market for the poor and an entirely different theory for the nonpoor. "The" theory of the labor market should encompass both groups.

The model also illustrates the importance of institutional constants and marginal change. Rosen derives a wide variety of operational hypotheses from assumptions about the existence of several different "types" of jobs, some of which provide learning opportunities and some of which do not. He does not seek to explain the origin of those differential job types, however, for that would involve, as he writes [1971, p. 61], a "rather more complete theoretical foundations that I have been able to devise so far." Rosen's model clearly illustrates the central importance of models of maximization and choice, finally, for it provides a means of explaining nearly all the most evident symptoms of current poverty and underemployment as functions of individual maximization. The distribution of human capital is determined by the market process, not by the *deus ex machina* of inheritance or ability. Poor and underemployed workers have "chosen" not to invest in jobs with learning opportunities because it was not profitable for them to do so. It is merely necessary to assume a set of precedent technologies and job structures, leading to stratified price structures for learning opportunities, in order to "explain" the distribution of investments. And given that distribution, with its freely-chosen inequalities, poor workers are likely to earn less and work more unstably than other workers solely because they have acquired less human capital. The presence of poverty and underemployment can be seen, through this approach, as a simple aggregation of individual lifetime income-maximizing decisions among workers. According to the analysis, in short, it becomes possible to understand poverty, underemployment, and inequality by proceeding *as if* all workers and employers act rationally in pursuit of their individual self-interest and *as if* the outcomes were optimal outcomes in light of the existing organization of work.

4   Dual Labor Market Theory

Toward the end of the last decade, some economists began to argue that a dual labor market theory could best explain the phenomena of urban poverty and underemployment. The theory suggested that a dichotomization of the American labor market had occurred over time, forging two separate labor markets—a "primary" and a "secondary" market—in which workers and employers operate by fundamentally different behavioral rules. One could understand little about urban poverty and underemployment, according to this perspective, without first tracing both the sources and the effects of this emergent dualism in the U.S. economy.

The dual labor market theory arose gradually out of a series of relatively informal studies of local labor markets and individual establishments. It grew without pretensions toward more sweeping generality. It has never been intended to explain very much about labor market behavior in other historical periods; it is, in other words, a "time specific" set of hypotheses. Despite these intentions and purposeful limitations, however, the theory has begun to play an important role as a participant in the emerging competition among theoretical perspectives on poverty and underemployment. Its proponents have intended that it replace a few central features of orthodox theory, first of all; they tend to share, consequently, a subjective sense of competition with at least one of the other perspectives. The theory also implies some corollary hypotheses about the determination and distribution of income in the United States at present, although most of its articulations have not stated these hypotheses in any very explicit ways. Most concretely, the notion of "dualism" has provided a very tangible "exemplar," in Thomas Kuhn's terms [1970c], with expanding influence on the perspectives through which economists begin to study the phenomena of poverty and underemployment. By providing this "exemplar" without demanding a fuller involvement in the more general disciplinary matrices of either orthodox or radical economics, the dual labor market theory has become a very important paradigm in the competition with which this book is concerned. As a kind of intermediate point between the two more general views, it helps clarify many of the most important differences between those two perspectives.

As an explanation of urban poverty and underemployment, the dual labor market theory grew first from a series of relatively casual, qualitative impressions of local labor markets. Four different groups were pursuing these studies over the same period of time without much contact among them. One group studied the Boston ghetto labor market, summarizing many of their first impressions in a report to the Labor Department (Doeringer et al. [1969]). Another group had been working in Chicago; two different reports emerged from that city, both the study of "dualism" by Baron and Hymer [1968] and some of the reports of the Chicago labor market study (reviewed by Rees [1968]). A third group, associates of the Michigan Institute of Industrial and Labor Relations, had been studying Detroit; several different essays followed (Ferman [1967], Fusfeld [1968], Bluestone [1970], and Wachtel [1970]). A fourth group worked in Harlem, leading to a summary report by Vietorisz and Harrison [1970].[1]

Based on many of these studies, and sometimes published simultaneously with their reports, some more formal articulations of the dual labor market theory appeared. Piore provided some of the first and clearest direct articulations [1968, 1969, 1970], working with an explicit dual labor market model. Bluestone chose to articulate a "tri-partite model of the labor market" [1970], although his three sectors could be collapsed into the "primary" and "secondary" markets of the dualistic version. I pulled together a few of the disparate formulations (in D.M. Gordon, ed. [1971, Chapter Two]) in order to begin comparing the theory with orthodox views. Doeringer and Piore [1971] explored the intersections of the dual labor market theory with their analysis of "internal labor markets," a much more detailed theory of behavior within "structured" labor markets. Although these versions of the theory had developed without reference to other kinds of analysis, some connections could later be drawn to analyses of dualism in development economics,[2] and to some analyses of dualism in the American industrial structure.[3] Although a consensus among all these different permutations of the theory had not yet been explicitly proclaimed, it appears that the several seminal groups acknowledge the essential similarity of their views.[a] The following pages infer a consensus and extrapolate some conclusions from all of these overlapping pieces of work.[4] The first section surveys the specific hypotheses of the explicit dual labor market analyses while the second extracts its essential implications for the determination and distribution of income.

Specific Hypotheses

To some of those economists studying ghetto labor markets in the 1960s, it often appeared that characteristics which economists had conventionally associated with "productivity"—like years of schooling and vocational training—had almost no influence on the employment prospects of large numbers of urban employees. In many instances, those who were rejected for jobs seemed nominally as "qualified" as workers who were hired. The important differences among

---

[a]One piece of evidence for that claim is that almost all the individual proponents were able to read a preliminary draft of this book and did not raise any vociferous objections to its allegations of consensus.

ghetto workers often seemed to center around their work preferences. Some workers frequently refused to consider jobs to which they were referred. These more particular applicants often had "better" qualifications than those who were hired, and yet chose to remain unemployed or out of the labor force. One began to guess, in this respect, that the range of jobs available to these workers was much narrower than the range of their "capacities" or nominal qualifications. Given that narrow range of jobs, the determinants of labor force status—whether a worker happened to be employed, unemployed, or out of the labor force—sometimes appeared to be relatively random.[b]

At least partly as a result of these perceptions, increasing attention was focused on the characteristics of jobs to which many ghetto workers seemed confined. With few exceptions, these jobs were typically menial, requiring little mental or physical dexterity. Instability of the work force seemed not only to be accepted by employers in these job categories but often encouraged by them. The jobs paid low wages and conferred minimal status. The quality of working conditions was poor. Most important, apparently, the jobs seemed completely isolated. They were not connected to job ladders of any sort. No matter how long an employee worked at these jobs or how clearly he demonstrated his diligence or skill, there seemed to be no fixed channels through which he could rise above his original job.[5]

There seemed to many to be a critical interdependence between the characteristics of "secondary" workers and "secondary" jobs. The structure of jobs often seemed to the workers to prevent them from improving their wages or status on the job. In response, they often quit their jobs to earn money another way. This pattern of instability fit into a more general pattern of life in the ghetto (and perhaps even caused it).[c] Secondary workers tended to continue their instability by habit or instinct even in those rare instances where stability might have mattered. Simultaneously, these patterns of behavior led employers increasingly to organize the structure of work and production in such a way that

[b]Many of these impressions were reinforced by data collected in the Boston ghetto labor market study, reported by Doeringer et al. [1969]. Data on job referrals by neighborhood manpower centers suggested, for instance, that there were no statistically significant differences between workers hired on jobs and workers rejected by employers. Nor did there seem to be significant differences between the jobs for which workers were typically hired and those for which they were rejected. Those who refused to report to interviews or refused to accept job offers were in some respects, according to the report [Doeringer et al., 1969, p. 84], "a 'superior' group [with respect] to the 'hires' and 'rejects.'" They were slightly older, on the average, had more years of work experience, and had generally worked on better jobs in the past.

[c]Three different aspects of life in the ghetto merged with this pattern of work instability: the welfare system, the "training economy," and the world of crime and "hustling." For some extended surveys of these aspects of ghetto life, with bibliographies, see D.M. Gordon, ed. [1971, Chapters Two, Four, and Five.] For a useful review of the interconnections among these three sectors and the "secondary" labor market, see Harrison [1972, Chapter Five].

worker instability did not disrupt production or reduce efficiency, further prompting them to separate these jobs from the rest of the establishment. The attitudes of employees and employers seemed symbiotically to adjust to developing behavioral patterns. And once these attitudes were fixed, employee and employer expectations combined to intensify the patterns to which they were initially responding. Keyed to these behavioral trends, a separate market appeared to emerge in which both secondary workers and secondary employers were forced to operate.

These impressions gradually forged a more formal analysis of the dichotomization between the "primary" and the "secondary" markets. In general, as Piore argues [1971, p. 91], the two markets display distinct and identifiable features:

... the primary market offers jobs which possess several of the following traits: high wages, good working conditions, employment stability and job security, equity and due process in the administration of work rules, and chances for advancement. The ... secondary market has jobs which, relative to those in the primary sector, are decidedly less attractive. They tend to involve low wages, poor working conditions, considerable variability in employment, harsh and often arbitrary discipline, and little opportunity to advance. The poor are confined to the secondary labor market.

Doeringer and Piore [1971] describe three distinct kinds of employment situations in the secondary market: completely unstructured employment, classically competitive; clusters of secondary jobs with a bit of internal job structure, as in foundry work; and secondary jobs with no internal job structure which are attached to primary markets, like wood yard jobs in pulp and paper mills.

Piore [1970] makes five connected arguments which he intends to explain both the historical separation between markets and the differences in behavior between them. First, he suggests, "the most important characteristic distinguishing jobs in the primary sector from those in the secondary sector appears to be the behavioral requirements which they impose on the work force, particularly that of employment stability." Secondary workers are generally barred from primary jobs not because they lack certain "work skills" but because they tend to work unreliably and intermittently.

Second, "certain workers who possess the behavioral traits required to operate efficiently in primary jobs are trapped in secondary markets because their superficial characteristics resemble those of secondary workers." Two kinds of discrimination seem important. There is discrimination "pure and simple" where employers simply dislike employing workers with certain characteristics. There is also "statistical discrimination." In this case, employers tend not to employ members of certain groups because their superficial characteristics seem to be statistically associated with undesirable behavioral traits like unreliability. As Doeringer and Piore [1971] are careful to note, of course, many workers in the secondary market will work stably despite the extent to which their jobs encourage instability.

Third, the distinction between sectors is not so much technologically as historically determined. Many kinds of work can be technologically performed in either sector. "Work normally performed in the primary sector is sometimes shifted to the secondary sector through subcontracting, temporary help services, recycling of new employees through probationary periods" and so on. Different jobs within the same plant can share the characteristics of either or both sectors. But once jobs come to be rooted in one sector or another, through a process of historical or institutional evolution, "shifts in the distribution [of jobs between sectors] generally involve changes in the techniques of production and management and in the institutional structure and procedures of the enterprises in which the work is performed." Since these changes are difficult and expensive they are infrequently made.

Fourth, "the behavioral traits associated with the secondary sector are reinforced by the process of working in secondary jobs and living among others whose life style is accommodated to that type of employment." Those who are channeled into the secondary sector as a result of discrimination "tend, over time, to develop the traits predominant among secondary workers." This grows both from work patterns on the job and from life style in the ghetto or in the family.[d]

Finally, a wide variety of historical forces have interacted to increase the likelihood of sharp separations between the two markets. (The following hypotheses draw largely from Piore [1968] and Doeringer and Piore [1971].) The increasing importance of skills acquired through on-the-job training has raised the incentive to employers to retain some (stable) employees, and has tended to create a division between those jobs and other jobs which do not require such employee retention. Trade union organization and federal social welfare legislation may have "operated in the postwar period to sharpen the distinction between stable and unstable jobs." The rise of federal social legislation—and particularly of minimum wages, "the income ceiling upon the tax base of social insurance programs, the ceiling on the tax rate in the experience rating for unemployment insurance taxation, and the limited coverage of the legislation" [Piore, 1968, p. 26]—has tended to encourage employment stability in those industries affected because the "employer has an incentive to minimize the number of people on his annual payroll and avoid absenteeism, turnover, and fluctuations in demand which disperse the wage bill over a larger number of workers." [Piore, 1968, p. 26] The differential rise in union strength among different industries, and the differential industrial coverage under the National Labor Relations Act also tend

---

[d]For instance, "reward and punishment in the work place are continually based upon personal relationships between worker and supervisor" in the secondary sector. In that setting, "workers forget how to operate within the impersonal, institutional grievance procedures of the primary sector and when they do gain access to primary jobs, are frustrated by the failure of the system to respond on a personal basis and their own inability to make it respond on an institutional basis."

to separate industries into those with stable and those with unstable work arrangements. And most important, the interactions between the process of economic growth and the changing behavioral characteristics of disadvantaged workers have accentuated these trends. Disadvantaged workers, especially those recently off the farm, have always had trouble responding to the discipline required of them in industrial organizations. That transition was traditionally abetted by the "stick" of the sharp penalties attached to unemployment and the "carrot" of the example of successful transition by previously assimilated groups. As Piore writes [1968, pp. 28, 29-30]:

Earlier migrants made their transition at a time when the penalties for unstable work habits were more severe. Public welfare programs have since reduced the cost of life without work and rising wage levels the threat which unemployment, especially temporary unemployment, poses to subsistence. . . . The completion, by a greater and greater portion of the total labor force of the transition to industrial work, combined with the effects of union organization and social welfare legislation, has tended to create a discontinuity along the spectrum. If workers (and jobs) of intermediate stability have not been completely eliminated, their numbers relative to those with unstable work habits may have been greatly reduced. This implies, in turn, a decline in the alternative behavioral models to which the very unstable are exposed and in the number of social groups that can serve as waystations in their transition to stable life styles. For Negroes, suburbanization combined with segregated housing patterns may have had an even stronger adverse impact upon the contacts necessary for the development of stable work habits.

This analysis would also apply to women (although the dual market analysts refer to the employment problems of women only implicitly). Women are much less able than previously "disadvantaged" workers to identify with "advantaged" workers and to follow their model in the transition to stable work. Further, the social defintion of family and sex roles continues to undercut employment stability among women. And, as the percentage of women in the labor force continues to increase, some employers seem more and more likely to move many jobs into the secondary market in response to the (expected) behavioral characteristics of secondary women employees.

In their book, Doeringer and Piore [1971] elaborate many of the institutional forces within the firm which tend to produce highly "structured" internal labor markets, characteristic of the primary sector, and tend also to widen the gap between those markets and "unstructured" secondary markets. They especially emphasize trends tending to increase the skill specificity of primary jobs, the importance of on-the-job training as a medium for skill acquisition, and the influence of custom (and intra-firm sociological forces) on internal labor market procedures. They argue that the historical interaction of factors which orthodox economists normally hold constant—like technology, custom, job structure, worker preferences, and labor force composition—helps explain the separation of markets, and through that separation the different behavior of individuals within each market [1971]:

Employment in the secondary labor market fails to provide the kinds of job security, wages, and working conditions required to stabilize the work relationship. This may occur because employers in the secondary sector cannot economically establish internal labor market conditions which are conducive to reducing turnover or because the technical aspects of the jobs are such that the reduction of turnover has little value to the employer. Second, the attitude and demographic traits of the secondary labor force may be such that workers place little value upon job security in particular enterprises. These two explanations, while examined separately, are not independent. Unstable and undesirable jobs may encourage workers to place low value upon job security while a work force prone to turnover may make the costs of reducing turnover prohibitively high.

Both Bluestone [1970] and Harrison [1972] further emphasize the probable importance of the sources of the hypothesized dichotomization in a changing industrial structure. Highly-concentrated industries can afford to pay higher wages, develop more highly-structured internal labor markets, and invest more in workers' training because they can pass on their costs to consumers. Their profits are relatively untouched, according to this argument, by the expensive requisites of market structure in the primary sector.

General Hypotheses

The concrete postulates of the dual labor market theory suggest some more general hypotheses about income determination and distribution in the United States. These general hypotheses are central in helping elucidate this theory's relation to the other two competing paradigms.[e]

According to the theory, a variety of social and economic forces have tended over time to produce a dichotomization of the American labor market. Given that historical separation, one must analyze the determination and distribution of income in two separate stages. At the first stage, one must explain the distribution of workers between the primary and the secondary labor markets. Given a central hypothesis that there is very little inter-sectoral mobility in the course of individual labor market careers, one should be able to approximate the present distribution of workers between markets by projecting the distribution

[e]This summary of general hypotheses has been inferred from the several separate discussions of the dual labor market theory. The hypotheses seem to me to arise logically from the theory's specific observations about the labor market. They are being offered here as hypotheses which might be tested empirically, not as conclusions drawn from specific empirical research. Their relation to reality and to the hypotheses of the other paradigms will be discussed in Part 3. This set of inferential hypotheses relies especially on Doeringer and Piore [1971].

of workers between sectors as they begin their careers. A worker's first job in the labor force, in other words, should predict the sector in which he presently works with some accuracy. (Dual market analysts would admit, it appears, that white males may be able to move out of secondary jobs they hold as teenagers.) According to nearly every version of the theory, finally, race and sex will probably serve as fairly accurate predictors of inter-sectoral allocation as workers enter the market. Both minority group workers and women are much more likely to begin their careers in the secondary sector than white males. Years of schooling may also constitute an important predictor of inter-sectoral allocation upon labor market entry. Since more and more Americans are continuing in school beyond the high school diploma, one might speculate that those who drop out of school before college are increasingly likely to appear to employers as potentially unstable employees.

At the second stage of the analysis, one must develop different behavioral models to explain the determination and distribution of income within each of the two markets, for the interaction of job and worker characteristics in each market over time has fostered different kinds of worker behavior and personality traits in the respective sectors. One should not propose—the dual market theory seems to suggest—a single set of behavioral hypotheses for both markets. The attitudes, personality traits, and behavioral rules to which individuals in either sector conform will probably differ widely. Although dual market analysts have not yet developed the separate sectoral models very fully, one can begin to sketch the rough skeleton of their general hypotheses for each.

In the primary market, the dual market theory would suggest, individuals' incomes are largely determined by their respective access to different job clusters, by the relatively rigid pattern of wages attached to the job structures through which they respectively move, and by the speed with which they pass through those structures. Differential access to internal job structures is mediated primarily by relative years of formal schooling, the influence of which derives as much from the role of education as a screening device—as a way of saving money on more complicated search, screening, and hiring procedures—as it does from its direct influence on worker "productivity." The wage patterns attached to varying job structures depend primarily on the historical influence of technological change and labor market custom—both manifested through internal "job evaluations" more than through external price influences; the influence of external economic forces of supply and demand is much less pronounced. The speed at which workers move through the job structures depends primarily on their attitudes and on the state of economic conditions, much less on worker merit or productivity in its narrow traditional sense. Everything else equal, workers' wages will tend to increase with age as the simple effect of institutional seniority privileges, fixed through bargaining and custom.

In the secondary market, variations in total individual incomes are likely to depend more heavily on variations in hours than in wages, for variations in the former will be large and variations in the latter are likely to be extremely slight. Employers act as if all present and potential employees have more or less equal productivities—or, in more classical terms, as if secondary labor is homogeneous—and behave as if employee turnover is costless. As a result, wages will generally not reflect variations in individual characteristics but will be largely determined by the aggregate balance of supply and demand in the secondary market. Wages will also tend, consequently, to gravitate toward some homogeneous wage level, dampening wage variations among workers in that sector. Given this aggregate sectoral wage level, individual income will depend primarily on the number of hours worked, while variations in individual hourly wages will depend very little on variations in individual "capacities" like aptitude, reasoning, and vocational skill. Individual hourly wages will increase very little with steady employment at the same job; if they do increase, they increase mainly as a result of historically-determined seniority scales within secondary job clusters rather than as a result of "productivity" increases from experience or on-the-job training. Labor supply functions are relatively indeterminate. Workers make decisions about turnover fairly capriciously, depending on their moods, their personal relations on the job and with the employer, and their inclinations toward alternative income sources. Their supply decisions depend only slightly on wage variations, primarily because those variations are usually so slight. Their supply decisions probably do depend quite directly, however, on the relationship between their family size and their total household income; those with relatively larger families and lower household incomes, *ceteris paribus*, may tend to work longer hours if they can.

Although the dual labor market theory seems sufficiently coherent to permit these concrete hypotheses about income determination and distribution, many pieces of the theory remain less certain. Several different kinds of questions are raised directly by the structure of the theory and have often been raised by its critics. Some mention of these questions seems useful, for they help clarify the boundaries of the theory and its relation to both radical and orthodox views.

First, the dual labor market theory places great emphasis on job stability as a source and an index of the division between the two markets. This difference between markets is only approximate, however, for not all workers in the primary market labor steadily at a single job and many secondary workers stay with a single job all their lives. Simple measures of job stability will not suffice to capture the distinctions between markets. The nature of the hypothesized separation seems more complicated and therefore more difficult to test. The separation arises from differences in the *potential* rewards for job stability—both objectively and as mediated by subjective evaluation. However intractable, some decent measures of this more precise formulation of the differences between sectors will be necessary in order to make very precise tests of the theory. (See D.M. Gordon [1971b] for some further discussion of this issue.)

Second, dual market analysts have not yet reached very firm agreement about the relationship between the job and individual composition of the two sectors. In some instances, analysts suggest that the division corresponds only to differences in job characteristics and that the inter-sectoral distribution of individuals in various groups—like race and sex groups—does not provide a very accurate picture of the dual market structure. Although many minority group workers, women, and teens work in secondary jobs, in other words, this view suggests that the intra-sectoral composition of workers can be fairly heterogeneous. In contrast, some others seem to equate the dual market structure with occupational segregation by demographic characteristics. According to this view, those jobs which are dominated by minority group workers, women, and teens are secondary jobs, while those jobs dominated by prime-age white males comprise the pool of primary jobs. One assumes that some balance between these two views will emerge, but the contours of that consensus have not yet grown evident.

A third and related problem concerns questions of emphasis. In some formulations of the dual labor market theory—especially some of the pieces contributed by Piore [1968, 1969, 1970]—heavy emphasis has been placed on the historical importance of changing individual attitudes as a primary source of the emergent dualism. In some other discussions—especially in Bluestone [1970]—emphasis has been placed primarily on the role of changing industrial and job structure as a primary source of the dichotomization. Once again, both suggestions seem important and one expects some resolution of the differences in emphasis to unfold.

Finally, the dual labor market theory poses a challenge which economists have not yet begun to meet. Its most important hypotheses are explicitly historical; they concern the dynamics and dialectics of changes in jobs, people, and labor market operations over a period of fifty or more years. Most of these hypotheses have not arisen from historical research, however, but have been adduced from local labor market investigation and cross-sectional analysis. The dual labor market theory suggests a methodology, in other words, which its proponents have not been applying in its conception. This problem will also be confronted very soon, I suspect, as more economists turn to historical research for the answers they seek.

While the dual labor market theory is currently providing some useful perceptual tools for the study of poverty and underemployment, it may have a short half-life as an integral paradigm in economics. Many of those who helped develop the theory have begun to incorporate it into a more general radical framework, convinced that the dual market hypotheses can be generated by radical theory and that radical theory provides some important historical foundations for the specific conclusions of dual market analysis. A number of orthodox economists have also begun to incorporate the dual market perspective into their own work, developing a series of orthodox explanations for the dual market structure and some projections of its implications. Some of the dimensions of these attempts at incorporation will be discussed in Part 3.

5 Radical Economic Theory

There has been a resurging interest over the past few years in radical and Marxist economics, especially in the United States. Many economists—notably a group of younger economists working through the Union for Radical Political Economics—have begun to develop and shape a paradigm which seeks directly to confront the reigning ideas of orthodox economic theory. Radical economic theory—or radical political economics, as it is also called—has not yet been pulled together into a fully embellished theoretical system. Individual strands of radical economic analysis have begun to interweave, but many of the features of the eventual fabric have not become entirely clear. So far, much of the analysis has not even been precisely formulated, much yet published; it continues to flow through conversations, letters, and unpublished notes.

And yet, however confusing this emerging analysis may appear, it seems to constitute a self-contained scientific paradigm in both of the senses in which Thomas Kuhn applies his concept. As I argued in chapter 2 above, radical economists have begun to share both a broader "disciplinary matrix" and some specific analogical "exemplars" which frame their work. The radical paradigm draws heavily on a precedent Marxist tradition, but it has molded and recast classical Marxism in response to modern social and historical developments; much of the classical Marxist methodology has been retained while some of the substantive generalizations of nineteenth-century Marxism have been revised to fit current realities.[a] Both some general radical constructs and a variety of specific applications have begun to emerge from this effort.

As radical economics has been developing, the problems of urban poverty and underemployment have drawn considerable attention. Gradually over the past several years, radical economists have tried to apply the nascent radical paradigm to explain the current phenomena of ghetto employment problems. Many of

---

[a]It seems important to emphasize some of the principal differences between the more recent radical analysis and an older Marxism which seemed to crest in the 1930s. The older Marxist literature spent much of its time arguing about the specific content of Marx's own work, worrying about the internal contradictions of *Das Kapital* and doggedly debating the political implications of different interpretations of the master's work. The more recent tradition seems to be concentrating on an application of the basic Marxist or radical framework toward an understanding of current social and economic problems. Many in the more recent tradition share Ernest Mandel's criticisms of the old [1968, pp. 15, 17]: "The fact is that, for nearly fifty years, Marxists have been content to repeat Marx's teaching, in summaries of *Capital* which have increasingly lost contact with contemporary reality." He laments the "inability of the Marxists to repeat in the second half of the twentieth century the work that Marx carried through in the nineteenth."

those who were making these applications at the end of the last decade tended to accept the dual labor market's description of and specific hypotheses about the behavioral processes of the ghetto (or "secondary") labor market. Their efforts concentrated on moving beyond the dual market theory, trying to establish the connections between that concrete piece of analysis and the broader context of radical political economics.

In order to relate that effort to the analyses of the two competing paradigms, I have organized this chapter on radical theories of poverty and underemployment in three sections. The first provides some general notes on the kind of methodology underlying radical political economics; there has been frequent misunderstanding of the radical analysis because its methodological framework has been misinterpreted. The second section outlines the general values, models, and inclinations of the radical "disciplinary matrix," developing those principal features of radical political economics which frame its specific application to the problems of poverty and underemployment. The third section sketches a number of specific hypotheses about the historical dynamics of American capitalism which suggest some obvious explanations of the present problems of poverty and underemployment. These hypotheses constitute a direct application of the more general paradigm to a specific set of developments.[b]

Methodology

Radical economists work within a central methodological framework provided by *dialectical materialism*. Some useful expositions of this framework are easily accessible (see, for instance, Cornforth [1968]), but some serious misconceptions about the methodology remain.

The first concerns the complexity of analysis which a materialist framework permits. Trying to counter impressions of what they often call "vulgar Marxism," radicals argue that it is impossible to develop a simple, historically permanent and universally determinant theory about economy and society. As societies change, so must theories about society change. The economic mode of production plays a determinant role in economic history, according to general radical perspectives, but economic and social relationships are always *specified* in their historical contexts; economic relationships can never be abstracted from those concrete manifestations. The "superstructure" of an individual society, as Marx and Engels first called it—the society's customs, religions, and politics, for instance—will affect both the relative importance *and* the form of the economic

---

[b]This chapter is somewhat longer than the summaries of the other perspectives for two reasons. Much of the analysis in this chapter has not been pulled together, first of all, and much of it is undoubtedly unfamiliar to the reader. Second, many of the hypotheses advanced in the third section represent my own, relatively original attempt to develop the radical model; as original contributions, they require somewhat more exposition. Needless to say, there has been some exaggeration of the coherence and consensus inherent in the radical paradigm throughout this chapter. Just as there are some important areas of disagreement within the orthodox and the dual labor market perspectives, so are there some important differences within the radical view. Points of essential agreement have been emphasized here.

determinants. Engels himself argued against the mindless economic determinism of many following Marx. "The economic situation is the basis," Engels noted [Marx and Engels, *Selected Works*, II, 1951, pp. 488-89], "but the various elements of the superstructure . . . also exercise their influence upon the course of the historical struggles, and in many cases preponderate in determining their *form.* . . ." The economy is determinant only in the "last instance," Engels argued—and, as Althusser puts it [1970, p. 113], "From the first moment to the last the lonely hour of the 'last instance' never comes." Historical circumstances constantly change, changing with them the forms in which and the institutions through which the economic relationships are manifest. All history must be studied on its own terms, for, as Althusser asks [1970, p. 104], "are we not always in exceptional situations?"[c]

Given these cautionary methodological notes, one must formulate a radical theory of income determination and distribution—and, in the context of this book, its specific application to the analysis of poverty and underemployment—at two quite different levels of analysis. First, one must formulate some *general* hypotheses about the dynamic ways in which the economic mode of production is likely to affect the determination and distribution of income in any capitalist economy. One must then postulate a series of historically *specific* hypotheses about the process through which the relations of production have manifestly influenced the determination and distribution of income in a given instance, isolating those changes in the "superstructure" through which the influence of the relations of production has been mediated. The general hypotheses are *applied* to a specific historical situation, in effect, through a series of historically specific hypotheses.[d] The following two sections—the first on the general disciplinary matrix of radical theory and the second on the specific application of that framework—may be seen as an illustrative replication of those two stages of analysis.[e]

---

[c]Engels added [loc. cit.]: "Marx and I are ourselves partly to blame for the fact that the younger people sometimes lay more stress on the economic side than is due to it. We had to emphasize the main principle vis-á-vis our adversaries, who denied it, and we had not always the time, the place, or the opportunity to allow the other elements involved in the interaction to come into their rights."

[d]Engels spoke [loc. cit.] of Marx's *applications* of the general theory in exactly the same methodological sense, referring particularly to works like *The 18th Brumaire . . .* [1963a].

[e]An analogy with the methodology of post-Freudian psychoanalysis might help clarify these general methodological points. After Freud, there was some danger that Freud's work would gradually be distorted by a kind of "vulgar Freudianism," by a literal, mechanistic, and simplistically deterministic application of his basic theories. Erik Erikson has tried to rescue psychoanalysis from that kind of application, arguing forcefully that one cannot apply the psychoanalytic perspective without studying the ways in which a society's culture (in its broadest sense) mediates some general psychological tendencies. In Erikson's view, as it were, the cultural "superstructure" *specifies* the relative importance of personal psychology and the forms in which the subconscious affects personality development. Thus, Erikson insisted that the personality development of American Indians be understood exclusively in terms of their own cultural history—rather than in terms of "Western" cultural history and some psychological categories rooted in the Western tradition. See especially Erikson's *Childhood and Society* [rev. ed., 1968] and Coles [1970].

The second misconception has involved a distorted view of "dialectical" analysis, with its focus on "contradictions" as driving social forces. Many critics of Marxist analysis have conventionally misunderstood the different levels of analysis at which and the intentions with which radicals have applied their study of contradictions. They have taken Marx's classic hypotheses about the inherent contradictions of nineteenth century capitalism as the singular example of analysis through the dialectical framework. Two consequent distortions of that analysis illustrate the central problems. First, fixed and universal schema of dialectical analysis cannot be applied to each and every social situation; Marx's analysis was conditioned upon a particular social reality and a particular level of study. As Cornforth writes [1968, pp. 95-96] :

We can never deduce what will happen in any particular case, or how a particular process can be controlled, from the universal idea of contradiction. . . . the dialectical method does not consist in applying some preconceived scheme to the interpretation of everything, but consists in basing conclusions only on the 'concrete analysis of concrete conditions.'

Each kind of process has its own dialectic, which can be grasped only by the detailed study of that particular process.

The intent of dialectical analysis is also frequently misperceived. An examination of contradictions in social processes does not permit any definitive predictions about the outcomes of those events. Contradictions may be resolved in society in many different ways. The importance of the analysis lies in its implication that the social processes cannot continue indefinitely in their present form; some qualitative change seems likely to occur. Although one can begin to isolate those contradictory forces which seem likely to generate change, one cannot forecast the character of the new, qualitatively different contradictions which will characterize the processes unfolding from the "resolution" of the original contradiction—at least not with perfect foresight and unerring accuracy.

The Disciplinary Matrix

Radical economists begin from six clusters of generalizations or hypotheses about capitalist economies. The radical theory of income determination and distribution cannot adequately be understood without first understanding these basic components of the disciplinary matrix defining the radical paradigm.[1]

Modes of Production

Every economic mode of social organization since primitive times has been characterized by a *social division of labor*, by a division of work responsibilities among different social groups. This social division of labor is determined through, and society is therefore characterized by, the society's *mode of production*. The mode of production reflects the social relations of production in an economy. As Tucker puts it [1969, p. 14] , ". . . inasmuch as the social relations of production have so far in history been successive forms of the division of labor in production, the various historical modes of production may be described as forms of productive activity within the division of labor." In ancient society the mode of production was slave labor, in feudal society it was serf labor, and in capitalist society it is wage labor. Dobb further elaborates the definition [1963, p. 7] : "By mode of production Marx did not refer merely to the state of technique—to what he termed the state of productive forces—but to the way in which the means of production were owned and to the social relations between men which resulted from their connections with the process of production."

Classes and Class Conflict

The social division of labor, characterized by social relations of production, creates a division of society into economic classes. These classes inevitably clash with each other, and the course of history is determined through the growth and resolution of class conflict. Despite the absolutely central role of class in the Marxist and radical tradition, however, the concept of class has been rather inconsistently defined. In the writings of Marx and Engels in particular, as Ossowski points out [1963, p. 71] , the concept has a fairly "variable denotation." For the purposes of this discussion, it seems important to clarify the two predominant senses in which radical theory deploys the concept of class.

First, following Marx, radicals argue that economic classes are defined *objectively* by the social relations of production. Groups of individuals sharing the same functions within the process of production constitute an *objectively-defined class*, as it were, despite themselves. (Marx called this a *Klasse an sich*.) "In the social production which men carry on," Marx wrote, "they enter into definite relations that are indispensable and independent of their will." [Quoted in Bottomore, 1966, p. 14] As Marx and Engels amplified this meaning of class in another context [*The German Ideology*, 1963, p. 49] , ". . . the class in its turn achieves an independent existence over against the individuals, so that the latter find their conditions of existence predestined, and hence have their position in life and their personal development assigned to them by their class, become subsumed under it." The central import of this concept of objectively-defined class is that an individual's economic class constrains his activities whether or not he is aware of his membership in that economic group. In that the members of a given class share objectively-determined common circumstances and activities, they also share common economic interests (in strictly objective terms), for the economic rewards accruing to any individual within a class will depend in part on the total share captured by his class in competition with other classes. To quote Marx once more [*The 18th Brumaire* . . . , 1963a, pp. 124], "In so far as millions of families live under economic conditions of existence that separate their mode of life, their interests, and their culture from those of other classes, and put them in hostile contrast to the latter, they form a class."

Second, radicals argue that an economic class does not fully constitute a class until its members develop *subjective* identification with the class. Marx helps evoke the importance of this concept of *subjectively-defined class (Klasse für sich)* in *The Poverty of Philosophy* [1963b, p. 173] :

Economic conditions had first transformed the mass of the people of the country into workers. The domination of capital has created for this mass a common situation, common interests. This mass is thus already a class as against capital, but not yet for itself. In the struggle . . . this mass becomes united, and constitutes itself as a class for itself. The interests it defines become class interests. But the struggle of class against class is a political struggle.

Ossowski concludes his summary of Marx's analysis of class [1963, p. 139] :

. . . Marx, in calling a class without class consciousness a 'stratum' or a 'class in itself' . . . in contrast to a 'class for itself' . . . , was expressing his conviction that a class fully deserves the name of 'class' only if members are conscious of class interests and feel class solidarity.

These two definitions of class play complementary roles in the development of radical theory. The relative emphasis with which each is applied depends in part on the historical sweep of the analysis. On the one hand, for instance, radicals may choose to concentrate on the role of class conflict in the long-run change from one mode of production to another. Since such conflicts began in primitive societies, the principal class division in society has involved the struggle between those who own the means of production and those who do not. With the very early development of social cooperation in production and with primitive technological innovation, individual men first become capable of producing more with their own labor than is necessary to sustain themselves and their families. They begin to produce a "surplus product." At different stages in different societies, a single ruling class, the owners of property, appropriate some of the surplus product of the producing class, providing for their own luxury, living off the surplus product of those whose labor they control. Through this appropriation, class division inevitably becomes class conflict. Mandel writes [1968, p. 175] :

The producers have never accepted as normal or natural that the surplus product of their labour should be seized by the possessing classes, who thus obtain a monopoly of leisure and culture. . . . The history of mankind is nothing but a long succession of class struggles.

On the other hand, one can concentrate on various class divisions within a specific historical epoch, given a specific mode of production. At this level, depending on historical circumstances, one can conceivably identify many economic classes, "each competing for power in a society with a multi-divisional structure." [Ossowski, 1963, p. 84] These struggles do not necessarily focus exclusively on the division of economic product, for they may involve conflict about the conditions of work or the structure of institutions. They may develop, as Ossowski puts it [1963, p. 84], as "struggles between classes with different interests . . . antagonisms which are not confined to situations in which the appropriation of the 'surplus value' is involved." In the objective sense, Marx would label these groups, divided from each other by their relations to the process of production, as "strata."

At either level of analysis, radicals emphasize that social class structure and class conflict must be viewed as dynamic processes rather than as static outcomes. As Bendix and Lipset conclude in their analysis of Marx's theory of social classes [1966, p. 9], "This . . . makes it apparent that Marx thought of social class as a condition of group-life which was constantly generated (rather than simply given) by the organization of production." E.P. Thompson has provided the clearest recent statement of this dynamic perspective [1966, pp. 9-10, emphasis in the original] :

By class I understand an historical phenomenon, unifying a number of disparate and seemingly unconnected events, both in the raw material of experience and in consciousness. I emphasize that it is an *historical* phenomenon. I do not see class as a 'structure,' nor even as a 'category,' but as something which in fact happens (and can be shown to have happened) in human relationships.

More than this, the notion of class entails the notion of historical relationship. Like any other relationship, it is a fluency which evades analysis if we attempt to stop it dead at any given moment and anatomise its structure. . . . The relationship must always be embodied in real people and in a real context. . . . We can see a *logic* in the responses of similar experiences, but we cannot predicate any *law*. Consciousness of class arises in the same way in different times and places, but never in just the same way.

Two notes should be added to help clarify the use of the concept of class. First, Marx's notion that capitalism could be viewed increasingly as divided into two (rather than many) classes represented an analytic prediction, based on a series of historical assumptions, the fulfillment of which did not pose an ultimate test of the viability of the concept of class itself. One can use the Marxian concept of class and class consciousness to analyze an historic past which witnessed several classes, and equally to predict the rise or continued presence of many economic classes in the future. Second, it is also unnecessary to document a total and overriding class consciousness among the capitalist class to assert their existence as a class. Based on their objective role in society, and on the manifold ways in which their existence is supported by "system-defining" institutions, capitalists constitute a class whether they have all developed full class consciousness or not. (See Edwards, MacEwan et al. [1970] for some further comments on this point.)

Given these definitions of class, radicals suggest that the evolution of society—of its relations of production and its "system-defining institutions"—can most fruitfully be analyzed in terms of the dynamics of class conflict, in terms of the dialectics of struggle among classes with opposing interests. The very structure of the relations of production themselves may change over time in response to the balance of power among several different economic interests. Those structures cannot be taken as "data" but must be analyzed themselves in order to understand the behavior of individuals or of individual classes.

The Drive for Capital Accumulation

In their analyses of the dynamic development of capitalist societies, radicals pay special attention to a central driving force—the unceasing attempt by owners of capital continuously to increase their absolute and relative share of capital by nearly any means. The forces of competition among capitalists, whether among small independent shopkeepers or corporate giants, inevitably spur owners of capital to protect themselves against their competitors by producing more goods and accumulating more and more profit. Marx sometimes referred to this drive for accumulation as the "werewolf hunger" of capitalists. As Mandel describes it [1968, p. 133, emphasis in the original], "the capitalist mode of production thus becomes the first mode of production in the history of mankind the essential aim of which appears to be *unlimited increase in production.* . . ." Because this dominates the priorities of the society, as Edwards, MacEwan et al. put it [1970, p. 356], "human needs become subordinated to the needs of the market and to capital expansion."

System-defining Institutions

In any society, no matter what its mode of production, a basic set of system-defining institutions, rooted in the relations of production, helps define and determine the nature and content of social relations among individuals in that society. In capitalist societies, the most important and most distinctive feature of the mode of production is its organization of labor by means of the wage-contract. As Dobb writes [1963, p. 7]:

Thus capitalism was not simply a system of production for the market—a system of commodity-production as Marx termed it—but a system under which labour-power had 'itself become a commodity' and was bought and sold on the market like any other object of exchange. Its historical prerequisite was the concentration of ownership of the means of production in the hands of a class, consisting of only a minor section of society, and the consequential emergence of a propertyless class for whom the sale of their labour-power was their only source of livelihood. Productive activity was furnished, accordingly by the latter, not by virtue of legal compulsion, but on the basis of a wage-contract.

Recent anthropological evidence has made clear that this basic organization of work and labor originated historically with capitalist societies, that antecedent societies organized work in different ways. (See especially Polanyi [1968].) Writing about this singular characteristic of production in capitalist societies, Marx himself said [*The Class Struggles in France* . . ., 1967b, p. 46], "Without it [there is] no capital, no bourgeoisie, no bourgeois society."

In addition to this central institution, Edwards, MacEwan et al. isolate four other system-defining institutions in capitalist societies [1970, p. 353]:

. . . control of the work process by those who own and control capital, including the concomitant loss of control by the worker over his activities during the hours of work; the legal relations of ownership, by which income distribution is determined through payments to owners for the use of their productive factors; *homo economicus*, the system of personality traits characteristic of and functional to capitalism, including especially the system of individual gain incentives; and the ideology which abstracts and organizes 'reality' in such a way as to justify and facilitate the operation of the other institutions.

Together these institutions frame the specific historical processes through which different capitalist societies develop. They also considerably reinforce the power of the owners of property to fulfill their basic objectives.

The State

The state, in the radical view, operates ultimately to serve the interests of the controlling class in a class society. Since the "capitalist" class fundamentally controls capitalist societies, the state functions in capitalist societies to serve that class.[2] It does so either directly, by providing services only to members of that class, or indirectly, and probably more frequently, by helping preserve and support the system of basic institutions which support and maintain the power of that class. In general, as Sweezy summarizes the radical view, the state may fulfill those roles in three ways [1968, p. 249]:

In the first place, the state comes into action in the economic sphere in order to solve the problems which are posed by the development of capitalism. In the second place, where the interests of the capitalist class are concerned, there is a strong predisposition to use the state power freely. And, finally, the state may be used to make concessions to the working class provided that the consequences of not doing so are sufficiently dangerous to the stability and functioning of the system as a whole.

Edwards, MacEwan et al. clarify the essentially passive manner in which the state is able to fulfill its functions in a mature capitalist society [1970, p. 359] :

If, as according to our hypothesis, the state is dominated by the capitalist class, then the operations of the state should reflect the needs of the capitalist class. In modern capitalist states, when the basic institutions have been thoroughly established, the maintenance and preservation of these institutions upon which the structure of class and privilege depends is of the greatest importance to the capitalist class. The uninhibited operation of the economic institutions will continue to bestow power, wealth, and prestige upon the capitalists. They do not need the state to enhance their position, only to assure it.

Internal Contradictions

The specific evolution of capitalist societies is heavily influenced by three internal contradictions, by three instances of an historical tendency which generates a contradictory historical tendency so fundamentally in conflict with that initial trend that some kind of qualitatively new historical process must develop. The nature of the ultimate resolution cannot be anticipated a priori, but depends on the specific dynamics of the concrete situation.

1. In the Marxist view, man achieves his fullest self-realization through work, through production, through the creative development and application of all his capacities. Increasingly in capitalist societies, man is denied this self-realization by the progressive division of labor. Owners of capital, locked in competition, seek constantly to improve efficiency and increase their control over the work process by mechanization and specialization within the process of production. Instead of providing opportunities for workers' "all-round development," as Marx put it, the capitalist dynamic tends increasingly to transform the "worker into a crippled monstrosity, by forcing his detail dexterity at the expense of a world of productive capabilities and instincts. . . ." [Marx, *Capital*, I, 1967a, p. 360]

As the division of labor proceeds, radicals hypothesize, man becomes increasingly alienated from his product, increasingly oppressed by the contradiction between the constraints of specialization and his desire for creative, unspecialized production. The one process—the division of labor—creates an opposing process—the increasing dissatisfaction of workers with their lives in production. As Marx put it [*Capital* I, 1969b, p. 645], the divisions of labor in capitalism "multilate the labourer into a fragment of a man, degrade him to the level of an appendage of a machine, destroy every remnant of charm in his work and turn it into a hated toil. . . ." The sociologist William Foote Whyte has put the problem succinctly [quoted in Bell, 1960, p. 244] : "The satisfactions of craftsmanship are gone, and we can never call them back. If these were the only satisfactions men could get out of their immediate work, their work would certainly be a barren experience."

This contradiction requires some kind of resolution, for the workers cannot continue their increasing dissatisfaction forever. Marx had predicted that it would result in the revolution of the proletariat. One could equally predict that capitalists will attempt increasingly and continuously to provide compensatory satisfaction for workers, especially through their lives as consumers. As Herbert Gintis has argued [1970a], for instance, the "dialectics of economic growth" provide the constant promise to workers that their own or their childrens' futures will provide them with more goods and therefore with greater happiness, making up for their present unhappiness. The resolution of the contradiction obviously depends on its specific historical manifestation, on the development of class consciousness and the relative strength of different classes.

2. Through the quest for accumulation, capitalists develop increasingly complex productive institutions. These institutions lead more and more to what Mandel calls the "objective socialization of production." Men no longer work individually, producing for their own needs. The division of labor, the evolution of corporate structures, and the expansion of markets under capitalism all effect an increasing interdependence among men as producers. Mandel writes [1968, p. 170] : "The work of each is indispensable to the survival of all, so that each can survive only thanks to the work of thousands and thousands of other men."

But this objective interdependence creates a complementary and ultimately contradictory requirement. If capitalists are to retain their fundamental power, they must try to prevent objective interdependence among workers from generating subjective cooperation against capitalists; if such cooperation developed, if classes attained a *subjective definition*, then the joint power of workers might threaten the privileges of capitalists. So, in various ways, capitalist institutions encourage an individualistic ideology, based on individual gain incentives and frequently ruthless competition among individuals. Brought into objective relationships of social cooperation in production, men are induced subjectively to compete against those with whom they cooperate.

Increasingly, in short, workers cooperate and compete at the same time. Some kind of resolution becomes increasingly necessary to dissolve the heightening tensions of that contradiction. On the one hand, workers might try, as Marx predicted, cooperatively to seize the control of the means of production so that competition among classes was more or less eliminated. On the other hand, in quite different ways, one could predict that workers (or potential workers) might try to avoid the tensions by avoiding the cooperative work process all together. In an overwhelmingly competitive world, they might try to avoid the tensions of objectively cooperating in work with others against whom they must also compete. They might "drop out," bumming for a living or seeking to work at crafts by themselves.

3. In capitalist societies, enormous increases in social wealth finally create the possibility that class conflict could cease. Society begins to produce enough so that *everyone* in society could acquire opportunities for leisure and creative activity. Mandel explains this development clearly [1968, p. 177]:

> It is the capitalist mode of production that, by the extraordinary advance of the productive forces which it makes possible, creates for the first time in history the economic conditions needed for the abolition of class society altogether. The social surplus product would suffice to reduce extensively the working time of all men, which would ensure an advance of culture that would enable functions of accumulation (and management) to be exercised by the whole of society.

√ But capitalists depend on the preservation of class privilege in order continuously to maintain or increase their relative shares. Given their basic power within the context of capitalist institutions, they are able roughly to maintain their privileges and their share of surplus product. Workers become more and more conscious of the gap between their actual standards of living and their potential standards of living under more egalitarian distributions. (Sociologists have installed this notion as the concept of relative deprivation.) The basic contradiction between the size of the pie and its distribution—between the actual leisure of a few and the potential leisure of nearly all—intensifies, and some resolution of the contradiction seems necessary.[3] On the one hand, workers may rebel, as Marx predicted, and eradicate the contradiction by providing everyone equal shares according to need. On the other hand, to pick another kind of potential resolution, the quality of life available for consumption through leisure may deteriorate so rapidly that leisure becomes a relatively unattractive good of which lower classes are not quite so jealous. Through externalities like noise and pollution, the quality of life may grow so undesirable for everyone—including the "leisure class"—that class competition for that undesirable good tends to diminish.

All of these general hypotheses frame the formulation of a general radical theory of income determination and distribution. According to orthodox theory, as noted above, wage equals marginal product in equilibrium, and the distribution of wages corresponds to the distribution of marginal products. In radical theory, there are two stages to the determination and distribution of income. First, a complex set of individual, social, economic, and technological forces determines an individual worker's productivity (expressed as average productivity) on a specific job. This average productivity varies both with the worker's "capacities" and with the characteristics of his job. Second, the relative power of employers and employees determines the share of the worker's total product paid to the worker in wages. He receives some of the product as wages and the employer receives the rest as surplus product. The worker's final wage thus depends *both* on his individual productivity *and* on the relative power of the class to which he belongs.

The radical theory thus combines the radical concept of class with orthodox notions of supply and demand. In many of the same ways as orthodox theory postulates, radical theory expects that supply and demand, reinforced to a certain extent by the forces of competition, will affect an individual's productivity; the market price of a product, for instance, obviously affects the value of an individual's marginal product in the radical model just as it does in the orthodox model. But the radical model also postulates that the class division in society and the relative distribution of power among classes will affect the distribution of individual income as well. An individual's class, ultimately, will affect *both* his productivity, through the allocation of social resources to investment in the workers of his class and through the differential access of different classes to different kinds of complementary capital, *and* his relative share of final product.

As radicals emphasize again and again, the entire process is dynamic. Employers seek to affect two different kinds of variables, since they seek constantly either to increase or at least to maintain their relative share of total product: they hope both to increase their workers' average products, *ceteris paribus*, and to decrease (or hold down) their workers' share of that product. Workers seek to increase their income—and thus either to increase their relative productivities, *ceteris paribus*, or to increase their shares. The capitalist drive for accumulation and the internal contradictions of capitalism all bring continuous changes in the institutions of a given capitalist society. At the same time, continuous changes in a society's "superstructure" affect the distributions of productivity and of class power. At any moment, capitalists may find it in their collective long-run interest to intensify their exploitation of workers if they can, trying more rapidly to increase their share of total product. At another moment, capitalists may find it in their long-run interest to permit a slight increase in relative wages—in order to foster higher standards of living among workers, and, through better nutrition and health, develop more productive workers; in order to undercut worker dissatisfaction by allowing higher consumption; or in order to intensify competition among different classes of workers by allowing the relative shares of some classes to rise. The fact that capitalists compete with each other over product market shares does not obviate the simultaneous dynamic of their collective class interest. The relative shares of all capitalists are increased, for instance, if workers compete among themselves (along racial lines, to pick one possible dimension), rather than presenting united demands of the capitalists; if the state refuses to provide legislation enabling unionization; if the state fails to provide a decent income maintenance program so that some workers are still driven by what Weber called the "whip of hunger"; or if state-supported schools instill all workers with an orientation toward monetary rewards and with some general "productive" skills required in employment, especially if the schools are financed not by the capitalists alone but by all citizens.

Mandel captures some of the dynamic flavor of the radical model in the following passage [1968, p. 145] :

In fact, it is not the absolute level of wages that matters to capital. The latter prefers, certainly, that wages should be as low as possible in its own enterprises—but it wants at the same time to see wages as high as possible paid in competing enterprises or by the employers of its customers! What matters to capital is the possibility of extracting more surplus labour, more unpaid labour, more surplus value, more profit from its workers. The growth in the productivity of labour, which makes possible the growth of relative surplus value, implies the possibility of a slow rise in real wages . . on condition that the equivalent of these increased real wages is produced in an ever shorter period of time, i.e. that wages rise less quickly than productivity . . .

The rise in real wages does not follow *automatically* from the rise in the productivity of labour. The latter only creates the *possibility* of such a rise, within the capitalist framework, provided profit is not threatened. For this potential increase to become actual, two interlinked conditions are needed: a favorable evolution of relations of strength in the labour market . . . and effective organization . . . of the wage workers which enables them to abolish competition among themselves and so to take advantage of these "favourable market conditions."

The general radical theory can be further illustrated and described, but it cannot be further specified. In the abstract, the model is indeterminate because its specification depends on the flow and circumstances of history. As Sraffa [1960] and Bhaduri [1969] have pointed out, the orthodox model achieves a certain determinacy at the macro-level by fixing the "rate of exploitation" as a constant. The radical model argues that the "rate of exploitation" cannot be held constant but is determined by social forces just as clearly as the rate of profit and the wage rate—that it is all one big simultaneous system.[f] Further specification and determination of the model awaits discussion of a particular historical period; it depends both on the stage of capitalism being considered and on the "superstructure" of the society in question.

Advanced American Capitalism

I have attempted in this section to specify the general radical theory of income determination and distribution by formulating some hypotheses about the development of advanced American capitalism. The hypotheses cover roughly 100

---

[f]To quote Bhaduri [1969, p. 538], "Marx left open the question of how the rate of exploitation is determined. He viewed it himself in terms of the balance of class forces. . . ."

years of history, from 1870 to 1970. They are intended to help explain the process of income determination and distribution in the United States at present by deducing that process from a series of hypotheses about the ways in which the capitalist mode of production has developed in this country and the ways in which the American "superstructure" has influenced that development. I am offering these speculations as *hypotheses* rather than conclusions because they have not yet been "tested" historically. I believe, nonetheless, that we have sufficient historical evidence available to consider these hypotheses "reasonable." Where it seems appropriate, some of this evidence will be mentioned in passing.[g]

The hypotheses begin with the last third of the nineteenth century in the United States because capitalism in this country had not effectively reached its "industrial" phase until after the Civil War. The problems of the transition to capitalism were finally being solved, it appeared, and a new stage of advanced capitalism was being launched. I would argue, in general, that Maurice Dobb's characterization of late-nineteenth century England applies with roughly equal accuracy to the United States during the same period [1963, pp. 265-266] :

The survival into the second half of the nineteenth century of the conditions of domestic industry and of the manufactory had an important consequence for industrial life and the industrial population which is too seldom appreciated. It meant that not until the last quarter of the century did the working class begin to assume the homogeneous character of a factory proletariat. Prior to this, the majority of the workers retained the marks of the earlier period of capitalism, alike in their habits and interests, the nature of the employment relations and the circumstances of their exploitation. Capacity for enduring organization or long-sighted policies remained undeveloped; the horizon of interest was apt to be the trade and even the locality, rather than the class; and the survival of the individualist traditions of the artisan and the craftsman, with the ambition to become himself a small employer, was for long an obstacle to any firm and widespread growth of trade unionism, let alone of class consciousness. . . . As late as 1870 the immediate employer of many workers was not the large capitalist but the intermediate sub-contractor who was both an employee and in turn a small employer of labour. In fact the skilled worker of the middle nineteenth century tended to be in some measure a sub-contractor, and in psychology and outlook bore the marks of this status.

Not until the late-nineteenth century, that is, did American capitalism finally resemble the classical Marxist characterization: homogeneous and disciplined industrial labor and capitalist control over working conditions. A single *objectively-defined* class of workers was finally emerging, in the sense of the radical

---

[g]Most of these hypotheses obviously also apply to other advanced capitalist countries in one way or another. I have limited my remarks to the United States because I assume that the combination of events would have demanded different emphases, and that the "superstructural" influences in different societies would have effected different kinds of results.

theory, but the proletariat had not yet become a united *subjectively-defined* class.[h] Income was more or less determined as Marx described it: wages clearly depended in part on worker productivity, since either the piece-rate system or the wage bonus system was quite common in manufacturing;[4] and the relative share of the working class depended in large part on the size of the pool of surplus labor. Most jobs were fairly dirty and exhausting and, although the division of labor was proceeding apace, the skills required of workers were relatively "general" (in the orthodox sense) and did not require too much "specific" training on-the-job. Some mechanisms were being established, gradually, to ensure the steady assimilation into the disciplined industrial labor force of whatever steady streams of foreign (and typically "disadvantaged") workers were continuing to enter the country.

From that beginning point in the United States—from the last third of the nineteenth century—the epoch of what I am calling "advanced capitalism" was launched in the United States. As the advanced capitalist system evolved, several important (relatively independent) developments brought about some fundamental changes in the economic relations of production. American capitalism became "monopoly capitalism," as Baran and Sweezy call it [1966], creating enormous concentrations of economic power and huge corporate units of production. In their constant quest for profits, capitalists exhausted many traditional markets and developed many new ones. In particular, American capitalists began to move out of "goods" and into "services." Changes in technology produced increasingly interdependent processes of production. As a result of changes in technology, the increasing importance of the services and the increasing importance of the government sector, the percentage of the work force in white-collar occupations increased rapidly.[i]

At the same time, some important changes in the "superstructure" occurred, with important eventual effects on the determination and distribution of income. For the purposes of this book, several developments seem especially important. The American frontier was finally exhausted as an outlet for exploration and expansion (although intra-national geographic redistributions continued); the United States became a "closed economy," in effect, with important psychological effects on the dynamic of worker migration and hopefulness. A series of migrations brought a steady stream of workers into the labor force, with partially noneconomic causes: first through the successive waves of

---

[h]E.P. Thompson's classic book [1966] has taught us that the working class was beginning to develop class consciousness much earlier in England, as early as 1800. Whether the same seeds had been sown so early in the United States is not entirely clear.

[i]To summarize two of the most important trends statistically, the industrial share of the "service" industries rose from 19.2 percent in 1870 to 54.8 percent in 1965 [Fuchs, 1968, pp. 19, 24]; and the proportion of nonagricultural workers in operative and laborers jobs in mining and manufacturing fell from roughly 31-33 percent in the 1870-1900 period to 14 percent in 1960 [U.S. Bureau of the Census, *Comparative Occupational Statistics...*, 1940, pp. 104-108; and Census, 1960 *Final Report* PC(1) 1C, pp. 1-219].

white European immigrants, then through heavy migration of black (and other minority workers) from the South (and from Puerto Rico and Mexico). Almost simultaneously, some partly cultural changes fostered rapid increases in the labor force participation rates among women and teenagers. The joint influence of democratic ideology and industrial work requirements, further, brought about a rapid expansion of formal educational institutions and substantial increases in median years of schooling. Both the Great Depression and several wars, finally, helped effect a substantial expansion of government influence over the economy.[j]

An important element of the dynamic of the class struggle, radicals would hypothesize, provided a final backdrop to the evolving process of income determination and distribution. Given the character of the late-nineteenth century economy, the capitalist class as a whole was severely threatened by the possibility that the proletariat would develop a united *subjectively-defined* class of all workers. As Marx and Engels predicted, workers were being drawn together in large work places and were enduring increasing specialization of labor. A priori they seemed fairly likely to begin to perceive their common interests and to begin to demand better working conditions and a larger share of total product. Given some fairly solid democratic traditions in the United States, it was unlikely that capitalists could expect perpetually to suppress those latent demands with sheer force.[k] If some basic institutions defining class did not change, in other words, the stability of the system seemed in danger. The capitalists faced the increasing necessity of forestalling the development of class consciousness among the entire proletariat. Unions were developing, the socialists were making advances, and the economy's instability wasn't helping matters at all.[l]

The interactions of these three sets of forces—changes in the economic relations of production, in the "superstructure," and in the dynamic of class con-

---

[j]Again to summarize some of the important trends statistically, the portion of the population living in urban areas rose from 25 percent in 1870 to 70 percent in 1960 [U.S. Bureau of the Census, *Historical Statistics . . .*, 1962, p. 9; 1965, p. 1]; and the labor force share of white males over 20 years old fell from exactly two-thirds in 1890 to less than half (or 49.6 percent) in 1969 [U.S. Bureau of the Census, *Historical Statistics . . .*, 1962, p. 72; *Monthly Labor Review*, August 1970, p. 96].

[k]They tried, of course, for a little while, *viz.* the Haymarket events and others in the late nineteenth and early twentieth centuries. See, for instance, Adams [1966].

[l]Weinstein [1968] has developed interesting evidence that many capitalists were indeed fearful for the stability of the system and decided, quite consciously from 1905 to the outbreak of World War I, to forestall the impending workers' revolution by engaging in a series of social reforms and cooperations with the more conservative craft wing of the union movement. A private memorandum circulated in 1914 in the Industrial Department of the National Civic Federation—the moderate business organization of the day—expressed the fears of business quite clearly [quoted in Weinstein, 1968, p. 128]: "In view of the rapid spread in the United States of socialistic doctrines, . . . it is important that there should be a carefully planned and wisely directed effort to instruct public opinion as to the real meaning of socialism . . . if our American political system and its underlying economic institutions are to be preserved."

flict—were extremely complicated, yet they clearly combined to have some critical effects on the process of income determination and distribution. I have formulated a set of detailed hypotheses about those cumulative effects, outlined in the following sections. In order to try to clarify the nature of the hypotheses, I have separated them into three sections: the first summarizing hypotheses about effects of these developments on the determination of worker *productivity*; the second describing hypotheses about effects on the process of *class definition and the distribution of relative class power*; and the third pulling together those two separate sets of hypotheses into a summary set of hypotheses about changes in the mechanisms of American income determination and distribution. As the third section suggests quite clearly, the current dimensions and character of poverty and underemployment seem quite natural outgrowths of the past hundred years of American economic history as interpreted by the radical perspective.

Effects on Productivity

Three closely related hypotheses about changes in the determination and distribution of productivity seem most important for understanding present labor market operations.[m]

1. It seems likely that variations in worker productivity have grown increasingly dependent on the amount of time workers spend on their specific jobs. In the first phases of nineteenth century industrial capitalism, a generalized kind of work stability was necessary. The entire work force had to be disciplined to accept orders, report to work, and respond to wage incentives. But it did not take a worker long on any particular job to achieve the maximum productivity possible in that job. Since then, production processes have grown increasingly complex, hierarchical, and interdependent. Two related effects have become important, each of them helping cause the growing importance of on-the-job training. First, the "general skills" of many workers have become increasingly insufficient as measures of their relative "productivity," for many skills must be adjusted to the requirements and procedures of the specific work place before they have any value. Traditionally, many physical skills could be applied in similar ways in many different settings. Gradually, this has changed as production grows more interdependent. A machine worker must learn not only how to operate his machine in general but specifically how to operate it within a given production process, for the machine's operation may be modified by its relationship to other machines in the individual establishment.[5]

---

[m]Most of the hypotheses in this section are similar to some of the observations in Doeringer and Piore [1971]; indeed, the radical theory is similar to the dual labor market and internal labor market analyses of the determinants of *productivity*, but differs from them in its simultaneous emphasis on the importance of *class*.

Second, many of the specific skills that workers must learn on the job in order to be productive can be learned, increasingly, *only* through simple and continuous tenure on the job; the time necessary for learning them cannot be reduced by formal instruction on the job. Each individual member of an inter-dependent production process must learn to relate to his fellow employees, as Maurice Dobb puts it [1963, p. 359]: "with a discipline that is something akin to that which co-ordinates the separate instruments of an orchestra." Workers, like orchestra members, cannot be taught the common rhythm in the abstract, but must pick it up by working together. To be more productive, in other words, every worker must understand the requirements not only of his job but of the entire work process. Assembly-line workers can learn quickly how to turn a screw, but it takes time for them to learn enough about the entire process to be able to spot other defects and to identify the sources of defects. (See Rapoport [1967] for one example.) Many white-collar workers often perform extremely menial tasks most of the time, the skills for which they can learn quickly. They may answer phones, run errands or stamp forms. But their value to the firm depends increasingly on the subtlety of their knowledge of the firm's operations. If a form doesn't come across their desks on schedule, they must know where to look for it. If a secretary needs to arrange a meeting on quick notice, she must know where to find the participants. (See Crozier [1971] for some interesting evidence.)

In general, potential job stability has probably become an increasingly impor-tant criterion to employers in filling many jobs, for workers are likely to become increasingly productive *on that job* the longer they remain on the job.[6]

2. It becomes increasingly useful, at the same time, for employers to try to organize job structures and to define the nature of job clusters in such a way that those jobs requiring employee stability are clearly separated from those which do not. The devices necessary to ensure stability often become expen-sive—through whatever special work adjustments and monetary incentives may prove necessary—and it becomes increasingly efficient for employers to confine those extra expenses to the narrowest range of jobs they can. They would rather avoid, in other words, being forced to spread those expenses over all their jobs. Ideally, if they have the freedom to act rationally, they will try to calculate the "costs and benefits" of different clusters of jobs in order to try simultaneously to minimize the costs of devices necessary to ensure stability and to minimize the efficiency losses from unstable workers. Given the rise of complex produc-tion processes and the continued presence of some jobs in which stability is *not* important, it therefore seems likely that employers will seek to balkanize the labor market, defining different clusters of jobs for which they establish quite different entry requirements. The entry requirements, in turn, will emphasize or de-emphasize potential stability depending on the job cluster. To pick a notable example, employers have found it increasingly convenient—I would hypoth-esize—to separate secretarial jobs into two clusters: to create typing pools in

which women do nothing besides typing, in which job stability makes almost no difference, and for which evidence of job stability is not particularly important; and to separate those jobs from more conventional secretarial jobs—like the "personal secretary"—for which specific skills like typing are probably less important than simple job stability, and for which entry requirements tend increasingly to emphasize characteristics associated with potential stability.[7]

3. Given the increasing importance of job stability for many (relatively more "productive") jobs, it has probably become more and more difficult for a firm to devise tests which accurately measure a worker's potential productivity. If a worker is supposed to shovel dirt, brute strength can be tested fairly easily. If an assembler must use his hands with dexterity, his skill can be tested by presenting him with round pegs and round holes. If a secretary must do nothing more than type letters, spelling and typing abilities can be tested quite precisely. But when an employee's potential contribution to the firm will depend ultimately on how long he stays with the firm, it becomes extremely difficult to test for that "skill." Psychological tests are probably too insensitive to differentiate potential stability among broad classes of workers. It becomes increasingly likely that employers will often rely on superficial characteristics as approximate predictors of potential stability. If it has been generally true in the past that certain demographically-identified groups have had relatively low average job stability, employers will be more and more likely to discriminate against those groups in filling jobs requiring stability. The more identifiable the demographic criterion, the easier it is to apply.[8]

Effects on Class Definition and Class Power

At the same time, five hypotheses about changes in the process of class definition and the distribution of class power seem especially important. In slightly different ways, each of these hypotheses "predicts" that employers will find it more and more in their interest to attempt to forge a highly-stratified labor market, with at least several *objectively-defined* economic classes, in order both to fill secondary jobs and to forestall the development of revolutionary class consciousness.

1. Gradually through these 100 years, the (putative) homogeneity of labor in the late nineteenth century began to dissolve. At the beginning, around 1870, much of the nonagricultural work force was moving into operative and laborer jobs in mining, manufacturing, and transportation, a harbinger of Marx's expectations that an industrial labor force would fuse. Before that trend culminated in complete proletarian homogeneity, however, other industrial and occupational trends took over. Service and white-collar employment grew much

more prominent, even within manufacturing. The labor force became increasingly dispersed over a wide variety of industries and occupations.[n]

This dispersion was likely to have two closely-related effects. First, the nature of work itself no longer so clearly defined the working class, for a wide variety of working conditions became common within the labor force. Since some jobs offered "better" working conditions than others—were somehow cleaner or less exhausting—and since firmly-established patterns of assimilation were beginning to make it possible for those in the less desirable jobs to identify with those in more desirable (principally white-collar) jobs, it probably became rather more likely that those in less desirable jobs would develop a consciousness about their working conditions, demanding better working conditions or threatening to quit for better work. Second, to the extent that blue-collar workers did in fact develop a certain class consciousness, unionize, and demand some of the perquisites of more attractive jobs, there was a danger that their demands would be satisfied in such a way that all workers, even those without class consciousness, would benefit at the expense of employers. It became likely that the relative share of all workers would increase, in other words, rather than the shares of those more limited numbers who demanded better conditions.

As a result, employers were likely to try to develop a stratified labor market in order to accomplish two complementary objectives. They were likely to seek, on the one hand, to minimize the extent to which those in jobs with less desirable working conditions could identify with those in more desirable jobs. If they could, they would try to segregate white-collar workers from blue-collar workers, create or permit the development of a class identity among more advantaged white-collar workers to distinguish them from blue-collar workers, and to impose some sharp barriers between the different kinds of jobs, like educational requirements. To the extent that employers could accomplish this stratification, it became more likely that blue-collar workers would accept their poorer working conditions (relative to those of white-collar workers) because they did not have the necessary credentials and education to move on to jobs with better opportunities. And employers were likely to seek, on the other hand, to sharply segregate those blue-collar or secondary workers who could potentially identify with white-collar workers—and who might therefore develop class consciousness—from those blue-collar or secondary workers who were not likely to develop class consciousness, in order, obviously, to limit the potential costs of concessions to workers who made determined demands. Employers would seek to do this in two ways. First, they would seek to stratify jobs in order objectively to separate job clusters from each other and consequently to establish "fire trails," as it were, to limit the potential spread of costly concessions. Second, they were like-

[n]Indeed, in statistical terms, the evidence suggests that conditions also became much more heterogeneous even *within* occupations; many indices of dispersion and inequality suggest that intra-occupational heterogeneity—given standard occupational categories—has been increasing for some time. See D.M. Gordon [1972].

ly to try to fill the worst jobs with those who were least likely to identify with advantaged workers. Gradually, as the composition of the American labor force changed, it became relatively easy for employers to reserve the most "secondary" jobs for teens, women, and minority group workers with quite confident expectations that they would not identify with more advantaged workers and develop a common consciousness about the disadvantages of their jobs.[9]

2. Trends in urbanization and migration tended to create precisely the same employer requirements. Traditionally, the disadvantaged status of many workers had been justified and reinforced by the rigidity of social distinctions by birth: in the late nineteenth century, the distinctions between native-born/English-speaking workers and foreign-born/foreign-language workers seemed sharp and effective. With the steady process of migration, increasingly complex urban social structures, and continuing infusions of disadvantaged foreign (or southern) migrants into northern industrial cities, the traditional distinctions probably began to erode. Regular patterns of assimilation were established and, at least among white immigrants, some firmly-rooted, relatively continuous avenues for upward mobility and social assimilation (either intra- or inter-generationally) became quite manifest. As with the trends described in section 1, these mobility patterns raised the likelihood that less advantaged workers would identify with those ahead of them, demand better working conditions, or leave their less desirable jobs in order to train themselves. And employers were equally likely to respond by trying to stratify markets, to create subjective distinctions among groups of workers, and to channel into secondary jobs those workers who were least likely to identify with more advantaged workers.

By the mid-twentieth century, these trends had acquired a momentum of their own; employers were somewhat caught in their own dynamic. Since the frontier had closed and the waves of foreign migration had ceased, blacks in northern ghettos were tending increasingly to regard themselves as the last immigrant group; no one else was coming along to fill in behind them at the bottom. (See the brief comments on the "promised land effect" in chapter 1.) And yet, because their skin color made it relatively unlikely that they would identify with more advantaged white workers ahead of them, many blacks—especially younger males—probably began to respond to these perceptions by developing even more unstable work habits than previously disadvantaged groups; they saw little hope that they could climb above the bottom rungs by working stably and diligently to better themselves. Women, for different reasons, were also likely to continue working intermittently, given the requirements of the family, the kinds of expectations molded in them by their experiences in school, family and labor market, and the small probability that they would identify with other previously disadvantaged groups of male workers who had moved upward by developing stable habits. Teenagers, finally, were increasingly likely to expect that they would continue through school and to work as teens solely to pick up spare cash. This meant that they cared less about retaining the same job for very long and developed increasingly unstable work habits over time. And, as all three of these groups increased their share of the labor force, employers found themselves left, quite frequently, with only the most unstable elements of the work force with which to fill many different kinds of jobs. Some employers were undoubtedly forced, on many occasions, to organize an increasing proportion of their employment around the behavioral patterns of unstable employment.[o] And once these organizational adjustments were made, they reinforced, in turn, the burgeoning instability (or expectations of instability) among those three secondary groups.[10]

3. The rise of unions, obviously, also encouraged employers to seek to stratify the labor force and the relations of production in such ways as to limit the potential extent of unionization. They were encouraged to establish separate pools of secondary employment, for instance, which permitted and even encouraged such unstable patterns of behavior among their workers that they were unlikely to develop a common class consciousness toward unionizing themselves. This would also mean that other unions found it increasingly difficult to organize those pockets of workers. Employers were encouraged, as well, to emphasize the differences among different groups of workers—particularly between blue-collar and white-collar workers—in order to limit the extent to which non-unionized workers would identify with those already in unions. It probably encouraged them, in particular, to stimulate or reinforce a sense of "professionalism" among many white-collar workers in the hopes that that emergent occupational identity would lead many workers to seek to differentiate themselves from unionized, primarily blue-collar workers. And, finally, it also encouraged them to fill the least desirable jobs with workers toward whom union members had reason to feel hostile, in order to try to limit the energy with which union members would move toward increasing their ranks.[p]

4. With technological change, there is always a danger of increasingly high unemployment (at constant levels of demand and constant levels of labor force

---

[o]Perhaps more frequently, employers chose to place new types of jobs or clusters of jobs in the secondary market when they first developed. This seems to have been the case with keypunch operators.

[p]It may not, of course, be coincidental that white male unionists felt a certain hostility toward blacks and women in the jobs below them, for they may have been encouraged to feel threatened by the competition of lower-wage workers—encouraged, at least, by the use of blacks as strike-breakers in the period around World War I. See Spero and Harris [1968]. For more general historical discussion of the union movement, which supports some of these observations, see Ulman [1961]. This phenomenon has probably been widespread. Many mechanisms in our society, radicals suggest, serve the function of inducing workers in the lower and middle strata to tolerate their conditions because they feel superior to those below them. Wilensky [1966] refers to this as the "consolation prize hypothesis" and Lockwood speaks of the "deferential" mode of consciousness among workers; "deferentials" are very conscious of status gradations in society and are adept, he writes [1966, p. 253] at discovering "groups with an even lower status than their own." For more general comments on these functions of inequality, see Weisskopf [1972].

participation). Also, new technology sometimes creates new skill requirements which general institutional education can often meet better than specific on-the-job training. Both of these trends make it convenient for employers to increase the (often arbitrary) general education requirements they impose as hiring standards for jobs of constant skills. Encouraging the labor force to stay in school through higher levels can then serve a dual purpose. It cuts down the amount of time any potential worker will spend in the labor force, therefore reduces the potential size of the pool of the unemployed, and therefore undercuts some potentially threatening developments to the system as a whole. It also imposes on the general public the costs of certain kinds of training, freeing private firms of these costs. *But*, the longer most workers remain in school, the less effective are traditional stratifications between those with no schooling and those with some. It becomes necessary either to adjust relative educational distinctions upward (establishing college as a new boundary between groups of workers, for instance), or to devise new forms of distinction on the job or within labor market institutions (to replace previous distinctions created by education).[11]

5. Finally and perhaps most important, the nature of work incentives has changed radically over time, with probably fundamental implications for the ways in which employers seek to organize the "relations of production." Formerly, as noted above, industrial workers were frequently paid by a piecework or wage bonus system of remuneration. Under those systems, employers hardly had to worry about the clarity and impact of incentives for employees to labor well and hard. If a worker produced more, in a given period of time, he would earn more. With the switch to bureaucratic and more complicated modes of production, an individual's contribution to output gradually became less distinguishable from that of other workers, for it became increasingly difficult to identify an individual worker's "piece." Wage incentives, one would therefore hypothesize, tend to become less effective as a result. Employers can no longer precisely measure the productivity of many individual workers in strictly quantitative terms, and must increasingly depend on their own relatively qualitative judgments about relative worker merit and productivity. Especially under automation, Daniel Bell writes [1960, p. 270], ". . . . with continuous flow, a worker's worth can no longer be evaluated in production units." But if employers singled out individual workers for monetary reward on the basis of those (relatively more arbitrary) qualitative judgments, workers might become much less willing to respond to those (relatively more arbitrary) incentives, and grow relatively more offended by them. Since workers have been taught to orient themselves toward monetary gain incentives, they probably tend to develop a sense of equity about how those rewards are tossed around.

One important alternative for employers, as a result, is to establish hierarchical incentives to replace monetary rewards. They can reward "more productive" workers with higher status and better jobs rather than with more money. The advantage of these incentives is that employers can more easily justify the application of their qualitative judgments of workers as a basis for reward; they can justify their singling out of certain workers on a qualitative basis because they, the employers, are the only ones who know the requirements of higher jobs and must make their own projections about which employees would perform better on those jobs. Workers themselves are much less able to evaluate the accuracy of the employers' judgments, and are relatively less likely to be offended by them.[q]

This means, of course, that employers must create a desire among employees for higher status and better jobs. It becomes increasingly likely that employers will seek to develop in the labor force a kind of "hierarchy fetishism"—a continual craving for more and better job titles and status, the satisfaction of which leads eventually to intensified hunger for still more and better job titles and job status. The objective is best satisfied, as David Lockwood has written [1966, p. 254] by a "widespread consensus about the rank order of status groups in the community, so that lower strata regard their lowly position less as an injustice than as a necessary, acceptable, and even desirable part in a natural system of inequality."

And in order to satisfy this "hierarchy fetishism," employers probably find it increasingly useful to create constantly and perpetually differentiated job categories—if for no other reason—in order to provide new and relatively compelling fodder for the fetishistic craving. This incentive–utility of job hierarchies and the increasing division of labor may or may not converge with the dictates of efficiency criteria on strictly technological grounds. Whatever the relationship between the two kinds of criteria for job design and organization, hierarchical job structures and specialized labor attain an independent rationale, over and above efficiency rationale.[r]

And, in order to create hierarchical incentives without providing too many mobility opportunities—in order to satisfy "hierarchy fetishism" without simultaneously establishing a continuum of relationships among workers along which they can develop common class consciousness—employers may find it useful to forge hierarchical ladders within clearly differentiated job clusters. For incentive reasons alone, that is, they may seek to "balkanize" the labor market and to proliferate job titles within each "balkanized" cluster.[1 2]

---

[q]As unions become more powerful in manufacturing, however, this kind of incentive works less effectively because the unions begin to stabilize the criteria for promotion and define qualifications for jobs. So, for instance, employers play around with the work environment to see if they can make workers happy enough to work more efficiently—*viz.* the Hawthorne Experiment at Western Electric. For some general comments on these problems of motivation in blue-collar work, see Bell [1960] and Friedmann [1955].

[r]The analogy with Marx's concept of "commodity fetishism" is obviously intended, for both desires, if inculcated, serve similar purposes in resolving the tension among workers about their lives as producers.

Cumulative Effects

The joint effects of the first two sets of hypothesized trends seem obvious and fundamental. I have summarized those effects in five separate clusters of summary hypotheses.

1. It becomes increasingly likely that employers will seek to balkanize the labor market, creating highly stratified clusters of jobs quite distinctly separated from each other. These stratifications have independent utility by productivity and class criteria. In addition, it seems especially likely that some of the separate strata will be organized to permit and encourage highly unstable work behavior, both to limit the expenses of devices necessary to ensure worker stability and to limit the potential spread of class consciousness among the most disadvantaged (and secondary) workers.

2. It becomes equally likely that employers will seek to fill the most disadvantaged and unstable jobs with minority group workers, women and teenagers, for three separate reasons. First, as employers have had to rely increasingly on statistical discrimination, they have undoubtedly found it easiest to discriminate by race, sex and age; these characteristics can hardly be disguised by workers very easily, and—at least until very recently—society has tolerated implicit and explicit discrimination against these groups. Second, these groups have all developed quite independent expectations of (and relative resignation to) secondary and unstable work patterns. Third, these three groups are least likely to identify with more advantaged groups and to develop a class consciousness about their relatively "oppressed" working conditions.

   In short, the functional economic importance to employers of general economic discrimination by race, age, and sex has probably grown increasingly important over time.[5] The creation and preservation of stratified, secondary work clusters has therefore probably developed an independent utility to employers, and their ability generally to fill those jobs with a relatively resigned secondary labor pool satisfies their needs quite precisely.

3. Whether or not it is required by technological change, it seems increasingly likely that the specialization of labor will continue. Apart from efficiency criteria, *ceteris paribus*, the specialization of labor is justified by and quite useful for the stratification of the labor force and the establishment of limits to the spread of class consciousness. As Harold Wilensky writes in this context [1966, p. 27]: "Advanced specialization has made for finer distinctions of status and a multiplication of occupational worlds."

4. Whether or not it is required by technological change, equally, the hierarchi-

---

[5]This is *not* a hypothesis that actual discrimination in fact increased, but only that—relative to other devices for satisfying some employer objectives—such discrimination became more critical as a potential recourse. Contradictory forces may also have countered such attempts.

cal organization of work is likely to continue. Employers probably find it more and more useful to create relatively meaningless and arbitrary status distinctions on the job and within the productive process, for at least three related reasons. Hierarchies establish a new and effective kind of incentive to replace the wage incentive under piece-work and wage bonus systems. Hierarchies also help ensure that workers will stay on the job longer, and thus develop certain kinds of productivities which cannot be acquired except through simple and continuous tenure; to promote stability, in other words, employers find it partially sufficient to create the illusion of mobility by creating trees of artificial job positions which workers can climb branch by meaningless branch. Third, the erosion of several traditional class divisions (like language and place of birth) have created the need for new stratification mechanisms. Both educational stratification and hierarchical stratification on the job serve equally to replace those traditional mechanisms.

5. The importance of job characteristics in determining relative income among workers has undoubtedly grown in importance, as a result of all these trends, for job structures have probably tended increasingly to dominate relative opportunities among workers for skill acquisition. The more that skills must be developed within specific job situations, the more the structure and distribution of those job opportunities tends to affect the distribution of skills among workers. Abstract, generalized individual abilities (like reasoning and reading abilities) become less and less important in determining or explaining variations in labor market status and income.

All of these summary hypotheses, derived from more specific hypotheses about 100 years of American economic history, directly predict the phenomena of poverty and underemployment described in chapter 1.[13] They suggest an increasingly discontinuous labor market. They suggest, further, that certain strata in the labor market will be dominated by unstable work patterns, and those strata will tend increasingly to be dominated by minority group members, women, and teens. They provide insight into the process through which potential stability becomes a keystone to differences between sectors in the labor market. And among those in the secondary sectors, the analysis implies a distinct and critical powerlessness which is likely to prevent their capturing a very large share of their product in wages and is also likely—both through their instability and their weakness—to preclude any kind of obvious relationship between income and productivity.

To summarize all these hypotheses in the language of the general radical theory, it seems likely that members of the capitalist class have sought increasingly to encourage and permit the development of several *objectively-defined classes* in the American labor market, each in objective competition with the others, in order to heighten the stratification of the labor force. It seems equally likely that employers have found it in their collective interest to encourage and permit the evolution of the more advantaged of those classes into *subjectively-defined classes*—through the development of class consciousness—particularly insofar as members of these subjectively-defined classes identify their "enemies" as those within the less advantaged classes of workers.[t] Finally, it seems likely that capitalists have tried especially to prevent the emergence of the lower strata as *subjectively-defined classes*—to prevent the development of class consciousness among lower-class workers—in order both to forestall revolutionary impulses among the most thoroughly exploited and to preserve some classes of workers who will continue to fill the most secondary, unstable, and undesirable jobs.

The entire set of hypotheses described above suggests that recent phenomena derive at least partly from a pursuit by the capitalist class of their own collective interests. As many critics of radical analysis point out, however, the analysis assumes that capitalists have been able *successfully* to fulfill their objectives. And that raises two final questions about the radical theory. First, was it necessary for capitalists collectively to conspire in order to fulfill their interests? And second, how much power do capitalists have, either collectively or individually, to enforce their will?

The radical responses to those questions are complicated, but they can be suggested quite briefly. First, it has not always been necessary for capitalists to conspire in order to perceive their common interests and pursue them. To the extent that changes necessary to achieve their objectives have also tended to serve the interests of some classes of workers, and particularly the more advantaged classes, it has been relatively easy for them to let nature run its course. And to the extent that some of the changes necessary to preserve the stability of the system have also tended to promote economic efficiency and to increase total product—if, indeed, hierarchies are efficient, for example—then their collective interests will be satisfied with relatively little sacrifice required of individual members of the capitalist class.

But suppose that capitalists did need to try to enforce their will on society, as a collective class. How much power would they have to do it? Many of the changes required in the past century have involved changes in the relations of production, changes, that is, in the organization of work. Until unions develop considerable power in any industry, capitalists have full control over working conditions and have fairly consistent capacity to make changes in job design and the organization of work. And most of the changes required during the last century were intended for sectors which had not yet been unionized, so that capitalists had fairly free rein in that respect. What about changes in schools, which radicals hypothesize have tended consistently to serve the basic requirements of

---

[t]This has been, I think, an important strain in American economic history, illustrated by many. It provided, of course, one of the major themes of Cash's classic study of the mind of the South [1960], and it has fueled the feelings of white building trades members in the North. Wilensky made the generalization [1966, p. 35] that ". . . the upper strata are more class conscious. . . ."

the capitalist class? One has considerable evidence that the schools have historically responded to the requirements of the industrial sector. And now that the
American polity is so fragmented between central city and proliferating suburbs,
a stratified educational system, producing different classes of workers for different strata within the relations of production comes almost as a matter of course,
without requiring exertion by the capitalists.

In short, the radical paradigm provides a framework within which one can
"explain" the recent phenomena of urban poverty and underemployment. The
hypotheses seem plausible and relatively consistent with the real world. Just as
hypotheses generated by the other two paradigms must be subjected to much
more detailed comparison with evidence about the real world, however, so must
the hypotheses developed in this chapter. Their plausibility and coherence does
not guarantee their consistency with data about social reality, and it is to those
kinds of comparisons that the discussion will now turn.

Part 3: Comparing the Theories

The Task of Translation

Part 2 of this book provided some brief summaries of three competing economic theories of poverty and underemployment. The separate chapters outlined the major methodological and substantive components of the three disciplinary matrices—the shared values and ideas to which their respective proponents are committed. The summaries also sketched some of the specific hypotheses about income determination and distribution through which each of the paradigms seeks to explain the current phenomena of urban poverty and underemployment in the United States. Except for some scattered comparative remarks, the summaries reviewed neither the important differences among the three paradigms nor their relative consistency with data about the real world. Part 3 provides some of these comparisons. In this chapter some of the more fundamental differences among the three theories are discussed. In chapter 7 and 8 the theories are compared with pieces of empirical evidence in order to weigh their relative accuracy and fruitfulness. Based on these comparisons, chapter 9 makes some suggestions about further research objectives and strategies.

The task of comparing the three theories, as I warned in chapter 2, is complicated and difficult. The theories speak different languages. To many who have tried to work within and among them, the paradigms seem "incommensurable," as Thomas Kuhn would put it. In order to begin to evaluate the comparative validity of the three theories, we must begin to develop some guides for translation. This chapter reviews some of the most important differences among the theories as a step toward spurring that translational effort. Four principal areas of difference among the theories offer the most fruitful terrain for exploration, I would argue, for an understanding of these four areas of difference will help clarify many other subsidiary disagreements as well. By establishing some standards of language through which these differences can be clarified, in other words, we can begin to clarify other less fundamental differences much more easily.

In the first section of this chapter, I outline these four principal areas of incommensurability. The second section makes use of that discussion to provide another kind of clarification. Many attempts to evaluate the apparent conflicts among these theories of poverty and underemployment have concentrated on their policy implications—on their analyses of policy alternatives and program design. These attempts at comparative discussion have usually failed, it appears, because they have ignored the incommensurability of the paradigms; they have tried to compare policy implications, that is, without developing some standards for translating one set of recommendations into another. In this brief concluding section on policy, I have tried to apply the lessons of the first section's discussion of principal paradigm differences toward an elucidation of the contrasting policy views.

Differences Among the Theories

Each of the three theories of poverty and underemployment seeks to explain reality in very different ways. One can best understand the differences in their explanations, I would suggest, if one begins by noting four principal areas of difference in their underlying theories of income determination and distribution. These differences cannot be formulated in some entirely neutral scientific language, but the ways in which each of the theories approaches these areas can be compared in some fairly concrete ways.

First, quite obviously, the three theories differ fundamentally in their analytic methodologies. These methodological differences help explain and cause many of the mutual misunderstandings and disagreements among them.

Orthodox economic theory, to begin with, concentrates on partial analyses. Its analysts are inclined to fix the institutional environment in order to model the choices which individuals make within that environment. The analyses value specificity and concreteness. That which cannot be precisely modeled is often relegated to a secondary or qualifying tier of the analysis. These methodological inclinations lead to fairly static analyses. They also place a heavy burden on the analysts' ability to hold enough about the world "constant" to permit model formulation. Even if the analyst admits that the world is changing, he must act, for the moment, as if it is not. (See Leontief [1971] for some useful observations on this problem.) Given the choice between an analysis which develops rigorous hypotheses and tests from an abstract, static model, on the one hand, and an analysis which develops much vaguer, more untestable hypotheses from a model emphasizing change, on the other, the orthodox analyst will generally choose the former. He will often try to show how individual choices will tend to preserve the world as it is or has been, restoring society to its natural equilibrium or reinforcing an existing equilibrium.

Quite in contrast, radical economic theory focuses on dialectical analysis. Radicals emphasize the interactions between individual choice and institutional change. They are willing to sacrifice "rigor" for some understanding of the dynamics of change. They concentrate on analyzing the internal contradictions in social processes which will tend to produce change. Given the conflict among social forces and the internal contradictions in any social process, they emphasize analyses illuminating the trends which will inevitably produce change. "A central tenet of dialectics," Zweig has written [1971, p. 49, emphasis in the original], " is that the prime energy for systemic change is *internal* to the developing system, not exogenously imposed." Radicals argue that orthodox economics involves an articial preoccupation with *harmony and equilibrium;* we should rather concentrate, they suggest, on *conflict and change.*

The dual labor market theory has a much less developed methodology, but some of its more informal predispositions have played an important role in its differences with orthodox theory and with the failure of many orthodox economists to understand its central model. Dual labor market analysts, like radical theorists, have decided to emphasize interaction and change. They have felt, in developing their models of dualism, that orthodox economists have erred in their interpretations of poverty and underemployment because they had kept too many variables outside the analysis and because they had focused on stability and the fixity of institutional environments. Dual labor market analysts argue that one cannot understand the changing character of poverty and underemployment without focusing on the dynamic nature of institutions and the interactions between institutional and individual change.

While these differences with orthodox analysis have led to mutual misunderstandings between orthodox and dual market economists, another important difference has helped prompt the attempt by many dual market analysts to incorporate the dual market theory into a more general radical framework. The dual market theory, however much it emphasizes the dynamics of change, does not provide an explicit analysis of conflict and is not oriented toward looking for the sources and effects of conflict in society. Without that focus, the theory began to seem to many radicals as a slightly ingenuous view of society; many of the dual market analysts' descriptions of change sometimes seemed to place too great an emphasis on the mutual delight of all parties with the emerging trends, as if a harmony of interest was driving the evolution of a dual structure.

The principal consequence of these methodological differences is that they complicate the task of translation, that they tend to obscure some more important substantive differences. Discussion about substance often dissolves into mutually recriminating rhetoric about science and religion. Radical economists try to counter the prevalent notion, as Stigler has put it [1959, p. 520], that "economics as a positive science is ethically—and therefore politically—neutral." Orthodox economists often insist that radical economics is hardly scientific at all, but rather more an exercise in religion and rhetoric. Dual labor market economists stand somewhere in the middle, accused either of sociological imprecision or political naiveté. Sooner or later, one suspects, most economists will accept the notion that methodologies in the social sciences can and do legitimately differ. When that happens, these debates about theories of poverty and underemployment can move beyond the incommensurability of their methodologies and begin to appreciate their real differences about substance.

Turning to substance, three critical differences seem most important. First, quite clearly, the three theories differ in their views about the concept of *economic class.* The concept of class plays a central role in the theoretical foundation of the radical analysis of poverty and underemployment through its formulation of a separate kind of interest with respect to which individuals calculate and by which individual behavior is at least partly determined. The dual labor market theory offers a specific analysis of the labor market which can be interpreted in class terms, but the dual market theory itself does not rely on the concept, does not link the distinction between primary and secondary markets to other potential class divisions, and does not consistently base its hypotheses on evaluations of the group interests of employers or employees in either market.[1] Orthodox economists, in general, are inclined to argue that class interests cannot be maintained in the face of conflicting individual interests and that, if individual and class interests are complementary, one gains no additional insights by positing the independent existence of class interests. Arrow has quite clearly summarized this orthodox inclination [1971, p. 25]:

Economic explanations for discrimination or other phenomena tend to run in individualistic terms. . . . Economists ask what motivates an employer or an individual worker. They tend not to accept as an explanation a statement that employers as a class would gain by discrimination, for they ask what would prevent an individual employer from refusing to discriminate if he prefers and thereby profit.

By itself, this difference among the theories is extremely difficult to evaluate directly and empirically. Two rather different kinds of research seem necessary to test the usefulness and validity of the radical concept of class, for there are indeed two dimensions to the radical axioms about class. On the one hand, radicals propose that class members *may* develop class consciousness and demonstrate an awareness of their group interests and the conflict of their interests with those of other classes. This kind of evidence about subjective identification can be developed only with the most delicate kind of historical research, as witnessed especially by Thompson [1966], and does not offer any immediate prospects for evaluation of the current competition among the theories of poverty and underemployment.[a] On the second level, radicals argue that the lives of different workers are *objectively* defined by their membership in a specific economic class, and that worker behavior, attitudes, and personality traits will vary substantially from one objectively-defined class to another. Since one presumes

---

[a]This process of research is just beginning in the United States. For a useful discussion of the problems of inference involved, see Thernstrom [1969]. Thompson [1966] helps define "consciousness" operationally, and offers some suggestions about the kinds of evidence which can begin to document the presence of class consciousness. The resistance to evidence of class consciousness will continue to be strong among orthodox economists, no doubt. One orthodox economist wrote the following comment about the first draft of this essay, in which I had implicitly criticized orthodox economists for ignoring the existence of class [letter to the author]: "I react to that particular accusation the same way I would react to the suggestion of a Catholic monk that I had not put enough weight on the existence of God. I understand that it is piety in the monk to emphasize God, just as it is piety in the intellectual grandson of Marx to emphasize class, but the monk and the grandson are going to have to show more than they have shown before I will take them seriously."

to be dealing with "objective" facts about behavioral differences, this latter kind of research should offer fewer problems than the former. In fact, however, it suffers its own particular kind of plague, since the boundaries of economic classes are likely to change gradually over the long run and one must be careful to compare behavior among appropriately defined classes at any particular point in history. In light of this problem, one must be able to establish some relevant measures of the boundaries of economic class before one can begin to compare behavior among classes and to test hypotheses about behavioral differences. Those measures have not yet been provided, and this strand of direct research must effectively await that identification. The problem is discussed in both chapters 8 and 9 below.

Second, with slightly less clarity, the three theories differ in the ways they consider the complicated relationships among *technology, jobs,* and *people.* Orthodox economists seem implicitly to suggest a kind of technological determinacy about the definition of job structure and job design. In their formulations of production function analysis, to be sure, they often postulate that the capital-labor ratio will vary with shifts in the price of either factor, and that the relationship of technology and capital to labor may change in response to shifts in the supply or price of labor. [Nadiri, 1970] At any given capital-labor ratio, however, they seem to suggest that there is a unique set of (most efficient) job definitions and job structures within which labor is hired and trained and by which workers make their decisions. In the short run, this often leads to the working assumption that job structure, job definition, and job responsibility are fixed parameters and that one should concentrate on an analysis of the choices that workers make in response to those fixed structures.[2]

Both the dual labor market theory and the radical theory tend to argue, somewhat in contrast, that the definition of job structures and job designs constitutes an independent economic parameter, separate from choices about either technology or labor, and that employer interests, employees, and technologies interact simultaneously in the long run to determine the characteristics of both jobs and people, defining the nature of the jobs and the behavior of the workers who pass through them. The dual labor market theory, rather informally, suggests that this interaction has constituted the central source of an increasing dichotomization of the labor market. Radical economic theory makes an even more general historical argument. Within the radical perspective, two separate and analytically comparable forces will influence the decisions of employers about job structure and job design. On the one hand, radicals agree with orthodox economists that employers will seek to develop the most efficient combination of job definitions given both the state of technology and the general availability of worker skills. On the other hand, radicals also argue that employers will be influenced in their decisions about the organization of work by "class" criteria—by considerations of class power and class consciousness. Marglin [1971] has suggested some of the ways in which this latter set of class considerations probably influenced the evolution of the structure of work in the early stages of capitalism, in the *transition* to industrial and manufacturing capitalism. Many of the specific hypotheses I formulated in chapter 5 above help suggest some of the ways in which these class considerations were likely to have influenced the evolution of the organization of work in the *advanced* stages of capitalism. In effect, the radical argument suggests that many comparably "efficient" organizations of work and definitions of job structure would be possible with a given technology and that the choice among those alternatives will be governed in part by class considerations.

The critical importance of this difference among the theories for the analysis of poverty and underemployment seems evident. If one concludes, for instance, that substantial changes in the structure of jobs and job ladders must take place in order to increase the availability of on-the-job training for the poor, then one might easily argue from the orthodox perspective that those changes could be effected by price subsidies to employers, altering the individual employer's terms of trade between capital and labor. [Thurow, 1969; Rosen, 1971] Especially according to the radical perspective, in contrast, these subsidies might have no substantial effect because they would not alter or affect the class dynamics governing employer choices about job structure and design. (The dual labor market analysis would make the same argument in a slightly different way. See Piore [1970].)

Despite the importance of this issue, economists are not yet in a position to evaluate the disagreement very directly. The subject of job definition and job structure, independent of technology, has been largely ignored in the economic literature, and little evidence on the issue exists. Moreover, it seems intrinsically difficult to develop direct measures of variations in job structure for these purposes, for at least two reasons. One must try to hold technology constant, ideally, and that seems an especially difficult task. One must also be able to develop some information about the subjective decision-making processes through which employer choices about job structure and job design emerge, another especially problematic assignment. Pending much more intensive research on this issue, one must at least initially rely on very *indirect* evidence, of a sort to be discussed in the chapters below, for some guides on this particular difference among the theories.

Third and finally, the three theories seem very sharply to disagree in the ways in which they analyze and interpret *discontinuities* in the labor market. Orthodox economists generally make two arguments about apparent discontinuities or imperfections. First, they usually assume that these departures from the conditions of perfect competition will tend to *erode* over time as a result of endogenous competitive pressures. Second, they suggest that such imperfections consist primarily of some walls erected artificially among groups of workers and that the behavior of workers in any given sector can be explained by the same sets of behavioral hypotheses as that of workers in any other stratum, that the characteristics, attitudes and personality traits of workers remain constant among sectors.[b] Both the dual labor market and the radical theories seem to differ with orthodox economists on both these points. They argue, on the former point, that some important endogenous economic forces have served recently to *intensify* at least one, if not several kinds of labor market stratification. More important, on the second point, they argue in slightly different ways that the basic behavior of workers in different sectors may differ quite fundamentally. Underlying this argument lie their hypotheses about the ways in which both worker behavior and worker attitudes are not determined totally exogenously of the economic system, and the ways in which some underlying and evolving differences in labor market structures among sectors will inevitably produce some underlying differences in behavior and attitudes among their respective workers through the interaction of job and worker characteristics. It is important to emphasize, in this regard, that the dual market and radical economists are discussing human behavior and personality at the most fundamental level possible; no facet of the human condition escapes the influence of economic institutions. (See Gintis [1969].)

Research on this third issue is confounded by several independent problems. First, since economists have traditionally held that tastes, personalities and attitudes are determined exogenously, they have not usually tried to develop any terms by which they could integrate research on personality traits with research on economic behavior. Second, when research has uncovered *apparent* differences in behavior among groups of workers, economists have usually postulated some hypotheses to demonstrate that these apparent differences actually stem from a common underlying behavioral response to dissimilar conditions; one does not very easily separate that kind of argument from the conflicting argument that the underlying behavioral response mechanisms are dissimilar. Third, the disagreements involve some subtle questions about the relationship between the short and the long run. If orthodox economists tend to take market discontinuities or imperfections as "data" or as "givens" in the short run, they may or may not always regard those imperfections as exogenously determined in the long run, depending on the nature of the forces involved. One needs very carefully to be able to separate historical from cross-sectional analysis in order to evaluate this problem.

---

[b]The most graphic recent example of this mode of analysis is in Holt et al. [1971], in which the authors postulate a "segmented labor market model" in which the existence of segments is taken as a given and the behavioral models describing worker behavior are the same for each segment. This insistence on universalistic models of human behavior has not always been true of orthodox economists. The classical economists placed great stress on the effects of different kinds of work on the human personality—on fundamental patterns of human behavior. Alfred Marshall wrote [1949, p. 1], for instance: ". . . . the business by which a person earns his livelihood generally fills his thoughts during by far the greater part of those hours in which his mind is at its best; during them his character is being formed by the way in which he uses his faculties in his work, by the thoughts and the feelings which it suggests, and by his relations to his associates in work, his employers or his employees."

Policy Differences

These principal differences among the theories provide some direct assistance in an evaluation of the policy implications of the paradigm competition. Disagreements about policy constituted some of the first confrontations among the paradigms, but the contours of those conflicts were poorly perceived. As the competition has begun to emerge more fully, some insight—or perhaps one ought to say "hindsight"—into those debates comes within the range of our imagination.

According to the orthodox paradigm, we should try nearly every possible policy to solve the problems of poverty and underemployment because nearly every strategy is likely to have some marginal effect. Under most sets of orthodox assumptions about the world, the labor market retains relatively high elasticities of substitution among different kinds of productive factors and among different kinds of labor productivity, at least in the long run. The analysis also assumes that individuals—both employers and workers—determine their behavior solely in terms of individual calculations about individual objective functions in response to the price parameters of the labor market. The analysis further assumes that individual incomes reflect marginal productivities under nearly all conditions, and that an increase in individual marginal productivity, *ceteris paribus*, will bring an increase in individual income. Since so many different components of marginal producitivity are useful in the labor market, nearly any kind of public policy which will increase the individual productivities of the poor should be pursued. And since, to cover the final step of the orthodox logic, education and job training have provided the major components of individual productivity (or "human capital") in the past, they can quite reliably provide marginal increases in productivities in the future. If there are imperfections in the labor market which tend to prevent an individual worker from realizing his full marginal product, then they can be overcome by adjusting the price parameters to which individual workers and employers respond.

This logic has dominated public policy in the past decade. As Ribich writes [1968, p. 1], "A major presumption of the war on poverty is that education and training are especially effective ways to bring people out of poverty." As R.A. Gordon has written more specifically [1968, p. 71]:

In addition to the gains to be hoped for from manpower, education, job-creation, and other programs directly aimed at the poverty-area jobseeker, we need to accelerate the movement of Negroes and other minority groups out of poverty neighborhoods—and also to improve housing, schools, and other public services in those neighborhoods. And much needs to be done also to provide better public transportation, as well as improved training, counselling and placement services, to facilitate the matching of jobseekers in the centers of our cities with the growing number of jobs available outside the urban centers.

Programs developed during the 1960s to encourage increases in nearly every kind of education and training among the poor and to erase nearly every kind of imperfection in the labor market. Each policy was designed on the assumption that it could have an independent, marginal effect toward increasing productivities among the poor or erasing imperfections in the market.

Both theoretically and realistically, some orthodox analysts realized that the logic described in the two preceding paragraphs might have an important flaw. Because of interactions and complementarities among many different kinds of productivity, and because of the critical roles of worker motivation and employer expectation in affecting worker stability, they argued, situations might arise in which productivity gains could not be translated into higher-paying work. This might be the case, for instance, because the only highly-paying jobs available require very specific productivities acquired on-the-job, thus requiring considerable employee stability, while disadvantaged workers could not be induced to stay on those jobs long enough to acquire those skills (as a result of negative expectations based on past experience) or employers could not be induced to hire and train workers who, they expect, are not likely to stay on the job. Citing the kinds of ingredients necessary to provide such training successfully, Thurow concludes [1968, p. 91], "The complementarities between these ingredients are large. One missing ingredient can make the others seem worthless."

When orthodox economists confront those kinds of complementarities and interactions, admitting that they may vitiate the effectiveness of attempts marginally to increase productivities among the poor, they tend to respond in either of two ways. On the one hand, they may conclude that highly-sensitive employer or employee subsidies can sufficiently outweigh the costs both of training and of inducing stability and can overcome "imperfections" in the market, eventually enticing employee or employer investment in "human capital." Based on quite different perspectives and assumptions about the causes of poverty and underemployment, both Thurow [1969] and Rosen [1971] resort to suggestions that an appropriate kind of subsidy program, subtly adjusting price parameters, might be able to produce desired employer and employee responses.

On the other hand, orthodox economists may simply respond by admitting that interactions in the labor market and technologically-determined discontinuities in job structures are insuperable, that wage or employer subsidies cannot feasibly be pegged high enough to overcome all the individual resistances to change. And at that realization, they tend to assume a kind of fatalism about possibilities. Since the market as they understand it cannot sustain changes or induce the desired changes in individual decisions, their theories do not permit judgments about "non-market" forces and institutions. Those judgments must be left to the politicians, because they are not variables which economists seek to explain. If discrimination lies behind all the problems, for instance, orthodox models do not suggest how to overcome discrimination unless price adjustments can have effect; if prices cannot effect different behavior among discriminators, then orthodox economists do not know how to change that behavior. As Arrow points out in particular [1971], economists are not prepared to make judgments about phenomena which serve the interests of an entire class of individuals, because traditional evaluations of price parameters can neither evaluate the nature of the class interest nor entice individual members of that class to violate that interest.

The dual labor market analysis differs with orthodox analysis over policy directions in three important respects. First, it *begins* by assuming that the behavioral interactions which have been forging market separation will substantially preclude the effectiveness of most marginal education and training programs under most circumstances. Within the secondary market, education and training have almost no significant influence on wages or work stability, according to the dual market view, so that increasing the education and training of secondary workers is not likely to improve their incomes in secondary jobs. And the barriers between the two markets are so firmly entrenched that, under most circumstances, marginal improvements in the "capacities" or "human capital" of secondary workers will not suffice to move them into primary jobs. The separation between primary and secondary work is so firmly rooted, in other words, the expectations of secondary workers and primary employers are so firmly entrenched, and the standard operating procedures for channeling workers among the two markets have such general utility to both primary and secondary employers that an opening of primary employment to secondary workers would entail too much disruption in the normal procedures of the establishment, the costs of which would be enormous. Second, because the dual market analysis regards the forces effecting market separation as endogenous phenomena and seeks to understand the causes of separation, it can more easily anticipate the kinds of indirect policy instruments which might, in the long run, either reduce the separation between markets or uniquely improve the quality of jobs in the secondary sector. (See Doeringer and Piore [1971].) Job design, job structure, and job characteristics are endogenous in the dual market model, by and large, and one can anticipate the kinds of social and economic policies which might, in the long run, have effects on the characteristics of jobs. There is no unique, technologically-determined organization of work within the dual market model, and different social circumstances can influence the choice among at least several alternative organizations of production. Third, the dual market analysis is constructed to anticipate and evaluate the costs and benefits to groups of workers and employers—over and above the aggregation of individual costs and benefits—through its analyses of the influence of custom and attitudes on work requirements and organization. As Piore has particularly emphasized [1970], the dual market analysis emphasizes the vested interests which primary employers, primary employees, and secondary employers all have in the preservation of current arrangements. This emphasis reinforces the prejudice of the analysis against marginal, direct policy recommendations about education and training, and in favor of indirect mechanisms which do not threaten the interests of those three major groups. To a very large extent, the dual market analysis points almost uniquely to policies to provide high-paying stable public service employment to secondary workers as the likeliest attack on their poverty and underemployment. (See especially the recommendations in Harrison [1972].)

Radical economic theory differs substantially from both paradigms in its suggestions about policy. It agrees with many of the dual market objections to orthodox inclinations, but reinterprets those objections in terms of the dynamics of class. It argues, essentially, that the dynamics of class division and class conflict have an overriding influence on the determination of income and individual productivity. It postulates that recent stratifications of the labor market and the increasing predominance of minority groups, women, and teenagers within the secondary labor markets serve some critical economic functions both for individual employers and for the capitalist class as a whole. And it argues that the capitalist class has a fairly strong and ultimately determinant influence over extra-labor market institutions like the schools, over the relations of production, and over the state. Since the ways in which productivities are currently distributed, both through the schools and through the relations of production, seem functionally important to employers (through their positive effects on worker incentives and their negative effects on class consciousness), it seems extremely unlikely, given current circumstances, that those mechanisms will change. And, in contrast to the dual market perspective, the radical analysis expects that the state will not act spontaneously to ameliorate the conditions of secondary workers as long as their current situations serve the interests of the capitalist class. Fully adequate government provision of direct public service employment, in the radical view, seems as unlikely as government provision of a truly adequate income maintenance program, for both would upset the current power of employers as a class. The economic functions of inequality seem too important, as Weisskopf has argued most directly, to permit much hope about comprehensive public programs to eliminate poverty and underemployment.

In short, the radical analysis argues that we cannot expect relative worker "productivities" to change very much in response to marginal investments in their "productivities." Given that expectation, it argues that we can therefore expect the incomes of the poor to improve only if their relative class share increases—if, and only if, through heightened class consciousness and more determined class action, they can increase their relative bargaining power. If and when they intensify their efforts radically to increase their power, given the current utility of secondary markets to the capitalist class, one can only expect that the struggle will be intense.

How do we evaluate or reconcile these policy differences? It seems quite obvious that we cannot settle them directly without settling the fundamental analytic issues dividing the three paradigms—without reaching some consensus about the differences discussed in the first section of this chapter. We must begin to understand the contours and economic dynamics of class (and class consciousness) in order to resolve disagreements about the class nature of public institutions. We must begin to resolve some basic issues about the social, economic, and class determinants of job structure and design—about the extent to which job design responds to endogenous economic forces—in order to clarify the responsiveness of the private labor market to public manipulation. And we must begin very clearly to appreciate the boundaries, intensities, characteristics, and economic functions of market "discontinuities" in order to assess the possibilities for public assaults on those divisions. The next two chapters review what we know and don't know about those critical questions.

7

Empirical Comparisons: The Aggregate Economy

Many of the economic issues dividing the three theories of poverty and under-employment involve some questions about the behavior of aggregate economic indices—about data at the level of macro-economic analysis. This chapter reviews many of these questions, comparing the expectations of the theories with information about the world.

Unfortunately, to issue a preliminary note of warning, the paradigm competition receives relatively little illumination from this discussion of aggregate economic data. Information about economic aggregates has rarely been organized or collected with the considerations involved in this competition fully in mind. The analyses conducted by economists involved in the respective paradigms have also rarely organized their information with these debates as guides. Orthodox analyses of aggregate income and employment indices have usually been insensitive to questions of stratification and structural change; they have tended to test for universal and continuous relationships over time, and have rarely tested alternative hypotheses about cross-sectional or historical discontinuity. At the same time, the dual market and radical theories have not yet proposed precise empirical specifications of the forms of stratification and the definitions of class implied by their analyses, so that one cannot precisely test for changes in the relative shares and status of different strata. Finally, the differences among the paradigms primarily involve micro-analytic issues—questions about labor market mechanisms and processes on which macro-data have relatively little bearing.

Nonetheless, a variety of macro-economic analysis exists, some of it partly relevant to the purposes of this book, and a few important macro-analytic research suggestions can be drawn from consideration of a series of specific issues and pieces of data at the macro-analytic level. I have divided the discussion into several parts, moving from a discussion of poverty and underemployment to more general measures of the income distribution.[a]

---

[a]Many of the summary comments will have a rather pointed tone. One gets the impression, from both the literature and from informal conversation, that many orthodox economists believe that aggregate data clearly resolve the debate in their favor. I believe that this conclusion is manifestly incorrect, for I believe that one cannot reach any firm conclusions about the debate at all from the aggregate evidence. Several of the following reviews of the data reflect this orientation, concentrating on dispelling some of the more obvious instances of orthodox self-confidence.

Poverty and Underemployment

Since the competing theories seek to explain the phenomena of poverty and underemployment in the United States, one should presumably begin with aggregate evidence about the extent, distribution, and changes of those variables for some first illuminations of the debate. One learns relatively little, in fact, except perhaps that the competition involves much more complicated structural issues than movements in these simple magnitudes can help explain.

Poverty

One of the ways in which orthodox theory has celebrated the continuity and competitiveness of the labor market has been to cite the significant impact of economic growth in the battle to reduce *absolute* poverty. Economists have often cited large drops in absolute poverty, both in the long run and since 1960, as demonstrable proof that, as Thurow has summarized the argument [1969, p. 47], ".... abundant job opportunities reduce poverty by providing employment and income for the unemployed, the underemployed, and those who are attracted into the labor market by the possibility of finding employment." *The Economic Report of the President* concludes [1969, p. 153], "With the general rise in family incomes in the postwar period, the incidence of poverty ... has declined sharply."[1]

Although orthodox economists suggest that the secular decline in absolute poverty supports their views, the amount of absolute poverty is not, in fact, especially germane to the competition among paradigms discussed in this book. Absolute poverty definitions refer only to absolute income levels and not to income distributions; they provide little information about the process of income determination. It seems quite plausible within either the dual market or radical vision of highly-stratified markets that the incidence of absolute poverty would decline over time; a decline in absolute poverty seems just as consistent with their theories as with orthodox theory. There is room in both theories, for instance, for arguments that an increase in aggregate demand can effect increases in income in all sectors, simply through the effects of rising product prices. Both models would insist, however, that declines in absolute poverty prove *neither* that the barriers separating sectors are especially permeable *nor* that economic growth tends in general to erode those barriers. Each would argue that quite detailed micro-data on the patterns of labor market careers would be necessary to sustain either of those (much stronger) interpretations about the relationship between growth and absolute poverty.

Despite that general disclaimer, three main arguments seem important about the evidence on absolute poverty. First, many economists, both orthodox and radical, have discounted the conventional arguments about the effect of growth on absolute poverty because they feel that the official government definition of absolute poverty represents much too low a level of income. (See Ornati [1966], Wachtel [1971], and Ackerman et al. [1971].) If one accepts some higher estimates of the absolute poverty standard, it appears that the declines in absolute poverty have been much less pronounced. Light [1970] has argued very tentatively, for instance, that a much more ample poverty definition reveals little or no decline in the incidence of absolute poverty, measured in percentage terms, since World War II.

Second, even making use of the official poverty definitions, one can argue that the secular declines in absolute poverty have been greatly exaggerated and that, despite rapid economic growth, the incidence of absolute poverty has declined nowhere as rapidly as many seem to believe. As I have argued at greater length elsewhere (in D.M. Gordon, ed. [1971, Chapter Four]), absolute poverty definitions should reflect changes in the commodity bundles necessary to maintain a "constant" standard of living. By those standards, Ornati has argued [1966] that absolute poverty remained almost perfectly constant from the end of World War II to 1960; according to his standards of minimum adequacy, 27 percent of the population was poor in 1947 and 26 percent was poor in 1960. (The Council of Economic Advisers, in contrast, backcast 1960 absolute poverty standards and concluded that the incidence of poverty had declined from 32 percent in 1947 to 21 percent in 1960. See *Economic Report of President* [1964, p. 57].) Examining more recent data, I suggested (in D.M. Gordon, ed. [1971, Chapter Four]) that some similar adjustments might well wipe out the vaunted declines through the prosperous years of the past decade.[b]

Third, the conventional analyses of the effects of growth on absolute poverty

---

[b]Official government figures report a substantial decline in absolute poverty in the United States between 1959 and 1968: from almost 40 million persons, or 22.4 percent, to slightly more than 25 million persons, or 12.8 percent. [U.S. Bureau of the Census, "Poverty in the United States, 1959 to 1968," 1969.] Although the government figures incorporated the effects of the rising price of food, they retained their preliminary assumption of a food/income ratio at one to three. This implied a constant composition of commodities among low-income families and uniform price changes across commodities. In fact, neither assumption seems valid. According to the most recent evidence (summarized in Haber [1966]; and Rein [1968]), there seems to have been a secular decline in the food/income ratio among low-income families; it had dropped, apparently, nearly to one to four by 1960. Further, price increases were obviously not equal across commodities in the 1960s. Between 1959 and 1968, for instance, the price of food at home rose by only 16.7 percent (according to the Consumer Price Index for July, 1968), while the cost of other commodities of special importance to the poor rose much more rapidly: the cost of public transportation rose by 38.5 percent, the cost of medical care by 45.1 percent (not all of it covered, by any means), and the cost of "general services" by 34.9 percent. For illustrative purposes, I incorporated both of these indications of secular decline in the food/income ratio by assuming a food/income ratio of one to three in 1959 (along with Mollie Orshansky) and a food/income ratio of one to four in 1968. Based on rough calculations, this suggests that the number of absolutely poor Americans was roughly 50 percent higher than the official estimates, at around 37.5 million. Harrington [1970] has apparently made similar heuristic calculations, and estimates equally that an additional 12 million Americans were absolutely poor beyond the government estimates.

LEWIS AND CLARK COLLEGE LIBRARY
PORTLAND OREGON 97219

abstract from the real movements of people in and out of poverty. They concern net rather than gross flows and disguise some important differences in the impact of gross movement on the "permanent" and the "temporary" poor. Kelly [1970] provides an interesting analysis of these gross flows and suggests a much more complicated picture than the earlier orthodox analyses had portrayed. Kelly concludes, in part, that the orthodox analyses have been misleading. He writes [1970, p. 47] : "Our analysis thus tends to cast some doubt on the wisdom of relying too heavily on aggregate demand or the job market as a means to combat poverty ... it is ... surprising to find such a large number of families whose economic status remained impervious to the general prosperity of the time." Although orthodox economists have never maintained that growth would alleviate all poverty, they have nonetheless inferred some much simpler relationships than Kelly's study, among others, would permit.

More relevant than data about absolute poverty are the data about relative poverty. That amounts, in part, to a consideration of information about the income distribution and its inequality; that information will be reviewed below. Concern about relative poverty also involves some concern with income-related aspects of inequality, however, aspects of the problem which income data do not themselves illuminate. Miller and Roby [1970] provide an excellent summary of these supplementary considerations. They argue that many different kinds of inequalities—in wealth, non-monetary remuneration, and access to services, for instance—are directly associated with pure income inequalities. While their evidence does not directly involve differences in expectations among the three theories (since each could explain such associations), the Miller-Roby analysis serves to emphasize the depth and complexity of the poverty problem. There may be some trends, as I hypothesized in chapter 5 above and Miller and Roby also suggest, for employers to substitute non-monetary for monetary inequalities. To the extent that this may be true, it underscores the importance of developing comprehensive measures of relative poverty and inequality in order to avoid some misleading conclusions.

Underemployment

There has been little agreement on some appropriate measures of underemployment—except that one needs something more comprehensive than the unemployment rate. Although a subemployment index was developed in 1966 for use in a single survey of ghetto areas, it has not been applied statistically since then.[c]

[c]I would surmise three explanations for the demise of the "subemployment" index. First, the substantive justification of the measure of "underemployment" involved some assumptions about workers' being employed "below" their "productivities." Some of the analyses which arose toward the end of the decade challenged these simple notions about "productivity." (See Harrison [1972] for more discussion.) Second, the increasing sensitivity to the problem of the Census "undercount" underscored the relatively arbitrary nature of any measure of "underemployment." In the 1966 surveys, half of the estimated "undercount" were assumed to be "underemployed"; any other assumption would have affected the estimates drastically. Third, as more recent events have revealed, the government is often reluctant to release politically damaging economic data.

One finds no discussion in the literature, moreover, about the possible design of a consistent underemployment index. In the absence of such an index, a survey of trends in underemployment is obviously impossible.

Even if we could agree on a measure of underemployment, however, and could develop some consistent historical time series of that index, it would probably provide little useful information for the competition. Any decent measure of underemployment would obviously include some kind of measure of job instability, for instance. But measures of job instability are extremely difficult to interpret. Suppose that a group of presumably "underemployed" workers, like black men in their twenties, has a relatively low average job tenure. (This particular group does, in fact, have relatively low average job tenure, so the example is not academic.[2]) This relatively low tenure could be interpreted in several different ways. Orthodox economists might argue that, in a period of rapid economic growth, hiring and promotion were moving rapidly down the queue and that previously secondary workers were finding new opportunities opening up for them, inducing them rather frequently to leave their jobs for new and better ones. The dual market and radical theories might argue, in contrast, that the closed and constraining confines of the secondary market, the insensitivity of wages or status to continued stability in secondary jobs, and some changing attitudes among black secondary male workers were producing an increasing propensity among that group to work rather randomly and intermittently, moving in and out of the labor force. To test the differing interpretations of the aggregate estimates, one would need immediately to move to quite detailed microstudies of labor market careers, in order both to control for education and other indices of labor market opportunities, on the one hand, and to make some reasonable comparisons among the mid-twenties labor market experiences of different age, race, and sex groups over time.[d]

It seems important to note, finally, that it is in discussions of aggregate poverty and underemployment trends that the problem of "missing persons" in the Census surveys most seriously compromises aggregate estimates. It appears, for instance, that nearly 20 percent of black males between 20 and 35 were "missing" in the 1960 Census (Wetzel and Johnston, 1969). Different assumptions about the poverty and employment status of those males would heavily influence any discussion of aggregate poverty and underemployment trends, but we

---

[d]One should add that the proliferating macro-analyses of unemployment rates themselves are little help in resolving the competition. Orthodox economists have often tested the "queue theory," for instance, by analyzing the relationship between aggregate (or "primary" group) unemployment rates and unemployment rates among disadvantaged groups (as in Thurow [1969], and Kalachek [1969a, 1969b]). As Doeringer and Piore especially point out [1971], however, those analyses are consistent with other labor market interpretations, similar to those of dual market theory, not relying exclusively on neoclassical, competitive, marginal productivity hypotheses. The unemployment rate is, unfortunately, rather insensitive to the range of hypothesized differences among labor market strata. The possible confusion over voluntary and involuntary unemployment further complicates the use of the measure. In general, many seem increasingly to agree with Hildebrand in concluding [1968, p. 270] that "the mutually exclusive categories of employment-unemployment over-simplify the dynamics of actual market behavior." Hall [1970a] provides another very helpful discussion of the problems with analysis exclusively of unemployment rates.

are able to learn remarkably little about the characteristics of those under-counted citizens in order to narrow the range of plausible assumptions. We also know nearly nothing about time trends in the size and characteristics of the "missing" population, so that inferences about changes in aggregate measures of discrimination must be made on a kind of faith that the undercount does not bias the results. And it appears, finally, that the undercount probably varies among cities, so that even cross-sectional analyses of aggregate variables seems prey to "undercount bias."[e]

One final comment about measures of underemployment seems necessary. Some orthodox economists, in responding to the dual labor market theory's very heavy emphasis on stability and instability as defining (and perhaps determining) characteristics of labor market status, have suggested that the focus on measures of instability may prove misleading. Many of the poor or undermployed seem to work stably, they argue, and one tends to ignore their poverty if one focuses only on those jobs featuring exceptionally high turnover. The response to this argument seems clear. Although many low-wage workers may work stably, sticking with their jobs for long periods of time, it may nonetheless be true that their jobs encourage instability—an enticement they resist. This kind of argument requires a very sensitive examination of job structures, promotion patterns, and tenure incentives. Those issues involve analysis at the micro-economic level and will be discussed in the next chapter.

Income Distribution Shares

Factor Shares

Wild controversies have raged in recent years over the neoclassical formulation of orthodox theories of the distribution of income among factors of production. (See the useful survey by Harcourt [1969].) Despite the confusion within the orthodox camp, nonetheless, one can isolate some important differences in the

---

[e]One example of the critical importance of "missing" population estimates should suffice. According to BLS estimates, 13.3 percent of the total black male population over 16 was "undercounted" in the Current Population Survey for July 1967 [Wetzel and Johnston, 1969]. Based on the plausible estimates by the "Riot Commission" report of total black "subemployment" for 1967 [National Advisory Commission . . . , 1968, pp. 264-265] and the BLS 1966 assumption that 50 percent of the undercounted are "underemployed," then one estimates that measured "subemployment" indices would understate true "subemployment" by roughly one-third of the true figures.

This sensitivity of aggregate estimates to "undercount bias" has especially profound implications for the frequently manipulated ratio of black to white median incomes. For some discussion of the dangers about using that measure in light of the "undercount," see Ashenfelter [1970].

Evidence on variations in "undercount" among cities comes from conversations with Census Bureau officials about their experiences with the Urban Employment Survey. For further discussion, see Root [1968].

analysis of changing factor shares over time among the three competing paradigms.

Orthodox theories argue in general that factors will continue over time to receive shares roughly proportional to their relative marginal products (as in an aggregate production function). Analyses of changes in factor shares of income concentrate on the effects of relative changes in supply and demand. (See Reder [1959], Kravis [1962], and Harcourt [1969].) In empirical analyses, orthodox economists have tended to argue either that labor's share has risen over the long run in the United States (for instance, Kravis [1962]), or that the share of labor income has remained remarkably and surprisingly constant despite substantial historic shifts in the relative supply and productivity of labor and capital [Solow, 1958].[3] In case of either interpretation, the explanation has concentrated on relative supply and demand. Kravis has a straightforward orthodox explanation for the appearance of a rise in labor's share [1962, p. 150]:

Our discussion thus leads to the view that the impetus to the rise in the labor share came from sharp increases in real wages owing to the lack of responsiveness in the supply of man-hours to the rising demand for labor attendant upon rapid economic growth. The use of relatively more capital was made possible by price-induced substitution and by price-induced capital-using (labor saving) innovations.

Solow [1958] suggested, as a possible explanation for evidence of constant factor shares, that industrial sectors with rising labor shares diminished in relative share of aggregate demand, and that those with falling labor shares increased their share of total output, effecting a (somewhat coincidental) statistical balance between the two trends.

Both the dual market and the radical theories would emphasize, first of all, that aggregate analyses of the shares of capital and labor become less and less relevant in the United States over time as the labor market grows increasingly stratified; they suggest that one ought rather to examine the relative shares of capital and of *different* groups of labor for evidence on competing theories of factor distribution. (See also Kerr [1957].) The dual market theory suggests, for intance, that the share of secondary labor has probably weakened over time in relation either to capital or to primary labor. Radical theory argues, in general, that the path of relative shares will probably follow variations in the relative strength of different classes. Since it appears that labor's aggregate strength increased from roughly 1920 to the end of World War II, but that it has generally remained constant since then as the union movement has tended to stagnate, radical theory would expect that labor's share would first have risen but more recently have remained fairly constant. More specifically, radical theory would argue that increasing competition among different laboring classes has recently helped protect capital's share from united labor demands; it would therefore expect some important variations in the relative shares of different working classes over time with respect to changes in occupational and labor force composition and the intensity of competition among the strata.

The aggregate evidence on factor shares seems murky, since the problem of statistical definition so complicates the estimates. If there has been a rise in the share of labor historically in the United States, it has not continued past World War II, apparently, for since then the share of labor seems to have remained roughly constant by several different measures. (See Kravis [1962], and Lebergott [1964].) Those general results seem consistent with all the paradigms. Although Kerr has argued [1957, p. 287] that "there is no evidence of any significant permanent effect" of labor unions on labor's share, his conclusion that unions have acted (in Galbraith's terms) as a "counter-vailing" power seems perfectly consistent with radical expectations. The statistical confusion about aggregate factor shares seems pointless, in any case, since the most interesting issues involve trends in shares among more disaggregated groups of workers. And these trends cannot adequately be explored until dual market and radical analyses specify the boundaries of the different strata.[4]

Pending that empirical specification, perhaps the most promising route toward some relevant comparison of factor share theories would pursue the initial experiments of Thurow [1968a, 1968c]. He differentiates estimated aggregate production functions to obtain empirical estimates of the marginal products of capital and labor (under assumptions of constant returns to scale) and compares those marginal products with actual average returns. He discovers that labor has consistently earned less than its marginal product since 1929 in the United States, while capital has earned considerably more than its marginal product. Although his results must be interpreted with caution, they provide some interesting initial support for the radical view. First of all, they produce some evidence of relative exploitation of labor by capital that is at least as consistent with the radical theory as with some ad hoc orthodox explanations involving disequilibrium. Further, the disaggregated results (for manufacturing, nonmanufacturing, and agriculture) conform closely to variations in labor strength in the disaggregated sectors: labor earns nearly 80 percent of its marginal product in manufacturing, and only 60 percent in nonfarm, nonmanufacturing. Orthodox analysis can be applied to explain many of Thurow's results (as Thurow indeed suggests), but it does not offer an automatic explanation. The results are suggestive and should be developed further, at least for the purposes of this competition. In particular, further studies could try to disaggregate the results even further, comparing industries with relatively homogeneous and concentrated groups of workers stratified by unionization, race, and sex in order more closely to approximate the radical hypotheses about variations in relative class strength and relative class consciousness.[5]

Income Size Distribution

Orthodox analysts generally conclude, however informally, that the size distribution of income in capitalist societies has grown more equal over time. (See especially Kuznets [1963, 1966].) One of the principle recent sources of this equalization is presumed to rest in the effects of education, particularly in the United States. Soltow has argued [1960, p. 453]: "Education shifts, although not as important historically as occupational shifts, will continue to be a strong factor in decreasing inequality of income as the average educational attainment is raised." With reference to a longer period, Kravis makes much the same kind of argument [1960, p. 416]: ". . . further economic growth, accompanied by the spread of education . . . produces a movement toward the more equal distribution of income." Or, as Kravis has put it elsewhere [1962, pp. 216-217]: "The rising level of education probably increased the ability of new recruits to the labor force to acquire skills and thus tended to increase the relative supplies of skilled workers."[6]

Dual market theory has more limited but essentially different expectations. Applied most clearly to the period in the United States since World War II, the dual market analysis suggests primarily that the size distribution of income from labor should appear increasingly bi-modal—that the relative bargaining strength of primary workers should increase their incomes relative to those of secondary workers (given certain plausible assumptions about changes in the composition of demand). This would tend to suggest, in general, a rising relative share of the middle and upper-middle ranges of the size distribution.

Radical theory expects changes in the income size distribution to correspond both to changes in relative productivities and to changes in relative strength among increasingly stratified workers.[f] It would expect, in part, that the incomes of more advantaged workers (or the size shares of more advantaged classes) may have been able to increase over the shares of less advantaged workers as the competition among strata has increased and as the class consciousness of more advantaged workers has risen. It would expect, in general, that the size distribution of income in the United States would change in roughly the same way as the distribution of income among factors; that if factor shares have remained roughly constant since World War II, for instance, so has the income size distribution as a reflection of an approximate constancy of relative class power.

Again, the evidence on the issue seems rather difficult to interpret. Long-run historical series on the income size distribution have been difficult to develop [Kravis, 1962; H.P. Miller, 1966]. More important, it has been difficult to relate historical data on income to historical data on labor force composition, occupation, and education. And finally, there has been some fairly wide variation in the measures by which analysts have expressed relative equality and inequality (see the discussion in T.P. Schultz [1969], and Budd [1970]).

Despite those difficulties, the very rough aggregate evidence seems slightly more consistent with the dual market and radical theories than with the orthodox view. Historically, the American income size distribution seems slightly to

---

[f]This assumes, obviously, that classes defined by the relations of production correspond more or less to classes defined by income. This is only partly true, but true enough to permit a radical assessment of the size distribution. For more on the problems of measuring the radical concepts of class, see Bowles [1970b].

have equalized up to and through World War II, a trend which fits equally with any of the theories. But since World War II, the evidence seems to support the dual market and radical views more closely. The aggregate shape of the distribution changed imperceptibly throughout the period since the war, whatever the measure of inequality employed (Miller [1966], Schultz [1969], Thurow [1970c], and Budd [1970]). Since average educational attainment increased substantially throughout the period, one would have expected, from the simple and partial analyses of some orthodox economists, that the distribution would have continued to grow more equal.[g] Schultz [1969], who most carefully controls for cyclical variations, seems to suggest that its failure to grow more equal can be explained primarily by the influx of women and teenagers into the labor force. Chiswick and Mincer [1971], in an extremely detailed application of the "human capital" model to an analysis of inequality over time, conclude that postwar changes in the level and inequality of age and schooling have been small and off-setting. Since their analysis does not backcast before 1939, it is difficult to compare the consistency of their analysis with prewar changes. Perhaps more interesting, the slight shifts within the distribution are also consistent with the dual market and radical explanations (although not necessarily inconsistent with plausible orthodox explanations). As Budd [1970] has most clearly shown, the most important shifts in the American size distribution since World War II have benefited the middle and upper-middle income classes at the expense both of the bottom half and the upper twentieth; Budd finds specifically that those earners between the 40th-50th percentile and the 90th-95th percentile have been able to increase their share of total income. Either the dual market or the radical analysis would explicitly predict that pattern.

That evidence still helps only slightly to illuminate the issues posed by the competition among paradigms, however. More clearly, to echo comments made about factor share analysis, one would want to be able to identify precise strata within the income distribution and to balance changes in their shares against changes in their "demand and supply" characteristics and their relative class power. At the moment, we are limited to analyses of income size distributions by family units, a dimension slightly inappropriate for these purposes. Once both the dual market and radical analyses produce more specified definitions of their hypothesized strata, the analyses of size distributions can proceed with more direction for the purposes of this competition.[7]

Occupational Differentials

Orthodox economic theory involves no precise empirical expectation about trends in occupational wage and income differentials in the short run, for it ex-

---

[g]To be specific, the median educational attainment of white males between 25 and 29 years increased from 10.5 years in 1940 to 12.6 years in 1969, while the median attainment of their nonwhite peers increased from 6.5 years in 1940 to 12.1 years in 1969. (From U.S. Bureau of the Census, *Historical Statistics . . .* [1962], p. 214; and U.S. Bureau of the Census, "The Social and Economic Status of Negroes . . ." [1970], p. 50.)

pects that those differentials will reflect underlying shifts in demand and supply. In the long run, however, orthodox economists seek to explain trends in differentials by "the competitive hypothesis" (as in Reder [1962]), and would expect, *ceteris paribus*, that differentials would tend to narrow in the very long run.

Dual market theory would seem to predict, *ex post*, that the wage differentials between primary and secondary occupations have probably widened since World War II, or at least that a longer-run trend toward equality has probably slackened, as a result of the market's increasing dichotomization. Its expectations about occupational differentials must be formulated quite carefully, however. Unlike orthodox theory, which tends to assume a considerable fixity in occupational structure over time, dual market theory expects that the structural and behavioral characteristics of different jobs will change quite substantially over time as technologies, customs, market forces, and employee characteristics all interact. This implies, most imponderably, that one can almost never isolate a group of occupations among which to conduct the necessarily partial analysis of trends in differentials, for the behavioral characteristics of those occupations will probably have changed.[h]

Radical theory views occupational differentials in similar ways. Like dual market theory, radical theory would expect a slackening of historic trends toward narrowing differentials—if not an actual widening of differentials—in recent years as a result of increasing consciousness among upper strata. It would also expect that the changing nature of different occupations over time—and particularly the changing patterns of relative class power and class consciousness among occupations—would substantially vitiate the precision of any simple historical analysis of differentials.

Regardless of the relative murkiness of the expectations of the three paradigms, the empirical evidence does not turn out to be very useful for these purposes, for two different reasons. First, the most careful analyses of wage differentials cannot seem to produce consistent pieces of evidence about trends in differentials based on roughly the same dimensions of occupational comparison. Reder [1962] concludes with persistent ambivalence that the evidence may confirm the competitive hypothesis, although he admits [p. 298] that it "can hardly be said to be firmly established as an explanation of wage phenomena even for long periods . . . " Hildebrand and Delehanty [1966] conclude from their much more detailed analysis of postwar occupational wages that the results are "mixed." Ulman reviews their results and those of other studies, concluding [1966, p. 317] that "the bag is mixed, the returns are not all in yet, and the authors' scrupulous caution may be complemented with reference to some mixed results of other studies."

---

[h]At the roughest level of detail, obviously, the behavioral characteristics of "service" workers have changed substantially over time. At much more detailed levels, the behavioral characteristics in many specific blue-collar occupations and white-collar occupations have probably also changed, as both blue-collar and white-collar jobs have become more stratified and hierarchical. I suggest (in D.M. Gordon [1972]), indeed, that aggregate occupational data reveal an increasing heterogeneity within Census occupational categories.

Second, the issues posed by the dual market and radical analyses suggest that the occupations among which differentials should be compared have been changing substantially over time. Many empirical analyses have traditionally concentrated on the differentials between blue-collar and white-collar or "unskilled" and "skilled" occupations. But as the labor market has grown more stratified in the United States, according to the dual market and radical views, differentials within any of those categories have tended to widen, raising the possibility that within-group differentials have varied more than between-group differences. This tends to undercut the possibilities for decent long-run historical analysis, and the implications of the orthodox view are not as clear for shorter periods. (See D.M. Gordon [1972].)

Clearly, as with the other measures of macro-income distributions, a clearer analysis of occupational differentials awaits some more precise specifications by the dual market and radical analyses of the particular dimensions along which they expect that stratifications have developed. Kerr had concluded his study of factor share evidence [1957, p. 297] by arguing that it is "probably becoming much more important to measure and to discuss size distribution than share distribution. . . ." One of the implications of the dual market and radical views is that, in fact, the dimensions along which we should seek to study factor share, income size, and occupational distributions are tending to merge. As the labor market becomes more and more stratified, in their views, the structural determinants of the three kinds of distributions will tend increasingly to coincide; factor share distributions will depend on the relative size and strength of different labor sectors, and so will income size and occupational distributions. And in all three cases, we do not yet seem to know enough about the specific dimensions of stratification to specify the precise formulae for these macro-analyses. Those specifications depend, quite precisely, on some answers posed most directly by issues in micro-analysis; only through some very complicated micro-analysis, of sorts to be described in the following section, will we be able to develop the definitions by which we can pursue the competition at the aggregate level.

Macro-economic Models

Some very brief comments seem appropriate, finally, about macro-economic models. Toward the end of the 1960s, the consistency and structure of many orthodox models of aggregate economic activity began to shift. (See R.J. Gordon [1970] and Perry [1970].) Some orthodox economists seemed inclined to explain those shifting aggregate relationships by reference to exogenous changes in tastes. In trying to explain the analysis by Perry [1970], which suggests an outward shift in the Phillips Curve during the 1960s, Charles Schultze expressed some frustration at being left with such arbitrary recourse [1970, p. 443]: "There is an alternate explanation of the phenomenon that gives Perry's results and that could explain some of the widening unemployment differences. . . . It is a sociological hypothesis—and it troubles my soul to dabble in sociology, particularly of this brand."

Recourse to sociology does not seem so necessary, given the perspectives discussed in this book. Both the dual labor market and the radical viewpoints would have predicted some of the shifts which Perry measures as a result of endogenous changes in labor market structures. The relative fruitfulness of those perspectives cannot actually be demonstrated until some specific definitions of sectors and strata are developed, but it seems useful to suggest their relevance for more orthodox attempts to explain the various conundra of late-60s aggregate economic activity.[i]

---

[i]Some extrapolation of the dual market and radical analysis at the aggregate level should be possible soon. I have been developing some tentative empirical definitions of market strata (in D.M. Gordon [1971b] and work in progress). When those definitions are completed, it should be possible to test for some structural shifts in the behavior of aggregate variables within strata over time and to compare those tests with the more aggregate evidence.

8

Empirical Comparisons: Labor Market Behavior

Many of the more central issues raised by this paradigm competition involve questions about labor market behavior—about issues of micro-economic analysis. This chapter reviews a variety of micro-analytic studies for their illumination of the competition. As with chapter 7, many of the studies seem to suggest little more than the need for further and better research. In several parts of the chapter, I have paid particular attention to the research lacunae revealed by the issues involved in the paradigm competition.

The chapter has three parts, focusing on the three main substantive areas of difference among the theories. The first section deals with labor market discontinuity, the second with the interaction between jobs and people, and the third with economic class.

Labor Market Discontinuity

The competition among paradigms involves some clear and important issues about the presence, intensity, and effects of labor market discontinuities. The implications of the paradigms and the relevant evidence can best be summarized in two different parts. On the one hand, one can consider general and summary evidence on basic labor market patterns in order to search for the general contours of labor market divisions. On the other hand, one can discuss evidence concerning the potential impact of marginal changes in labor market characteristics or behavior—on the part either of firms or of individuals—on the character and intensity of whatever divisions seem most important. Orthodox theory is prepared to admit that labor market imperfections may be our historical legacy, but the theory usually postulates that marginal adjustments will tend, through the competitive process, at least marginally to diminish the importance of those market divisions. If competition no longer entirely exists, the theory often seems to argue, we should be able to recreate it. In slightly different ways, on the other hand, dual market and radical analyses have not only built their analyses from the foundation of market stratifications but they have also anticipated that marginal changes in the individual characteristics or behavior of either firms or individuals will not dent the walls between strata.

General Labor Market Patterns

Most of the usual studies of labor market discontinuity do not help illuminate the competition. These studies typically examine the differences in outcomes

111

between two demographically-identified groups, like blacks and whites, and conclude either that discrimination remains or that it does not. The analyses rarely concern labor market *process*, the mechanisms through which those differences in outcomes are generated. (See Michelson [1968] for a useful taxonomic discussion of the relationship between outcome and process.) But the terms of competition among these theories of poverty and underemployment do not involve the simple presence of important inequalities, which each of the theories admits, so much as they involve the degree to which inequalities are exogenously determined or endogenously reinforced. Those questions cannot be answered by simple analyses of outcomes but must be explored through intensive analysis of basic labor market operations.

Since World War II, unfortunately, economists have made few attempts to provide a general view of the behavior of firms and individuals within identifiable labor markets.[1] Faced with the recent paucity of information, I have concentrated on the more general empirical questions raised by the competition and on only a few of the more suggestive pieces of information in the literature.

Relying on conventional assumptions and hypotheses about labor market competition, orthodox analysis usually presumes that a wide variety of labor market mechanisms tend to work against market stratifications, either preventing their rise or eroding them if they have arisen historically. Orthodox analysis seems to assume, first of all, that class stratification tends not to survive intergenerationally, principally because individuals are able to make schooling investment decisions quite rationally and competitively. Once individuals enter the labor market, moreover, orthodox economists place heavy reliance on the possibilities for individual investment in human capital (outside the school) and on labor mobility within or among sectors as market equilibrating mechanisms. Theoretically, for instance, Rosen [1971] proposes a mechanism by which workers make optimal lifetime investments in on-the-job human capital investment opportunities by switching from job to job throughout their careers. Empirically, earlier labor market studies (like Palmer [1954]) emphasized the amount of upward labor mobility within individual labor market careers. The nature of the "competitive hypothesis" itself implies, as Reder [1962] has emphasized, that labor mobility plays a critical role in the long run in preserving the forces of labor market competition. More than ever, the "new" micro-economics pursued by Phelps and friends [1970] postulates a wide variety of labor market mechanisms, especially through the impact of the economics of information and job search (and drawing heavily on Stigler [1962]), which tend, in the long run, to reproduce the conditions of competitive labor markets.

Both the dual market and the radical theories paint quite different general pictures of the labor market. They emphasize that the cumulative impact of a wide variety of institutional inequalities and discriminatory practices produces an effective stratification of the labor market, thoroughly resistant to the impact of competitive forces and individual decisions. The stratification persists, according to both views, because it underlies and is supportive of the functioning of labor market institutions. Without it, the ways in which firms are able to operate (and in which certain groups of workers are able to benefit) in the labor market would be fundamentally disrupted.

The two theories diverge a bit, however, in the details of their expectations about general labor market patterns. Both emphasize the rigidity of barriers among job clusters within the labor market. The dual market theory pays less attention to the relationship between labor market and extra-labor market institutions than the radical theory. Because the dual market theory does not employ the concept of class and does not postulate class influences on the state, or on state expenditures, it does not link labor market stratifications with educational stratifications as clearly and closely as the radical theory. Furthermore, dual market theory expects that the secondary job market is dominated increasingly by blacks, women, and teenagers and therefore tends to deemphasize, at least implicitly, the continuing influence of class on white males both within and outside the labor market. The radical theory expects, for instance, that class influences on educational attainment, educational quality, and attitudes toward schooling are nearly as powerful in affecting lower-class whites as in affecting minority groups, but that white males face rather less labor market discrimination than minority group members once they begin their labor market careers.

Quite obviously, it is extremely difficult to devise some rigorous tests of market stratification in order to compare the orthodox with the dual market and radical visions of the labor market. If one kind of labor market imperfection is erased, another is typically confronted, and orthodox theory can always claim that the remaining imperfections can also be eroded without fundamentally disruptive effects on labor market mechanisms. At best, available evidence can only be suggestive. Nonetheless, most of the micro-information we have, in the most approximate ways, tends to suggest strong and persistent labor market stratifications with pervasive effects.

Inferentially, to begin with, three recent individual labor market studies provide impressive evidence of intra-market wage differentials which the analysts themselves conclude are reflections of important labor market stratifications, of quite "separate" intra-metropolitan markets. Rees concludes from the Chicago Labor Market Study [1968, p. 247]: "Our work shows a number of different kinds of submarkets, marked by wage differences related to patterns of residential and non-residential areas, concentrations of particular kinds of industry, and concentrations of nonwhite population." M.S. Gordon and Thal-Larsen conclude, equally, that important sub-markets exist within the San Francisco Bay Area labor market [1969, pp. xx-xxi]:

Undoubtedly the most interesting of our wage findings relate to patterns of spatial or geographical wage differentials within the Bay Area. Not only do these findings appear to be consistent in many ways with those of the recent Rees-

Shultz study of the Chicago labor market, but they also strongly suggest that further research along these lines in large labor market areas would be very fruitful. Moreover, they indicate that differences in demand and supply relationships in various parts of a large labor market area play a significant role in explaining these spatial wage differentials. . . .

The results of an analysis of the Boston labor market, finally, produced strong evidence of at least two quite separate labor markets. (See Doeringer [1968], Doeringer et al. [1969] and Doeringer and Piore [1970].)

Second, labor mobility studies have, in general, found that many of the conditions necessary to support the assumptions of orthodox analyses have not frequently been present in those labor markets studied. Parnes concluded from his earlier survey of mobility research [1954, pp. 197-198] that workers' labor market information was usually poor; that workers were not often in the position of "comparing the desirability of two or more jobs, either of which they can have"; that wages provide only a small part of the motivation behind voluntary job changes; that wage differentials persist within labor markets; and that these differentials are "often reinforced by differentials in the nonwage attractiveness of jobs." Parnes and associates have since concluded [1970b] that labor market information is least ample when labor market entry decisions are made, and that, once those decisions are made, those in lower wage and status occupations are not often able to improve their income or status by job shifts.

Much more detailed evidence exists on the presence and strength of stratifications at different stages in workers' lifetimes. Evidence on the class stratifications of educational systems and of unequal lower-class and racial access to differential educational resources has been amply documented (see Guthrie et al. [1969] for a useful summary, and Bowles [1972] for discussion). Large racial differences have been shown to exist in the translation of educational attainment to first job [Blau and Duncan, 1967], as well as fairly substantial class differences among whites [Schiller, 1971]. Given first jobs, large racial differences in wage and status have also been substantiated, controlling for age and education. Parnes and associates found, for example, that among male operatives, 20-24 years of age with eleven years of schooling, whites earn an average $2.39 an hour, while blacks earn an average $1.72 an hour [Parnes et al., 1970b, p. 98]. And, of equal importance, there is evidence of substantial differences in the access to promotion *within* occupations. Blau and Duncan [1967] and Parnes et al. [1970a] have shown this effect on a national sample for broadly-defined occupational categories. And in one of the most revealing studies of labor market stratification in the literature (based on the Chicago Labor Market study), Taylor [1968] found that white material handlers earned more than black material handlers (controlling for education, age, marital status, job location, job experience, and establishment characteristics) essentially because they were considered "promotable." He concludes [1968, p. 389] :

White material handlers are considered promotable and hence are disproportion-
ately in positions in high-wage firms. Nonwhite material handlers are not generally in the promotable category and, through the allocational effects of discrimination, are to a larger extent employed by low-wage firms.

As a result, it seems insufficient to argue, as Bergmann in particular has suggested recently [1971], that racial wage and occupational differentials can be
explained primarily by the initial allocation of workers among occupations upon
labor market entry. Even after initial occupation has been determined, patterns
for advancement from first job vary widely between the races. Parnes and associates conclude [1970a, p. 118] of older males, for instance, that ". . . . the occupational differences between whites and blacks are greater in their current jobs
than at the beginnings of their careers."

Similar evidence abounds about women. Fuchs [1971] finds, for instance,
that one cannot reduce the income differentials between men and women very
much at all by controlling for variables which economists typically relate to income and productivity. Shea et al. [1970] conclude that large numbers of
women have been downwardly mobile during their careers, in considerable contrast to the career paths of men described by Blau and Duncan [1967]. Davies
and Reich [1972] review several independent measures of the barriers dividing
males and females in the labor force.

It seems much less clear whether there are significant class stratifications
among workers independent of sex and race distinctions. (See the general discussion in Bowles [1970b].) Schiller [1971] provides evidence that class distinctions have some influence on inequalities in first-job attainment, but his evidence
does not extend beyond career beginnings. Although Parnes et al. [1970a] had
available some interesting data about class (or family) background, they did not
make use of that information.

In my dissertation, I tried to develop some more systematic tests for the character and intensity of labor market stratification. (See D.M. Gordon [1971b].)
The variety of analyses and complexity of results confound simple summary, but
they do provide several interesting supplementary pieces of evidence about labor
market inequalities. First, they suggest that labor market inequalities develop
and intensify at each of several stages of individual labor market careers. For
both blacks and women, inequalities appear at the beginnings of careers, during
the process of movement from first jobs to present jobs, and, given present occupational status, in the determination of wages. Second, the analyses provide
some interesting evidence of fundamental behavioral differences not only in the
determination of status and income but also in the tenure response of different
workers to their relative status. Relying on what I call "the beginner's luck tenure hypothesis" and the "overachiever's tenure hypothesis," I provide some interesting evidence that more "secondary" workers develop a certain insensitivity
to their relative fortunes in the labor market; they seem to lose some of the

"ambition" so characteristic of primary workers. (See Kalachek and associates [1970] for some similar evidence from their study of St. Louis.) Third, in a way to be described below, they suggest some interesting pieces of evidence about class discrimination; certain groups of whites, properly defined, seem to behave quite differently in the labor market than the basic control group of "primary" white males.

Few of these pieces of evidence, however suggestive, provide any direct tests of the more specific dual market and radical hypotheses about the contours of stratification in the United States. Is there a clear and evident separation between "primary" and "secondary" markets, for instance, characterized by behavioral differences along the stability/instability axis? As I argue in my dissertation [D.M. Gordon, 1971b], it has not been possible to specify the dimensions of this primary/secondary division a priori because there have been some disagreements about the relative importance of personal and job characteristics in the evolution of the dual structure. (See the comments in chapter 4 above.)

In my dissertation, I sidestep the problem of a priori specification and develop a test for market duality which allows the data to speak for themselves. Making use of factor analysis and relying on some analogies with the factor analysis of intelligence test scores, I devise an explicit empirical test for market duality in which one is not forced to specify the parameters associated with that duality before the analysis. The test seems very clearly to confirm the dual market hypothesis. Controlling for a first factor reflecting the general distribution of income among jobs, one finds a second factor, which I label the "dual market factor," which reflects almost all of the predicted dimensions of difference among primary and secondary jobs—differences in stability, attitudes, worker characteristics, and labor market behavior. Ranking jobs by their scores on this "dual market factor," one finds that jobs are bimodally distributed along the factor score axis. One detects a clear division into two sectors, in other words, between which one can draw a line.

This division of jobs into primary and secondary clusters bears interesting fruit. Given that division among jobs, one can compare the labor market behavior and outcomes of different groups of workers in each sector. One finds some clear differences among workers divided both by demographic characteristics and by sector of work. Even among white males, for instance, there seem to be some interesting and important differences in labor market behavior between those who work in primary and secondary jobs. This set of results, as I argue elsewhere [1971b, Chapter Six], offers interesting possibilities for very explicit tests of some of the differences among the paradigms on this stratification issue. Taking off from those suggestions, the conclusions in chapter 9 summarize some of the most important implications of the current evidence and the paradigm differences for further research.

Marginal Change

Although evidence about general patterns of labor market discontinuity bears more directly on the paradigm competition, specific studies of marginal variations in one or another individual characteristic have often been drawn into the debate to support one side or another. Some brief reviews of those studies seem necessary, if for no other reason than to suggest their inconclusiveness as sources of information about the terms of the competition.

1. Education. The most extensive discussion of marginal improvement in the incomes of the poor concerns the potential marginal impact of improvement of the educational attainments of the poor. This focus has been intensified by the increasing popularity of human capital analysis within the orthodox perspective. And the differences between the orthodox perspective on the one hand and the dual market and radical perspectives on the other seem quite profound. These differences involve two different empirical issues: first, empirical expectations about patterns of monetary "returns" to years of schooling; and second, the structural mechanisms through which schooling improves income.

And one must probe these empirical issues quite carefully in order to develop some useful pieces of information for comparative purposes. All three paradigms expect that, in general, those with more education will earn more income, as they do indeed in the United States. The paradigms differ in their rather more precise expectations about the patterns of returns to education among different groups, and in their assumptions about the mechanisms through which the education/income relationship develops.

a. Monetary returns. Orthodox analysis—and particularly human capital analysis—would predict that all groups in the labor market should realize monetary returns to their marginal investments in additional education, *ceteris paribus*, for it is on that hypothesis that recommendations about the efficacy of education as an antipoverty policy instrument seem to rest. Dual market and radical analyses emphasize quite different empirical expectations. They suggest, in general, that secondary male workers (and especially blacks) will realize few, if any monetary returns to many incremental levels of educational attainment because they are typically channeled into secondary jobs in which educational attainment makes little difference, either in their manifest productivities or in their (negligible) chances for promotion. The two analyses would expect more evident patterns of returns to education among women, both because stronger discriminatory patterns against women within the labor market help reduce the bargaining strength of women (and permit employers to reward the more educated without fearing for greater mobility), and because many women work in a variety of white-collar clerical jobs for which some general educational skills are useful.[a]

Some initial evidence on returns to education among blacks tends to confirm the dual market and radical expectations. Weiss [1970] finds, in a national sample for 1960, that black males in three of four age categories did not realize any significant marginal returns to years of schooling, controlling for some other demographic variables. Hanoch [1967] found that blacks universally realized lower returns to education than whites, and that those returns were negligible for the 9-11 years of school category. Michelson [1968, 1969] shows, using the same kinds of specification as Hanoch, quite low or negligible returns for blacks in the intermediate educational ranges. More clearly, since the analysis is performed on local rather than national samples, Harrison [1971, 1972] has found quite low or insignificant returns to education for blacks in the ghetto and outside the ghetto. Harrison's results withstand considerable experimentation with different data bases and different model specifications. (And he finds that, in contrast, even those whites who still live in the ghetto realize significant returns to educational investment.) In my dissertation [1971b, Chapters Three and Five], I find widespread evidence that education bears few rewards for secondary workers throughout their labor market careers. Bergmann and Lyle [1970] and Friedlander [cited in *Manpower Report of the President*, 1971, p. 93] provide some interesting evidence that the labor market success of blacks across cities does not correspond very closely to variations in their relative educational attainments.

Perhaps most strikingly, Taylor [1968] found that, even within as narrowly-defined an occupational category as material handlers, whites realized statistically significant returns to years of schooling while "for the nonwhites, however, education does not contribute to the fit of the equation." Taylor draws two inferences from his result, both consistent with the dual market and radical perspectives [1968, p. 386]:

There may be two factors operating to produce this result. First, employers could be considering whites but not Negroes as potentially promotable to more skilled jobs, and their educational level is thus of some significance. Second, employers may view the educational attainment of Negroes as irrelevant because of their feelings, justified or not, about the quality of nonwhite schools.

Using a different measure of labor market success, finally, Blau and Duncan [1967] found that black males gained much less occupational advancement from incremental educational attainment than white males, even though they

---

[a]The only ways that statistically insignificant returns to additional educational investment could be predicted by the human capital model, it appears, would be by assuming a perfectly inverse correlation between years of schooling and quality of schooling among certain groups; by assuming investor irrationality; by assuming perfect complementarity between returns to education and returns to on-the-job training; or by assuming some unexpected and unusual shapes of or correlations between the demand and supply curves.

were measuring occupational status by a "socioeconomic index" highly corre-
lated with years of education. They found [1967, p. 210] in particular and in
surprising agreement with the economic analyses of education and income, that:

For nonwhites, however, the increment in upward mobility effected by higher
education is relatively small except for the college-educated.... Education, a
path to upward mobility for all, is not as effective a route up for nonwhites as it
is for whites. This pattern exists notwithstanding the lower social origins of nonwhites, which should make it easier for them than for whites, if other things
were equal, to attain upward mobility.

None of these scattered pieces of evidence provides any kind of finally conclusive evidence on the relative validity of the paradigms' expectations about returns to education, for two different kinds of reasons. First, as Thurow [1969]
particularly emphasizes and as Mincer [1971] also suggests, there are important
complementarities between education and later on-the-job investments in training, and one needs precisely to control for those later opportunities in order to
make proper inferences about the potential of educational advancement.
Thurow [1969] tries to measure the complementarities, concluding that the
racial inequalities in later investment opportunity far outweigh the inequalities
in return to education. For his results precisely to bear on the competition, however, it would be important both to try to stratify his results by different indus-
trial/occupational groupings (in order to test the stratification hypotheses) and
to break "on-the-job" experience down into "general" and "specific" components—which his data do not permit. Very few sources of data, in fact, permit
the kinds of detailed occupational histories which we would require quite precisely to test for differences in educational returns.

Second, and much more important, the analyses depend on some implicit assumptions about the structural relationship between education and income
which are rarely evaluated. The following paragraphs explore that issue.

b. The Structural Mechanisms of Education. Orthodox analyses assume, in general, that workers realize returns to formal education because they become generally more productive with increasing education. The analyses seem to assume,
further, that the specific dimensions of productivity which formal education is
especially likely to supply are those of general reasoning abilities, or cognitive
skills.[2] In contrast, both the dual market and the radical analyses have different
kinds of expectations about the structural role of education. Dual market analyses generally assume that education has little relevance for the analysis of productivity in most male secondary jobs; that it has some relevance for many fe-
male secondary jobs; that it has fairly little relationship to primary blue-collar
productivity—since, as Doeringer and Piore write [1971, p. 18], "by far the largest proportion of blue collar job skills are acquired on the job"—and that, for
many primary white-collar jobs, "formal education is often used more as a

screening device for selecting people with certain aptitudes and social backgrounds" [Doeringer and Piore, loc. cit.]. Radical analyses of education carry the same specific expectations about the structural role of education in the United States at present. They assume more generally that education serves two primary functions in capitalist societies: to help establish and preserve class divisions within the labor force; and to develop the sets of personality characteristics functional to the work requirements of the separate classes. (See Bowles [1972], D.M. Gordon, ed. [1971], and Gintis [1971].)

These differences, obviously, are extremely difficult to test, but a surprising amount of evidence is beginning to appear to support the dual market and radical views. Ivar Berg [1969] has summarized a wide variety of evidence that educational achievement (measured either by years of schooling or achievement scores) seems fairly unrelated to variations in worker productivity. He draws, basically, on two different kinds of evidence. He refers, first of all, to the work of Eckaus [1964], Scoville [1966], and others, who relate aggregate trends in educational achievement to aggregate trends in the educational requirements of jobs (as manifested in the Dictionary of Occupational Titles ratings); he concludes, in general, that [1969, p. 80] "educational achievements were changing much more rapidly than jobs..." and that, as a result, we cannot automatically assume a direct relationship between job requirements and educational attainments. Second and more important, Berg draws on a wide variety of (often unpublished) evidence which suggests that educational achievement (measured by grades or tests) bears surprisingly little relationship to measures of worker productivity on the job, especially as employers define productivity by merit ratings and promotions. Both in blue-collar and white-collar work, Berg cites numerous studies which suggest that "success" on the job has only rarely been related to superior educational achievement or attainment.

Still more rigorously, Gintis [1969, 1971] has summarized a wide variety of evidence which suggests that education produces a certain set of attitudes, compatible with the capitalist mode of production, much more directly than it produces productive cognitive achievement. He derives this conclusion from three different kinds of evidence. He shows, first of all, that several different studies of education, ability, achievement, and earnings all tend to support the hypothesis that the influence of education on earnings is independent of the influence of education on cognitive achievement (measured by standard tests); in nearly all those studies, the contribution of education to earnings is barely and often insignificantly reduced by the subsequent inclusion of a variable controlling for achievement scores. Second, Gintis cites a wide variety of studies, including some of his own original research, which show that a consistent set of psychological attitudes are much more closely related with performance in school, especially with grades in school, than cognitive achievement is related to performance in school. The set of attitudes roughly reflects the worker requirements in bureaucratic organizations: students in school are rewarded principally for the traits of "subordinacy," "discipline," "supremacy of cognitive over affective modes of response," and "motivation according to external reward." The most compelling of the several results draw from work by Gene Smith [1967], in which factor analysis shows that an attitudinal factor, roughly reflecting the student's "strength of character and especially his self-discipline," explains by far the largest portion of the variance in school grades, three times greater than the variance explained by a factor associated with high scores on achievement tests. Third, Gintis concludes from several surveys of worker performance on the job, several of them complementary to those cited by Berg, which equally confirm that worker attitudes bear a much closer relationship to performance on the job than do measures of educational achievement.[3]

In short, two fairly comprehensive surveys of the structural relationship between education and income conclude, as Gintis puts it [1971], "that the economic productivity of schooling is due primarily to the inculcation of personality characteristics." Those who fare better in school, and therefore tend to last longer in school, are those with the personalities most suitable to certain kinds of jobs in large organizations. Since it is presumably much more difficult to change personality structures than to change reading scores, one cannot very blithely assume that increasing the educational achievements of the poor will automatically increase their incomes.

These results are suggestive about the kinds of productivities, if any, which education tends to instill in workers. Another kind of evidence is just beginning to emerge to support the second half of the general radical argument about education: that education helps to reinforce class differences by instilling different kinds of attitudes and behavioral characteristics in the children of different kinds of parents, themselves segregated residentially or by tracking. Sexton [1961] and Friedenberg [1963] had provided earlier qualitative evidence that different schools emphasized different kinds of social behavior among their students depending on student socioeconomic states. Bowles [1970b, 1972] has carefully sorted the issues involved in the radical assertion and summarized a variety of evidence which tends very tentatively to provide support for the radical analysis.

At both these levels of analysis about the structural role of education, however, much more work needs to be done to provide differential evidence on the mechanisms of education affecting different classes. If the dual market and particularly the radical analyses are correct, then the behavioral and attitudinal requirements of work vary sharply among different classes within the relations of production, and schooling helps create those differences. As Gintis has argued [1971, p. 272n]:

Actually the personality requisites of job adequacy no doubt vary from level to level with the hierarchy of production, and different levels of schooling (e.g. grade school, high school, junior college, college) likely reflect these differential needs. Moreover, within a particular educational level, we would expect different types of schooling to subsist side-by-side (e.g. ghetto, working-class, and middle-class-suburban high schools), reflecting the differential positions in the production hierarchy that its students are destined to fill.

As with other issues, we need here much more carefully to explore the dimensions of stratification in the labor market in order most carefully to develop analyses of the relationships between attitudes developed in school and attitudes required on the job.

2. Institutional Training. Orthodox analyses have tended, at least until recently, to assume that general institutional vocational training, like education, will help raise the marginal productivities of disadvantaged workers and therefore help raise their incomes. Both dual market and radical analyses have placed much less faith in the strategy, although the differences between the paradigms have begun to diminish as everyone, from all three perspectives, is beginning to conclude that on-the-job training makes much more sense and carries much more promise than general institutional training. With Thurow [1968b], many orthodox economists have been concluding that institutional training programs have "not been very successful" at improving the employment prospects of disadvantaged workers. And many have also tended to agree with Doeringer and Piore [1971, p. 200] that

the responsibility of training for skills and abilities which are enterprise-specific . . . should rest with the enterprise. The structure of the internal labor market makes it difficult for workers outside the enterprise to gain direct access to many jobs utilizing these skills even if trained to perform them.

All three perspectives, to a certain extent, have reached those conclusions in response to scattered pieces of evidence about the performance of institutional training programs during the 1960s. Although many early studies of training programs seemed to show, in cost-benefit terms, that training was successful—that retraining, as Somers put it [1968, p. 7] "is a sound social investment"—some later reevaluations raised serious questions about the relevance of those results.[4] On one level, some serious methodological questions were raised about the usefulness of cost-benefit analysis for these purposes. (See Sewell [1967], Ribich [1968], Mills [1968], and Goldfarb [1970].) Second, there was some evidence that the participants in those programs studied had been, as Somers put it [1968, p. 12], a "select group, the cream of the unemployed." Third, there was some evidence that, if properly interpreted, the benefits of training flowed through its utility to employers as a screening device rather than through its effects on productivity. Solie concluded [1968, p. 225], "There is some evidence in both the present study and the West Virginia study which suggests that the benefits of training are rather short-lived and consist principally of facilitating a rapid return to gainful employment for unemployed workers." Main found in his study of a national sample [1968, p. 165] that "MDTA training had no effect on weekly wages for those who found full-time employment after training." Even within the orthodox perspective, assuming that wages equal marginal product, this would seem to suggest that training brought about little significant increase in marginal productivities of program graduates.

Since the earlier studies, there have been a few pieces of evidence about the effects of institutional training programs on ghetto participants, although these results have generally been plagued by follow-up problems. Doeringer et al. [1969] concluded that the effectiveness of institutional training was limited in the Boston programs they studied, and that it seemed most successful when the program was directly tied to a specific job upon graduation. Harrison [1972] finds little relationship between institutional training and income or occupational status among several samples of ghetto workers, although he often had too few training participants in his sample to warrant more than the most hesitant conclusions.

In general, many analysts working within all three perspectives view the potential of formal, institutional vocational training with a certain skepticism.[b] It seemed particularly evident that time spent learning some "skills" did not necessarily raise "productivities" and/or did not necessarily raise incomes.[5]

3. On-the-Job Experience and Training. As the interest in institutional training as an antipoverty instrument has declined, interest in on-the-job training has definitely increased. Those working in all three theoretical perspectives have seemed increasingly to underscore the importance of on-the-job experience and training as paths to higher income.

The differences among the perspectives come, by and large, from assumptions about the structural mechanisms through which greater on-the-job experience and "training" seem associated with higher incomes. Orthodox economists—and especially those using the language of human capital analysis—place great weight on the role of general experience and specific training in increasing workers' marginal productivities. (For various statements of this basic hypothesis, see Becker [1964], Thurow [1969], Mincer [1962, 1971], Rosen [1971], and Reder [1969].) The dual market and radical analyses qualify their assertions about experience and training with some differentiated observations about labor market sectors and strata. Within the primary market, both of them seem to assert, on-the-job experience and training often lead to higher incomes as a result *both* of their influence on productivity *and* as a result of the customary relationships of internal labor markets, through which those with seniority are customarily accorded higher wages whether or not they are more productive. Within the secondary market, in contrast, both dual market and radical analysts tend to assume that secondary workers will not be able to increase their income through

---

[b]Fein [1968, p. 9] has put the skepticism aptly: "On the one hand, on-the-job training was better for very specific training. On the other hand, general literacy training, it was suggested, is perhaps best undertaken in the regular high school where the economies of scale for that type of training are highest. What, then, is left in the middle?"

longer tenure (in the labor market at large or specifically on certain jobs) both because the relations of production do not provide them opportunities for more productive work and because their relative weaknesses as a worker group tend to preclude their capturing whatever higher productivities they develop in the form of higher wages. In general, therefore, both the dual market and the radical paradigms expect that the efficacy of on-the-job training as an antipoverty, anti-underemployment device hinges singularly on the structure of internal markets to which the underemployed have access. Enticing the underemployed to work more diligently or more stably will neither increase their productivity nor their income, in most cases, if they continue to work in secondary markets. And it seems extremely difficult, for historical reasons, to open primary jobs to secondary workers.

Unfortunately, the evidence on this issue is remarkably scant, given the importance which many economists place on these variables. Mincer [1971] has quite extensively examined the relationship of age to income (controlling for education), inferring an automatic relationship between higher incomes and higher productivities. His results have limited usefulness for the comparative issues discussed here, for two independent and important reasons. First, he has largely tested his results on an all white male sample, precluding some comparisons of race and sex differences in the patterns of returns to experience. Second, and more important, he has tried neither to separate general labor market experience from specific "internal" market experience nor to differentiate the patterns of returns among different industrial/occupational groupings to test for the relevance of internal structure in generating different kinds of relationships between income and "experience." Thurow [1969] makes use of similar techniques, and finds pervasive inequalities in returns to experience between the races. His results have little bearing, as well, because he is not able to separate the effects of "general" and "specific" experience; his only variable is total labor force experience.

The results of my dissertation [1971b] help fill in some of the holes. Using data from the federal Urban Employment Survey, I was able to develop some rough controls for both "general" and "specific" job experience. The former, as in other studies, could be reflected in a variable measuring total years in the labor force. The latter, given some information uniquely provided by the survey, could be reflected by some adjusted indices of the time a worker had spent on a specific job. The use of these two variables helps confirm many of the important implications of the dual labor market and radical views, for the returns to both general and specific experience seem to differ sharply between groups defined both by demographic and by sectoral characteristics.

Two other recent studies, finally, help support some of the implications of recent hypotheses about inequalities on the job. Both Alexander [1970] and Tucker [1970] show some important differences in the access to internal labor market mobility channels between both men and women and whites and blacks. Using quite different methods, they find it possible to control for some of the differences between general and specific experience for which earlier studies had not been able to control. Alexander [1970, p. 25] concludes, in particular, that "separate promotion ladders for whites and nonwhites is strongly supported by the data."[6]

4. Worker Attitudes. The three paradigms bear some important differences in their expectations about the determinants and effects of worker attitudes. Orthodox analysis tends to assume that individual attitudes are determined exogenously and that worker motivation can be described by a similar set of behavioral relationships across all labor force groups. Dual market and radical analyses emphasize the essentially endogenous character of workers' attitudes. They argue that emerging market stratifications have produced different kinds of attitudes across market sectors, and that one can directly attribute these attitudinal differences to economic factors.

Almost no useful evidence exists on this issue (except for a few studies of the effects of education on attitudes cited above). Michelson [1969] has provided one example of the way in which alternative preference structures might explain the decisions of blacks about education. J.P. Robinson et al. [1969] has surveyed some of the literature on occupational attitudes and confirms that there are substantial differences among workers in different occupations; his survey does not precisely help us divide the occupations up into appropriate categories, however. Some interesting work is in progress at Harvard, still in very early stages, which is seeking to develop some measures of attitudinal determinants of worker success on the job and to relate those attitudes to the kinds of attitudes which seem to be developed through and rewarded by education. As that research progresses, it will be important to try to relate it to alternative specifications of occupational classes or strata. (See Edwards [1972])

5. Enterprise Characteristics. All three paradigms, in their different ways, have focused increasing attention on the characteristics of the enterprise as they determine opportunities for on-the-job training and occupational mobility. Moreover, the dual market and radical views emphasize the probable importance of social and economic variables as influences on changes in job structures and job design over time. There have been some investigations of the industrial variation in income and employment variables, especially with emphasis on important characteristics like unionization and establishment size. Rosen [1969] studied industrial wage variations, for instance, while both Stoikov and Raimon [1968] and Burton and Parker [1969] studied inter-industry variations in quit rates for evidence of the determinants of job stability and job mobility.

Unfortunately, most prevalent analyses of industrial variations in income and employment characteristics seem extremely difficult to interpret for the purposes of this competition, for two independent reasons. First, orthodox economists assume that occupational structure is determined exogenously, and therefore usually standardize industry variables for their "skill mixes." As Rosen puts it in his analysis of inter-industry wage variations [1969, pp. 250-251], a failure to standardize industries by their occupational (and/or educational) characteristics would make it "necessary to incorporate a theory of occupational structure into the model. . . . Factors determining occupational composition are largely independent of the variables entering this analysis." Since dual market and radical theories emphasize the central *interdependence* of occupational structure and socioeconomic variables, most orthodox analyses of industrial characteristics rule out the central questions posed by the two other perspectives.[7]

Second, it seems more and more true that using the "industry" as the unit of observation for studies of enterprise characteristics begins to miss the central points. Several hundred giant corporations are increasingly dominating American industry; we are witnessing, indeed, a dichotomization of the market in purely enterprise terms as large firms buy up those in the middle (see Barber [1970], and Averitt [1968]). As conglomerate mergers tend more and more to characterize the nature of corporate mergers, it becomes increasingly true that large corporations have large shares in at least several different industries. There is strong evidence that large firms are particularly likely to have fixed internal job and wage structures.[8] There is also some evidence that, as local firms are acquired by national companies, their behavior changes in important ways with respect to personnel and hiring policies. The Bay Area Employer Survey found, for instance, that single unit establishments used rather different employee selection practices than branches or headquarter units of multi-unit firms. As M.S. Gordon and Thal-larsen write [1969, p. 283]:

We also found that single unit establishments were considerably less likely to use selection tests than branches or headquarters units of multi-unit firms. . . . Some of the comments of interviewees in branch establishments indicated that headquarters not only prescribed the use of tests but also specified cut-off points and tended to oppose any change in these practices.

All of these points are intended to suggest that it may be growing relatively more important to study variations in employment and income variables among and within groups based on corporate size and power—controlling for industrial product and price variations—rather than studying industrial variations and controlling for establishment size and market concentration. It may be, that is, that variations within industries (as conventionally defined) have begun to equal inter-industry variations in their importance for explaining the behavior of employers and the incomes of workers. The differences between giant corporations and single-unit establishments may effectively outweigh differences among industries.

In analyses not yet fully available at the time of writing, Bluestone [1972] is exploring most of these issues with some sources of data he has compiled merging individual and corporation characteristics. His initial results confirm the central importance of industry and corporate characteristics in the determination of wages, and some of his measures may help quantify the more informal notions of industrial stratification. Given that stratification, some comparisons of the effects of stratification by corporate and individual units may be possible.

6. Market Imperfections. Orthodox economists have often been inclined to place increasing emphasis on the probable importance of market imperfections in explaining some of the perversities of ghetto employment problems. In particular, some orthodox economists have paid special attention to locational and informational imperfections. Kain in particular has argued [1968, 1969] that housing market segregation, employment suburbanization, poor public transportation, and poor information have tended to isolate ghetto blacks from the expanding pools of primary employment in the suburbs. The implication is that black income and employment prospects could (at least marginally) improve if blacks could live in the suburbs or if their transportation access to suburban jobs were improved. Equally, many orthodox economists like McCall [1970a] have argued that informational imperfections—both among employers and employees—could substantially explain racial inequalities in employment and income. The implication in this case is that better job information and/or better information to employers could marginally improve the employment and income prospects of blacks.

Dual market and radical analyses disagree, essentially, because of their views of the importance of fundamental market stratifications. They argue that even with better locational access or better job information, blacks would still be trapped in secondary employment, more or less, because of the interactive effect of all their disabilities and the pervasive influence of discrimination. (They also argue, concomitantly, that ghetto blacks have much better, albeit "informal," transportation and informational access than they're given credit for.)

Some evidence does seem to be available on these points, and it seems primarily to support the dual market and radical views. Harrison [1972] has provided impressive evidence from his analyses of micro-data that the employment and income prospects of blacks do not improve even if they succeed in living in the suburbs (while the status and income of whites improve sharply), and that the monetary returns to education among suburban blacks are as low as among ghetto blacks. Further, initial reports on some transportation experiments seeking to transport blacks to suburban jobs indicate, very tentatively, that they did not substantially affect the possibilities for jobs in those areas [Floyd, 1968, Altshuler, 1969, and Harrison, 1972].[c]

[c]It should be noted that orthodox results do not disprove the contentions of the radical and dual market analysts. Kain (1968) is able to conclude from his results only that there is a relation between residential location and job location, not that blacks would get jobs in different areas if they had access to those areas. And Mooney [1969] concludes that the access phenomenon is of very small statistical importance in explaining inter-metropolitan variations in unemployment. And neither of their analyses is designed to test for the relationship between the actual structure of job opportunities in the suburbs and the actual likelihood that blacks could take advantage of those opportunities if they had better access to them. See Harrison [1972] for further comment on this issue.

The same fairly negative (though tentative) results seem to apply for informational imperfections. Kidder [1968] concluded that blacks do not suffer for lack of information about jobs and that they in fact search "more intensively" for work than whites of comparable education, occupation, and age characteristics. She concludes [1968, p. 26]:

Those black workers who do venture beyond well-worn paths of job search do indeed encounter discrimination. But few individuals attempt such a venture. Anticipation of discrimination, based on a rational appreciation of actual patterns of Negro employment in industries, effectively circumscribes the search of the majority of Negroes.

Doeringer and associates concluded from their Boston study [1969] that the establishment of neighborhood job information and referral centers did not noticeably improve the employment prospects of those in the ghetto, but seemed simply to provide them with information they were already getting themselves through "informal" channels. Harrison [1972] summarizes a wide variety of information suggesting that public information sources serve to reinforce the patterns of the secondary market; he writes, in general, that "public programs designed to promote mobility in fact serve as a recruiting instrument for employers in the secondary labor market."[9]

Jobs and People

The second critical difference among the three theories concerns the interrelationships among technology, jobs, and individuals. Many orthodox analysts seem to assume, for operational purposes, that the design of job tasks and job structures is determined uniquely by technological factors. Dual market analysis assumes that job design reflects not only technological requisites but also employer and employee characteristics—that the relative need for job stability, for instance, substantially affects job design. Radical economists argue, finally, that employers determine job design with both productivity and class considerations in mind—that they will design certain jobs, for instance, in order most efficiently to forestall the development of class consciousness among certain workers.

Economists have traditionally paid little attention to job structure and design, leaving the field to industrial engineers and sociologists. Economic evidence on job design is slim. The principal questions around which the competition seems to rest have not often been asked very directly. One needs to explore two basic issues. First, one needs to analyze the range of job design choices available to employers given a specific technological process. Second, if there is more than one job design set conceivable at any level of technology, what influences employer choice among the several sets?

Two kinds of evidence have been arrayed in response to the first question.

Some historical studies have been developed, first of all, which suggest that alternative job designs and structures have been feasible with a constant technology. Marglin [1971] reviews some of the historical evidence about the sources of the rise of the factory in nineteenth century England, for instance. He concludes, very tentatively, that technology did not dictate the factory form of production organization, for existing technology afforded several different job structures. Marglin suggests that the success of the factory model was largely due to the discipline and supervisory potential it provided employers in their relations with workers. In another way, Friedmann [1955] reviews a number of sources on employer attitudes about the changing possibilities for job design during the first half of the twentieth century. Friedmann suggests that employers have been especially sensitive to the range of possibilities available to them within their technological process constraints, and that, in particular, employers had begun to worry during the 1930s and 1940s whether work had not already been over-specialized. Some industrial experiments began to explore the possibilities for increased variation in work responsibilities, given a constant technology. Lockwood [1958] reaches some of the same conclusions from his study of the historical evolution of the clerical occupations. He argues that the evolving technology of bureaucratic production did not uniquely determine the changing structure of bureaucratic occupations. He suggests that a wide variety of concerns with occupational stratification and worker consciousness influenced the design of jobs. The continuing division of jobs and job titles was not prompted by technological imperatives, for instance, but by status considerations. Lockwood concludes [1958, p. 81]: "The proliferation of office titles is recognized by those expert in the human relations of the bureau as an inexpensive way of keeping staff content, through satisfying prestige needs and by furthering individualism."

A second kind of evidence about job design choices emerges from the industrial design literature. In response most frequently to employer interest, industrial engineers have often conducted controlled experiments in which they redesigned job tasks, using the same technology, in order to search for more efficient organizations of work. Disregarding the nature of their experiments for the moment, one can at least conclude from the literature that other organizations of work and jobs have been possible which afforded *at least* as efficient a production process as the reigning organizations of production; productivity per worker did not decline, in other words, despite the changes in worker tasks. Davis [1966] and Shepard [1969, 1970] provide some independent reviews of this literature, each of them reaching similar conclusions.

The second question poses much more difficult empirical problems. One has few reliable means for discovering employer motivation, especially about such delicate questions as the design of work. Inference must be indirect. Three kinds of inference seem possible, although none of them provides especially irrefutable evidence about employer motivation. First, one might be able to infer from some historical studies of choices about the organization of production that employers have chosen among alternative job design possibilities in order to satisfy other than purely efficiency objectives. Marglin [1971] provides the clearest example of this kind of argument, suggesting that employers made job design choices during the nineteenth century at least in part in order to "divide" workers and therefore to "conquer" them by forestalling working-class cohesion. Second, one might try to infer from industrial design studies that employers had chosen current modes of productive relations for certain reasons because, in comparison to comparably efficient alternative designs, the current modes shared certain characteristics. Working from the industrial design literature, one almost uniformly reaches the conclusion that current organizations of work feature much narrower definitions of job tasks than other (at least) equally efficient organizations of work. (See Davis [1966] and Shepard [1969, 1970].) One could hypothesize, in an effort to explain these results, that employers have had an historical incentive to design very specialized job structures in order to separate workers from each other and to permit internal stratifications of their employees. The evidence that current structures are very specialized, however, does not uniquely justify that hypothesis; it is merely consistent with it. Finally, one might try to infer from comparative studies some evidence about the direction of employer choices. Given firms which employ the same technologies in different social settings, one might try to adduce something about the consequences for job design of alternative social objectives. Two recent examples seem suggestive. Melman [1969] studied several pairs of firms in Israel, one partner in the pair producing a given commodity within the *kibbutzim* mode of social organization and the second partner producing roughly the same commodity within the capitalist-managerial mode of production, relying on hierarchical lines of authority within the plant. Since Melman found that the cooperatively organized plants in the *kibbutzim* were at least as efficient as the managerial firms—in output per worker terms—one could hypothesize that the hierarchical mode of job structure in the managerial firms had been motivated by other criteria than efficiency, and particularly by considerations of social and worker control. Similarly, Wachtel [1972a] reports on some comparisons of auto plants in Italy and Yugoslavia. Fiat had built technologically-comparable plants in the two countries. Those in Italy were administered by conventional capitalist means. Those in Yugoslavia were organized with workers' councils in charge of certain important productive decisions. In the Yugoslavian instances, there was much less division and stratification within the plant; one could hypothesize that the relative stratification of the Italian firms flowed from the capitalist "divide-and-conquer" imperatives.

There is a central difficulty in any of these kinds of inferential analyses. They concern the problem of employer "choice." The radical and dual labor market theories seem to suggest, in more formal orthodox terms, that there is a frontier of job design possibilities, given a specific technology, which promise equally efficient production in output per worker terms. Employers then choose a point of production organization along the frontier which satisfies some other objectives. One can easily hypothesize, especially from the radical perspective, that employers choose along the job design frontier in order to maximize the stratification of labor and to minimize class consciousness within the potentially most dissatisfied strata. But this kind of formulation implies that concrete choices are made at specific historical junctures. It suggests that employers are making those choices at this very minute, and that they are free to alter their organization of work in order to reflect changes in the job design calculus.

More properly, I suspect, one ought to view the process as an historically imbedded evolution. Organizations of work arise, presumably in response to fairly concrete historical situations, and they then begin to foreclose certain historical choices which may have been, at some original point, institutionally conceivable. Radicals might argue, for instance, that many workers have become so conditioned to hierarchical and specialized modes of production that they would not be able to function in other, equally efficient, less specialized, less hierarchical organizations. Employers are thus constrained at this moment, but they may have been less constrained at some other historical moment. One must view the question, it seems, through the framework of historical dialectics and not through the perspective of static, partial, marginal choices.

Class and Class Consciousness

The third general difference among the paradigms concerns the concept of class. Evidence about class and class consciousness seems especially difficult to develop in such a way that the paradigm competition can be illuminated. Several different kinds of evidence need to be considered.

First, one needs to ask whether there are qualitatively different life experiences among workers at different levels of the relations of production. This amounts to asking, in the language of classical Marxism, whether one can identify several different "objectively-defined classes" or "strata" within the labor force. Are "secondary" workers different from "primary" workers in this respect, for instance? For many years, economists have simply not paid any attention to this question because they have assumed that the "fundamental behavior" of all workers can be assumed to be qualitatively the same. Economists have failed to define, in other words, what criteria might characterize a difference in the underlying behavior and personality structure of workers.

Sociologists have often tried to compare the personality structures, aspirations and behavioral characteristics of workers at different levels of the social structure. Their analyses have often confused two different definitions of class, however, and their conclusions are difficult to reconcile with the imperatives of this competition. Sociologists often compare "middle-class" and "working-class" employees, relying on Weber's distinction between social-status or consumption classes, and they often compare "white-collar" workers with "blue-collar" workers, hoping that the office/factory distinction will reflect the Marxian distinction between workers at different levels of the relations of production.[10] Inkeles concludes [1960], for instance, that white-collar workers have a "special propensity to risk-taking" while manual workers "remain unmoved and stick to security." But their analyses have not tried, in any rigorous way, to sort out the inter-generational transmission of class through workers' positions in the relations of production. These connections between inter- and intra-generational class transmission-mechanisms, mediated through different kinds of institutions, need to be very carefully defined before some useful answers to the problems of this paradigm competition can be developed. (See Bowles [1972], D.M. Gordon [1972], and chapter 9 below for further discussion of this issue.)

Second, one needs to develop some standards by which to study and measure "class consciousness." If there are definable strata in the economy, are the respective members of these strata conscious of their common interests? This kind of question enters into very intractable empirical territory, for the analysis of subjective beliefs involves extremely difficult analytic and methodological questions. Thompson [1966] provides a useful discussion of the characteristics one might associate with a class consciousness on the part of the working class. Weinstein [1968] provides an interesting analysis of the strength of class consciousness among capitalists around the turn of the century in this country. Domhoff [1971, Chapter Four] provides a useful discussion of the degree of "cohesion" and "consciousness" within the American "upper class," arguing that one does not also have to demonstrate "conspiracy" in order to establish the subjective element of class existence. Leggett [1968] makes the most careful attempt to develop quantitative empirical measures of the degree of class "consciousness," expressed as "militancy," in a study of blue-collar workers. He finds substantial variations in the degree of class consciousness in his sample and finds that those variations conform to certain expectable patterns of variation in underlying worker characteristics.

Many of the radical arguments about class involve hypotheses about the role of the dominant classes in the activities of the State. Sweezy [1972] and Edwards and MacEwan [1972] summarize much of the radical argument. Domhoff [1967, 1971], Domhoff and Ballard, eds. [1968], and Wolff [1969] summarize both the arguments and the evidence for the radical contention. Studies of tax incidence and relative class benefits from government expenditures have played an especially important role in the radical argument, as in Kolko [1962], Gurley [1967], and Michelson [1970]. These explorations are very recent, however, and their evidence has not yet been very conclusive. As in most of the other issues described in this chapter, the current literature helps define some directions for future research more clearly than it helps settle the paradigm competition. Chapter 9 tries to pull together many of those central implications for further research.

9 Implications for Further Research

One of the central conclusions of the preceding two chapters has been that recent economic research has not provided us with empirical evidence which can ultimately arbitrate the competition among theories of poverty and underemployment with which this book has been concerned. Often the evidence has not been formulated in the right language. Often the empirical questions have been too intractable to permit easy answers. In the face of these problems, we have little recourse but to plunge back into empirical research, motivating the empirical questions we ask by the translational imperatives of this paradigm competition. In these brief concluding pages, I offer a few suggestions for some specific paths along which further research might follow.

I would emphasize, first of all, that the paradigm competition described in this book seems to raise a single critical issue for short-term empirical research—the issue of *labor market stratification*. Given some important hypothesized or demonstrated differences among groups of workers or groups of jobs, how should one characterize those differences: as the product of quantitative differences in the characteristics of workers, like years of schooling; as the result of some exogenous forces acting on characteristics distinguishing the workers, like racial prejudice; or as consequences of some at least partly endogenous differences in behavior, personality and attitudes among those different groups of workers?

With others, I have argued that these questions revolve around the empirical evaluation of a central hypothesis about *labor market stratification* (see Edwards, Gordon, and Reich [1971]). For empirical purposes, we would distinguish definitionally between *stratification* and *segmentation*. A *stratification*, we have proposed, constitutes a "difference between markets such that the fundamental character of worker *behavior* and *attitudes* differs between markets, . . . where both employees and employers in a given market expect and operate by completely different behavioral rules and develop completely different attitudes from those in another market." In the case of the dual labor market distinction between primary and secondary markets, for instance, "this definition of stratification focuses on the difference between stable, persistent, persevering working attitudes, behavior and relations of production in the former market and unstable, intermittent, capricious working behavior, attitudes and relations of production in the latter." This definition of stratification arises principally from the emphasis of the dual labor market and radical theories, which evolve from a central hypothesis, as we have written, "that worker behavior, attitudes and personality characteristics are not determined exogenously of the economic system, and that evolving differences in the demands and requirements of various jobs can help cause some fundamental differences in the behavior and personalities of workers in different jobs."

In contrast, we have defined a *segmentation* as a separate division within a *stratum*. Within any stratum, several different labor market segments may co-exist, resistent to the forces of competition, suggesting evidence of persistent wage differentials and little intersectoral mobility. In the context of this distinction, as we have written, "one assumes that worker behavior, attitudes and personality characteristics are similar among labor market *segments* within a given *stratum*."[1]

This distinction between stratification and segmentation obviously relates to each of the three main areas of disagreement among the theories of poverty and underemployment. It directly involves questions about the concept of economic class, since the radical concept of class effectively coincides with this definition of stratification. It indirectly involves questions about the determination of job structure and job design, since this definition of stratification involves some assumptions about the *interaction* of job and worker characteristics in the evolution of market stratifications. It clearly involves the disagreement over the nature and sources of discontinuities in the market, for its formulation draws on that particular disagreement. (See Wachtel [1972b] and Harrison [1972] for additional comment.)

Given this distinction between stratification and segmentation, one can immediately pose a number of critical empirical questions which do not depend on the final resolution of the longer-term questions. A variety of measures of labor market discontinuity, imperfection, or differential have been proposed to explain some of the phenomena of poverty and underemployment in the United States—measures of discontinuity by occupation, industry, establishment, job stability characteristics, job creativity characteristics, region, intra-metropolitan location, unionization, race, sex, age, and so on.[2] Do any of these dimensions of discontinuity define market *strata*, as we have defined them, or do they all reflect segmentations in the market? If one can identify some dimensions of market stratification, which of those dimensions are overlapping, independent, or congruent? If one concludes that certain measures of discontinuity reflect dimensions of stratification, can one develop some useful statistical measures of those dimensions in order to divide workers into separate strata and test for the hypothesized behavioral and attitudinal differences among them? If one can proceed that far, how should one best characterize those behavioral and attitudinal differences?

Three central hypotheses have been advanced in the past few years about the dimensions of stratification which currently divide the American labor force. First, several have argued that some fundamental divisions among firms and industries have helped frame some important differences among workers. Both

Averitt [1968] and Bluestone [1970] have suggested that a duality has evolved in industrial structure, effecting a distinction between what Bluestone calls "core" and "periphery" firms. These firms are distinguished by corporate power. The two different classes of firms display different relations of production, according to these arguments, and both hire and develop different kinds of workers. Bluestone [1972] provides some initial empirical attempts to define the distinctions between the two classes of firms.

Second, several have speculated and I have more firmly argued (in D.M. Gordon [1972]) that the interaction between job and worker characteristics has resulted in the evolution of three distinct modes of work in the relations of production—three distinct objective circumstances involving, encouraging, and often requiring different behavioral traits and personality characteristics on the part both of employers and employees. One dimension of distinction involves the dual labor market theory's hypothesis about primary and secondary work. A second dimension of difference, within the primary sector, involves some important differences between a "routinized" and a "creative" mode of work. Some primary jobs demand menial and disciplined subservience to a steady routine. Other jobs encourage creative, entrepreneurial activity. Together, these two distinctions define three hypothesized modes of work: secondary work, routinized primary work, and creative primary work.

Third, many economists have focused on demographic distinctions among groups of workers. Most have agreed that race, sex, and age differences constitute the most important dimensions of difference. Many have argued, for mainly heuristic purposes, that prime-age white males constitute a unique and advantaged group of workers, while minority group workers, women, and the young and old suffer serious discrimination in the labor market.

Given these three groups of hypotheses about labor market groups, how do the different groups overlap and entwine? Can one construct, for purely descriptive purposes, a taxonomic *tableau* illustrating the cross-distributions of workers along these three dimensions of difference?

Three main empirical techniques seem most useful for exploring the boundaries of the different groups involved in those hypotheses. First, one may be able to continue to make some progress through the use of micro-analysis of large data sources on the labor market history and behavior of individuals. D.M. Gordon [1971b], Harrison [1972], and Bluestone [1972] provide three examples of the use of such data for these empirical purposes. The use of factor analysis, as illustrated in D.M. Gordon [1971b], seems especially promising. Second, through the more intensive analysis of the personality correlates of individual worker performance, one may be able to begin to define behavioral differences among various groups of workers. Gintis [1971] and Edwards [1972] help clarify the measures which economists may be able to apply for these purposes. Finally, it seems most important to develop a series of historical studies to trace the evolution of various (hypothesized) dimensions of stratification and segmentation in local labor markets. All of the processes about which economists have speculated are historical, and it seems clear that historical research will provide the most direct evidence on the validity of the stratification hypotheses.

If some relatively fruitful definitions of the empirical boundaries of labor market strata can be developed, the next task will focus on the mechanisms through which those strata are developed and preserved. How important are the families, the schools, the extra-market institutions, and the market institutions through which individuals move during their lifetimes? A number of the essays in Edwards, Reich, and Weisskopf, eds. [1972] provide some useful discussions of the dimensions of these mechanisms and the kinds of evidence one needs to develop in order to understand them.

With those two steps as background, one needs finally to begin to explore the transition from stratification to class conflict. If strata can be shown to exist, what are the factors which permit or develop consciousness within those strata, which begin to define them as classes in the subjective sense?

Finally, if one can make those empirical advances, one must ask the most important questions of all. What are the internal contradictions in the historical evolution of classes and class conflict which will drive society toward important changes in the structure of the stratification processes? Through the perspectives afforded by the foregoing analysis of labor market stratification, can one isolate those central social forces which will produce new dimensions of social interaction and conflict?

Most of these questions would have seemed totally foreign to economists less than a decade ago. They have been raised in this book because economists have been raising them. They have flowed out of a new and abnormal period in economics, one in which fundamental debate has been raised about basic economic models. That debate has begun to focus, as Thomas Kuhn would put it, on which of many puzzles it seems most significant to solve—which of many questions it seems most important to answer. Only through the tentative provision of answers to these critical questions will economists begin to resolve the revolutionary debate which has erupted in their ranks. This book has merely clarified what had been obvious long before: that revolutionary debate—the emergent paradigm competition—can no longer be ignored.

Notes

Notes

Notes to Chapter 1

1. For several other discussions of these same trends, see Fusfeld [1968], Miller and Roby [1970], and the relevant chapters in Ferman et al. [1968], K. Gordon, ed. [1968], Kain, ed. [1969], and D.M. Gordon, ed. [1971]. For extensive bibliographies on the two problems, see D.M. Gordon, ed. [1971].

2. Those most widely credited with alerting the government were Harrington [1962] and MacDonald [1963]. On the evolution of early government concern, see Moynihan [1969], Sundquist, ed. [1969], and Kershaw [1970].

3. The most prevalent absolute definition was the Orshansky Social Security Administration definition [Orshansky, 1965]. This definition defined and priced a minimum food budget and multiplied that amount by a factor of three to estimate the poverty floor. Two principal relative definitions began to attract attention: the income share of the bottom decile or quintile of the income distribution; or a measure first proposed by Victor Fuchs [1965] —the percentage of families earning half the national median family income. Many revisions of the absolute definition were also proposed. One can trace the history of the absolute definition and its emendations through the following literature: *Economic Report of the President* [1964], Orshansky [1965], Rein [1968], Weisbrod and Hansen [1969], Watts [1969a, 1969b], and Morgan and Smith [1969]. For a general comparison of the three definitions and recent numbers on the magnitude and composition of poverty according to each, see Miller and Roby [1970, Chapter Two]. For a brief discussion of the sociology of knowledge of the two kinds of definitions, see Marmor [1971].

4. These categorical perceptions were manifest in the first wave of economic analyses of poverty, focusing on the effect of economic growth on poverty—on the "backwash" hypothesis, as it was called. See Anderson [1964], Gallaway [1965], Kershaw and Levine [1966], Aaron [1967], and Gallaway [1967]. The constructs did not correspond precisely to the boundaries of the measured "labor force," since some not in the labor force would presumably enter it as aggregate demand increased. See Mincer [1966], and Bowen and Finegan [1969].

5. Thus, some sought to measure annual flows into and out of poverty in order to separate the two groups; this was one of the purposes of the special OEO Survey of Economic Opportunity in 1966 and 1967. (See McCall [1970b], and Smith and Morgan [1970], for two discussions of such flows.) For economists, of course, the new categories made implicit reference to Milton Friedman's concept of "permanent" and "transitory" income components [Friedman, 1957]. Sociological definitions of poverty remained more constant, tending to speak of a "permanent" class or culture of poverty from the beginning. See, in particular, the survey by Rossi and Blum [1969].

6. See Mangum [1967a], Levitan and Mangum [1969] and Mangum [1971] for related summaries.

7. For some useful discussions of the relationships between macro- and micro-analysis of employment problems, see R.A. Gordon [1967], Holt et al. [1971], and R.A. Gordon [1972].

8. For much of this discussion, see Sundquist [1968] and Mangum [1971]. For a more specific example of earlier policy analysis, see Shultz and Weber [1966]. For greater detail on depressed regions, see Levitan [1964]. On the particular problems of unemployment and displacement as a result of plant dislocation, see Sheppard and Belitsky [1966] and Wilcock and Franke [1963]. For a later, more sophisticated discussion growing out of the same tradition, see Hammermesh [1971].

9. Indeed, the "New Economists" proclaimed the victory of demand explanations with exultant pride. To quote Gardner Ackley [quoted in Killingsworth, 1968a, p. 62], ". . . .the inadequate demand camp was right and the structuralists were wrong." Ironically, the late 1960s inflation raised some complicated questions about the reigning "New Economic" policy models, but these questions did not seem to prompt a reevaluation of the "structural argument" or a review of the original debate between the "aggregate demand" and "structural" schools. On the problems raised by the late-decade inflation, see R.J. Gordon [1970]. For an attempt to continue the structuralist argument, see Killingsworth [1968a, 1968b]. For a recent review of the problems, see R.A. Gordon [1972].

10. For both definitions and data from the first survey application of the measure, see the *Manpower Report of the President* [1967, pp. 74-75].

11. This was particularly true of manpower programs for the young, like the Neighborhood Youth Corps and Job Corps, sponsored initially by the Office of Economic Opportunity. For their history, see Levitan [1969]. For some interpretation of their purposes, see Thurow [1968b]. See also Doeringer, ed. [1969].

12. Almost all new programs had remedial training elements added to them. Many new programs hoped to provide new and better incentives to industry for on-the-job training, especially the MA-II/MA-III/MA-IV series of revisions of basic MDTA OJT subsidies after 1966, and the JOBS program associated with the National Alliance for Businessmen. See Sundquist [1968] and Levitan and Mangum [1969].

13. On varieties of these efforts, see Levitan and Mangum [1969] and the *Manpower Report of the President* [1969, 1970].

14. To try to combat employer discrimination, it relied on state fair employment laws, enforcement of government contracts, the adjudication of suits filed under the civil rights law, and the public relations effect of community hearings sponsored by the Equal Employment Opportunity Commission. (In general, see

Sovern [1966]. On specific programs, see Landes [1967, 1968] and the symposium on "Equal Employment Opportunity: Comparing Community Experience" in *Industrial Relations* [1970].) To provide better information, it installed a number of manpower referral centers in ghetto neighborhoods, designed to provide information on jobs which ghetto residents presumably knew nothing about. (For comments on one such effort, connected with Boston's CEP program, see Doeringer et al. [1969].) To improve accessibility to suburban jobs, HUD sponsored a series of experiments, funding bus lines to travel from the ghetto out to suburban industrial areas. (See Floyd [1968], Altshuler [1969], and Harrison [1972].)

15. The Nixon Administration spoke loudly about this tactic but seemed to carry a small stick. (For analysis of the idea, see Haddad and Pugh, eds. [1969], and Bluestone [1971].)

16. The clearest illustration of the fusion of concerns about poverty and underemployment appeared in the geographic specification of policy objectives. At the beginning of the decade, geographic areas of greatest concern to manpower policy seemed quite separate from those of greatest concern to poverty warriors. Indeed, the rank correlation between areas graded by the unemployment and poverty criteria was quite low [Levitan, 1964]. By the end of the decade, in contrast, areas with high poverty and underemployment seemed relatively congruent, with central city slum areas ranked high on both lists. Analysts were becoming increasingly aware, moreover, of the very direct and important causal connections between rural and ghetto labor markets. See Kain and Persky [1968], and N. Hansen [1970].

17. One of the biggest influences on this new orientation was the sociological literature—especially Liebow [1967], Dizard [1968], and Wellman [1971]—and the autobiographical—like Brown [1965] and Malcolm X [1966].

18. For one example of evidence showing the importance of inequalities in returns to experience, see Thurow [1969].

19. On ghetto crime, see the chapter on crime in D.M. Gordon, ed. [1971], and D.M. Gordon [1971a].

20. In New York State in 1970, for instance, a male head-of-household in a family of four needed to earn nearly $95 a week to equal the subsidies available to him under the State's Home Relief Program for New York City. At least a third of the jobs in New York City paid less than that. (See D.M. Gordon [1969].) See also Moynihan [1968], Durbin [1969], and Piven and Cloward [1971].

21. These points have been emphasized especially by the new analysis of "internal labor markets"—see especially Doeringer and Piore [1971]. For some more general comments on the importance of demand, see Sundquist [1968], Pascal [1971], and Bluestone [1970].

Notes to Chapter 2

1. References on discussion about paradigms in economics will follow below. For some discussion in sociology, see Gouldner [1970]; in political science, see Wolin [1968] and Euben [1970], and in psychology, see any of the works by R.D. Laing, like [1960].

2. See the essays in the *Review of Radical Political Economics* [1971], Gintis [1969], Sweezy [1970], Gurley [1971], and, from the orthodox view, Bronfenbrenner [1970].

3. For some general discussion from the orthodox side, see D.F. Gordon [1965], Coats [1969], and, much earlier, Friedman [1953]. Although Friedman does not use the term "paradigm," his discussion of "positive economics" is related.

Notes to Chapter 3

1. See especially Blaug [1962], J. Robinson [1965], and Friedman [1953].

2. An earlier literature had argued about the factual basis of the income/ marginal productivity hypothesis, but those arguments have not been continued for more than twenty years. See Lester [1946, 1947], and Machlup [1946, 1947].

3. The queue theory has tended to dominate almost all manpower policy planning and has provided the micro basis for most analyses of unemployment. See Thurow [1969], Kalachek [1969a, 1969b], and Doeringer and Piore [1971].

4. These assumptions are critical, for instance, to inter-industry and inter-regional studies of wage and employment variables, which make assumptions about the relationships between income variables, industrial structure variables, and aggregate individual variables like educational attainment; see, for instance, Thurow [1967a], Kee [1969], Rosen [1969], and Scully [1970]. On the basic theory of production functions, for instance, see Brown, ed. [1967].

5. The queue theory and the Phillips Curve, in fact, can usefully be viewed as the micro- and macro-sides, respectively, of much the same coin. For some basic discussion of the Phillips Curve and its applications to the American labor market, see Lipsey [1965], R.A. Gordon [1967], Thurow [1967b], and for some elaborations and extensions, see Hammermesh [1971].

6. For some theoretical discussion along these lines, see Reder [1969], and Tinbergen [1970]. For four different kinds of empirical counterparts to the theoretical argument, see Welch [1966], Hansen, Weisbrod, and Scanlon [1970], Fuchs [1967], and Hall [1970b].

7. Most analyses of on-the-job training have developed within the human capital perspective, as in Mincer [1962] and Rosen [1971]. But the traditional,

relatively more ad hoc incorporation of age as a variable explaining income always presumed the productivity effects of on-the-job experience. See, for instance, Morgan et al. [1962].

8. Tinbergen has come closest, it appears, to dealing with this problem without relying on the "language" of human capital analysis. See, especially, Tinbergen [1970].

9. One of the first attempts was Gilman [1965]. For later attempts see Duncan [1969], Wohlstetter and Coleman [1970], and Fuchs [1970]. For some interesting comments on these attempts, see Arrow [1971]. On male-female differentials, see Fuchs [1971].

Notes to Chapter 4

1. Underlying many of these studies by economists were some equally interesting studies generated by sociologists and some material culled from a proliferating autobiographical literature. See, on the former count, Liebow [1967], Dizard [1968], Wellman [1971], and H. Lewis [1967]; and, on the latter count, Brown [1965], Malcolm X [1966], and Cleaver [1967].

2. See, for instance, W.A. Lewis [1954], and Myrdal [1968].

3. See Averitt [1968] and Galbraith [1967].

4. Some similar conclusions are reached in Doeringer and Piore [1971] and Harrison [1972, Chapter Five].

5. For some interesting statistical evidence which seemed to help characterize the nature of these jobs at the time, see Bluestone [1968]. Doeringer and Piore [1971] give a good picture of the job ladder problem, with plentiful examples.

Notes to Chapter 5

1. For some other general summaries and discussions of the emerging radical view, see Bronfenbrenner [1970], Sweezy [1970], Edwards, MacEwan et al. [1970], Gurley [1971], Gordon, ed. [1971], various essays in the *Review of Radical Political Economics* [1971], and, most comprehensively, Edwards, Reich, and Weisskopf, eds. [1972].

2. For the most comprehensive discussion of the radical theory of the state, see Milliband [1969].

3. Many interpretations of the civil rights movement in the United States involved this kind of argument. The concept of "relative deprivation" was widely applied. Blacks saw the goods on television, began to taste a few of them, and wanted their equal share. For several statements of this argument, see Clark and Parsons, ed. [1967].

4. On wage systems see Dobb [1957] and Mandel [1968].

5. Doeringer and Piore [1971] provide many illustrations of this development.

6. Lockwood [1958] and Crozier [1971] have the most interesting general discussion and evidence of these trends for white-collar work. Doeringer and Piore provide some interesting illustrations for blue-collar work. In D.M. Gordon [1972], I have emphasized the similarities between developments in the office and factory worlds.

7. Lockwood [1958] provides a wide variety of illustrations of these developments in the office setting. He also provides some specific comments which reinforce this example of the evolution of the typing pool.

8. Doeringer and Piore [1971], and Piore [1970] provide some helpful expansion of these employer imperatives.

9. For some similar perspectives on some of these issues, see Blau and Duncan [1967], and Leggett [1968].

10. Leggett [1968] provides one of the most useful discussions of this theme, building his analysis around the concept of the "uprooted."

11. See Gintis [1970] and Bowles [1971, 1972] for useful discussions of these trends in the functional importance of education. On earlier history, see Katz [1968].

12. Lockwood [1958] has provided some illustrative evidence of some of these imperatives.

13. See Wachtel [1972b] for some related discussion.

Notes to Chapter 6

1. Piore [1970] speaks of the vested group interests of "primary" and "secondary" employers in terms which seem similar to the radical analysis, but does not resort explicitly to the class construct. Doeringer and Piore [1971] speak in similar terms.

2. Orthodox economists rarely talk about this issue, of course, so that it is difficult to be absolutely clear about their assumptions. For similar descriptions of orthodox theory and its assumptions about job structures, see Scoville [1969] and Marglin [1971].

Notes to Chapter 7

1. See much of the literature cited in footnote #4, chapter 1 above.

2. See Hamel [1967] and O'Boyle [1969]. For some similar indications about occupational mobility, see Saben [1967]. For some other measures, see Hall [1970a].

3. The differences in the contentions stem mainly from different statistical definitions of the share of labor. Kravis [1962] shows clearly that different assumptions and manipulations of the Census income data can produce quite different historical appearances.

Further, quite obviously, both the series on labor and the series on capital "undercount" their respective samples; labor income is understated by the amount of survey undercounts or unreported income, while capital income has been understated because of "missing" capital (as in R.J. Gordon, [1969]).

4. N. Simler [1961] claims to have shown that unions have had no effect on labor's share in the manufacturing sector over time, through an extended series of disaggregated inter-industry comparisons. His analysis seems strikingly inconclusive, unfortunately, since he does not control for any other variables (which might also influence labor's share) in his analysis.

5. Further suggestive support for the dual market and radical views can be found in the interesting analysis of Murray Brown [1966], in which Brown concludes that the net exploitation of labor by capital tended to increase from the end of World War II through 1962. Radical theory, in particular, would have predicted his result, based on the declining momentum of the labor movement and on increasing stratification among workers during that period. Brown's estimates, like Thurow's, draw from production function analysis; Brown works at a more disaggregate level than Thurow, exclusively within manufacturing.

6. A recent paper by Chiswick and Mincer [1971], still unpublished and available to the writer only at the time of final revision, provides a much more sophisticated discussion of orthodox expectations about trends in the size distribution of income. It has not been possible to digest and evaluate that discussion for these purposes.

7. See D.M. Gordon [1971b] for a detailed discussion of the kinds of data which would be most useful for these purposes.

Notes to Chapter 8

1. For two useful summaries of the earlier labor market studies, see Reynolds [1951] and Parnes [1954].

2. This has been true particularly in the analysis of "educational production functions," as in Bowles [1970a] and Hanushek [1971].

3. See the work in progress by Edwards [1972] for a useful summary of the dimensions of this empirical problem.

4. See Mangum [1967b], Somers [1968], Solie [1968], Page [1968], and Hammermesh [1971].

5. For a useful discussion of the political factors which may underlie some of this ineffectiveness of institutional training programs, for a discussion, in effect, of the "political economy of training," see Wachtel [1971] and Harrison [1972].

. For a useful summary and analysis of the failures of many attempts to provide more advantageous on-the-job training and experience to disadvantaged workers, see Cohn [1971]. See also Freedman [1969] and Shelley [1970].

7. Rapping [1970] has some similar suggestions about industry analyses in his discussion of the effect of unions.

8. See U.S. Department of Labor [1964], "Salary Structure Characteristics in Large Firms."

9. Similar issues are involved in the analysis of labor migration. For a discussion of the literature and some empirical results, see Bowles [1970c].

10. There has been a vast literature on social stratification in sociology, but that literature has not distinguished between different kinds of differences among workers. For a general and useful summary of some of the literature, see Miller and Roby [1970].

Notes to Chapter 9

1. This definition of segmentation corresponds to earlier orthodox analyses of balkanization in the labor market (see Kerr [1954] for the original statement) and to the "segmented" market model postulated by Holt et al. [1971].

2. On occupation, see Bergmann [1971]; on industry, see Bluestone [1970]; on establishment, see Doeringer and Piore [1971]; on job characteristics, see the summaries in Edwards et al. [1971]; on region, see Fuchs [1967b]; on intra-metropolitan location, see Kain [1968]; on unionization, see Doeringer and Piore [1971], and on the demographic characteristics, see the summaries in D.M. Gordon [1971b].

Bibliography

Bibliography

Henry Aaron [1967]. "The Foundations of the 'War on Poverty' Reexamined," *American Economic Review*, December 1967.

Frank Ackerman, Howard Birnbaum, James Wetzler, and Andrew Zimbalist [1971]. "Income Distribution in the United States," *Review of Radical Political Economics*, Summer 1971.

Graham Adams [1966]. *Age of Industrial Violence, 1910-1915.* New York: Columbia University Press, 1966.

Arthur J. Alexander [1970]. *Structure, Income, and Race: A Study in Internal Labor Markets.* Document R-577-OEO. Santa Monica: RAND, October 1970.

Louis Althusser [1970]. *For Marx.* Translated by Ben Brewster. New York: Vintage Books, 1970.

Alan A. Altshuler [1969]. "Transit Subsidies: By Whom, For Whom?" *Journal of the American Institute of Planners*, March 1969.

W.H. Locke Anderson [1964]. "Trickling Down: The Relationship between Economic Growth and the Extent of Poverty among American Families," *Quarterly Journal of Economics*, November 1964.

Kenneth J. Arrow [1971]. *Some Models of Racial Discrimination in the Labor Market.* Document RM-6253-RC. Santa Monica: RAND, February 1971.

Orley Ashenfelter [1970]. "Changes in Labor Market Discrimination over Time," *Journal of Human Resources*, Fall 1970.

Robert T. Averitt [1968]. *The Dual Economy.* New York: W.W. Norton, 1968.

Paul Baran and Paul Sweezy [1966]. *Monopoly Capital.* New York: Monthly Review Press, 1966.

Richard E. Barber [1970]. *The American Corporation.* New York: E.P. Dutton, 1970.

Harold Baron and Bennett Hymer [1968]. "The Negro in the Chicago Labor Market," in Julius Jacobsen, ed., *The Negro and the American Labor Movement.* New York: Doubleday Anchor Books, 1968.

Alan B. Batchelder [1964]. "Decline in the Relative Income of Negro Men," *Quarterly Journal of Economics*, November 1964.

Gary Becker [1957]. *The Economics of Discrimination.* Chicago: University of Chicago Press, 1957.

————— [1964]. *Human Capital.* New York: National Bureau of Economic Research, 1964.

————— [1967]. *Human Capital and the Personal Distribution of Income.* Ann Arbor: University of Michigan Press, 1967.

————— [1968]. "Crime and Punishment: An Economic Approach," *Journal of Political Economy*, March/April 1968.

Daniel Bell [1960]. *End of Ideology.* New York: The Free Press, 1960.

Reinhard Bendix and Seymour Martin Lipset [1966]. "Karl Marx's Theory of

Social Classes." in R.B. Bendix and S.M. Lipset, eds., *Class, Status, and Power*. New York: The Free Press, 1966.

Ivar Berg [1969]. *Education and Jobs: The Great Training Robbery*. New York: Praeger Books, 1969.

Barbara R. Bergmann [1971]. "The Effect on White Incomes of Discrimination in Employment," *Journal of Political Economy*, March/April 1971.

Barbara Bergmann and Jerolyn R. Lyle [1970]. "Differences amongst Cities and Industries in the Occupational Standing of Negroes in the Private Sector," University of Maryland, mimeograph copy, September 1970.

Amit Bhaduri [1969]. "On the Significance of Recent Controversies on Capital Theory: A Marxian View," *Economic Journal*, September 1969.

Kjeld Bjerke [1970]. "Income and Wage Distributions: Part I: A Survey of the Literature," *Review of Income and Wealth*, September 1970.

Peter M. Blau and Otis Dudley Duncan [1967]. *The American Occupational Structure*. New York: John Wiley and Sons, 1967.

Mark Blaug [1962]. *Economic Theory in Retrospect*. Homewood, Illinois: Richard D. Irwin, Inc., 1962.

_____, ed. [1968]. *The Economics of Education*. London: Penguin, 1968.

Barry Bluestone [1968]. "Low Wage Industries and the Working Poor," *Poverty and Human Resources Abstracts*, March-April 1968.

_____[1970]. "The Tripartite Economy: Labor Markets and the Working Poor," *Poverty and Human Resources*, July-August 1970.

_____[1972]. "The Wage Determinants of the Working Poor," Ph.D. Dissertation in progress, University of Michigan, 1972.

T.B. Bottomore [1966]. *Classes in Modern Society*. New York: Vintage Books, 1966.

William Bowen and T. Aldrich Finegan [1965]. "Labor Force Participation and Unemployment," in Arthur M. Ross, ed., *Employment Policy and the Labor Market*. Berkeley: University of California Press, 1965.

_____[1969]. *The Economics of Labor Force Participation*. Princeton: Princeton University Press, 1969.

Samuel S. Bowles [1970a]. "Towards an Educational Production Function," in W. Lee Hansen, ed., *Education, Income, and Human Capital*. New York: National Bureau of Economic Research, 1970.

_____[1970b]. "Schooling and Inequality from Generation to Generation," Harvard University, mimeograph copy, October 1970.

_____[1970c]. "Migration as Investment: Empirical Tests of the Human Investment Approach to Geographical Mobility," *Review of Economics and Statistics*, November 1970.

_____[1971]. "The Weakest Link: Contradictions in U.S. Higher Education," Harvard University, mimeograph copy, January 1971.

_____[1972]. "Unequal Education and the Reproduction of the Social Division of Labor," in R.C. Edwards, M. Reich, and T.E. Weisskopf, eds., *The Capitalist System*. Englewood Cliffs, N.J.: Prentice-Hall, 1972.

D.S. Brady [1965]. "Age and Income Distribution," *Research Report*, Social Security Administration, U.S. Department of Health, Education And Welfare, Number 8, 1965.

Martin Bronfenbrenner [1970]. "Radical Economics in America: A 1970 Survey," *Journal of Economic Literature*, September 1970.

Claude Brown [1965]. *Manchild in the Promised Land*. New York: The Macmillan Co., 1965.

Murray Brown [1966]. "A Measure of the Change in Relative Exploitation of Capital and Labor," *Review of Economics and Statistics*, May 1966.

————, ed. [1967]. *The Theory and Empirical Analysis of Production*. New York: National Bureau of Economic Research, 1967.

Edward C. Budd [1970]. "Postwar Changes in the Size Distribution of Income in the United States," *American Economic Review*, May 1970.

John F. Burton, Jr. and John E. Parker [1969]. "Interindustry Variations in Voluntary Labor Mobility," *Industrial and Labor Relations Review*, January 1969.

W.J. Cash [1960]. *The Mind of the South*. New York: Knopf, 1960.

Barry R. Chiswick and Jacob Mincer [1971]. "Time Series Changes in Personal Income Inequality: The United States Experience, 1939 to 1985," National Bureau of Economic Research, mimeograph copy, August 1971.

Kenneth Clark and Talcott Parsons, eds. [1967]. *The Negro American*. Boston: Houghton Mifflin Co., 1967.

A.W. Coats [1969]. "Is There a 'Structure of Scientific Revolutions' in Economics?" *Kyklos*, Vol. XXII, No. 2, 1969.

Jules Cohn [1971]. *The Conscience of Corporations*. Baltimore: The Johns Hopkins University Press, 1971.

Robert Coles [1970]. *Erik Erikson: The Growth of His Work*. Boston: Atlantic-Little-Brown, 1970.

Maurice Cornforth [1968]. *Materialism and the Dialectical Method*. Fourth edition. New York: International Publishers, 1968.

Michel Crozier [1971]. *The World of the Office Worker*. Chicago: University of Chicago Press, 1971.

H. Dalton [1920]. *Some Aspects of the Inequality of Incomes in Modern Communities*. London: Routledge, 1920.

Margery Davies and Michael Reich [1972]. "On the Relationship between Sexism and Capitalism," in R.C. Edwards, M. Reich, and T.E. Weisskopf, eds., *The Capitalist System*. Englewood Cliffs, N.J.: Prentice-Hall, 1972.

Louis E. Davis [1966]. "The Design of Jobs," *Industrial Relations*, October 1966.

Jan Dizard [1968]. "Why Should Negroes Work?" in Louis A. Ferman et al., eds., *Negroes and Jobs*. Ann Arbor: University of Michigan Press, 1968.

Maurice Dobb [1957]. *Wages*. Cambridge, Eng.: Cambridge University Press, 1957.

_____[1963]. *Studies in the Development of Capitalism*. New York: New World Paperbacks, 1963.

Peter B. Doeringer [1968]. "Manpower Programs for Ghetto Labor Markets," *Proceedings*, Industrial Relations Research Association, 21st Annual Meetings, 1968.

Peter B. Doeringer, Penny Feldman, David M. Gordon, Michael J. Piore, and Michael Reich [1969]. "Urban Manpower Programs and Low-Income Labor Markets: A Critical Assessment," Manpower Administration, U.S. Department of Labor, mimeograph copy, January 1969.

Peter B. Doeringer and Michael J. Piore [1970]. "Equal Employment Opportunity in Boston," *Industrial Relations*, May 1970.

_____[1971]. *Internal Labor Markets and Manpower Analysis*. Lexington, Mass.: Heath Lexington Books, 1971.

Peter B. Doeringer, ed. [1969]. *Programs to Employ the Disadvantaged*. Englewood Cliffs, N.J.: Prentice-Hall, 1969.

G. William Domhoff [1967]. *Who Rules America?* Englewood Cliffs, N.J.: Prentice-Hall, 1967.

_____[1971]. *The Higher Circles*. New York: Vintage Books, 1971.

_____and Hoyt Ballard, eds. [1968]. *C. Wright Mills and the Power Elite*. Boston: Beacon Press, 1968.

Otis Dudley Duncan [1969]. "Inheritance of Poverty or Inheritance of Race?" in D.P. Moynihan, ed., *On Understanding Poverty*. New York: Basic Books, 1969.

John T. Dunlop [1957]. "The Task of Contemporary Wage Theory," in J.T. Dunlop, ed., *The Theory of Wage Determination*. London: Macmillan, 1957.

Elizabeth Durbin [1969]. *Welfare, Income, and Employment*. New York: Praeger Books, 1969.

R.S. Eckaus [1964]. "Economic Criteria for Education and Training," *Review of Economics and Statistics*, May 1964.

Economic Report of the President [1964]. Washington, D.C.: U.S. Government Printing Office, 1964.

_____[1969]. Washington, D.C.: U.S. Government Printing Office, 1969.

Richard C. Edwards [1972]. "Alienation and Inequality: Social Relations in the Capitalist Firm," Ph.D. Dissertation in progress, Harvard University, 1972.

Richard C. Edwards, Arthur MacEwan et al. [1970]. "A Radical Approach to Economics: Basis for a New Curriculum," *American Economic Review*, May 1970.

Richard C. Edwards, David M. Gordon, and Michael Reich [1971]. "A Research Project on Labor Market Stratification: Background Paper," National Bureau of Economic Research, mimeograph copy, April 1971.

Richard C. Edwards and Arthur MacEwan [1972]. "Ruling Class Power and the State," in R.C. Edwards, M. Reich, and T.E. Weisskopf, eds., *The Capitalist System*. Englewood Cliffs, N.J.: Prentice-Hall, 1971.

Richard C. Edwards, Michael Reich, and Thomas E. Weisskopf, eds. [1972]. *The Capitalist System*. Englewood Cliffs, N.J.: Prentice-Hall, 1972.

"Equal Employment Opportunity: Comparing Community Experience–A Symposium," [1970]. *Industrial Relations*, May 1970.

Erik Erikson [1968]. *Childhood and Society*. Revised edition. New York: W.W. Norton, 1968.

J. Peter Euben [1970]. "Political Science and Political Silence," in P. Green and S. Levinson, eds., *Power and Community*. New York: Vintage Books, 1970.

Rashi Fein [1968]. "Introduction," in "Vocational Education," Report on a Conference published as a supplement to *Journal of Human Resources* 1968.

Louis A. Ferman [1967]. "The Irregular Economy: Informal Work Patterns in the Ghetto," University of Michigan, mimeograph copy, 1967.

————et al., eds. [1968]. *Jobs and Negroes*. Ann Arbor: University of Michigan Press, 1968.

Belton M. Fleisher [1970]. *Labor Economics: Theory and Evidence*. Englewood Cliffs, N.J.: Prentice-Hall, 1970.

Thomas H. Floyd [1968]. "Using Transportation to Alleviate Poverty: A Progress Report on Experiments under the Mass Transportation Act," American Academy of Arts and Sciences, mimeograph copy, paper presented at the Conference on Transportation and Poverty, June 1968.

Marcia Freedman [1969]. *The Process of Work Establishment*. New York: Columbia University Press, 1969.

Edgar Freidenberg [1963]. *Coming of Age in America*. New York: Vintage Books, 1963.

Milton Friedman [1953]. "The Methodology of Positive Economics," in M. Friedman, *Essays in Positive Economics*. Chicago: University of Chicago Press 1953.

————[1957]. *Theory of the Consumption Function*. New York: National Bureau of Economic Research, 1957.

Georges Friedmann [1955]. *The Anatomy of Work*. Glencoe, Ill.: The Free Press of Glencoe, 1955.

Victor Fuchs [1965]. "Toward a Theory of Poverty," in Task Force on Economic Growth and Opportunity, *The Concept of Poverty*. Washington, D.C.: U.S. Chamber of Commerce, 1965.

————[1967]. *Differentials in Hourly Earnings by Region and City Size in the United States, 1959*. Occasional Paper 101. New York: National Bureau of Economic Research, 1967.

————[1968], *The Service Economy*. New York: The National Bureau of Economic Research, 1968.

————[1969]. "Comments on Measuring the Low-Income Population," in Lee Soltow, ed., *Six Papers on the Size Distribution of Wealth and Income*. Studies in Income and Wealth No. 33. New York: National Bureau of Economic Research, 1969.

Victor Fuchs [1970]. "Wage Differentials in the United States, 1959," National Bureau of Economic Research, mimeograph copy, tabular summary, 1970.

_____[1971]. "Differentials in Hourly Wages between Men and Women," *Monthly Labor Review*, May 1971.

Daniel R. Fusfeld [1968]. "The Basic Economics of the Urban and Racial Crisis," *The Conference Papers of the Union for Radical Political Economics*, December 1968.

John Kenneth Galbraith [1968]. *The New Industrial State*. New York: Signet Paperbacks, 1968.

Lowell E. Gallaway [1965]. "The Foundations of the 'War on Poverty,' "*American Economic Review*, March 1965.

_____[1967]. "The Foundations of the 'War on Poverty': A Reply," *American Economic Review*, December 1967.

Herbert Gintis [1969]. "Alienation and Power: Toward a Radical Welfare Economics," Unpublished Ph.D. Dissertation, Harvard University, 1969.

_____[1970a]. "New Working Class and Revolutionary Youth," *Review of Radical Political Economics*, Summer 1970.

_____[1970b]. "Neo-Classical Welfare Economics and Individual Development," *Occasional Paper Number 3*. Ann Arbor: The Union for Radical Political Economics, 1970.

_____[1971]. "Education, Technology, and the Characteristics of Worker Productivity," *American Economic Review*, May 1971.

Robert S. Goldfarb [1969]. "The Evaluation of Government Programs: The Case of New Haven's Manpower Training Activities," *Yale Economic Essays*, Fall 1969.

David M. Gordon [1969]. "Income and Welfare in New York City," *The Public Interest*, Number 16, Summer 1969.

_____[1971a]. "Class and the Economics of Crime," *Review of Radical Political Economics*, Summer 1971.

_____[1971b]. "Class, Productivity and the Ghetto: A Study of Labor Market Stratification," Unpublished Ph.D. Dissertation, Harvard University, 1971.

_____[1972]. "From Steam Whistles to Coffee Breaks: Notes on Office and Factory Work," in Irving Howe, ed., *Blue-Collar World*, a special issue of *Dissent*, Winter 1972.

_____, ed. [1971]. *Problems in Political Economy: An Urban Persective*. Lexington, Mass.: D.C. Heath, 1971.

Donald F. Gordon [1965]. "The Role of the History of Economic Thought in the Understanding of Modern Economic Theory," *American Economic Review*, May 1965.

Kermit Gordon, ed., [1968]. *Agenda for the Nation*. Washington, D.C.: The Brookings Institution, 1968.

Margaret S. Gordon and Margaret Thal-Larsen [1969]. *Employer Policies in a*

155

Changing Labor Market. Berkeley: Institute of Industrial Relations at the University of California, 1969.

Robert Aaron Gordon [1967]. *The Goal of Full Employment*. New York: John Wiley and Sons, 1967.

———— [1968]. "Unemployment Patterns with 'Full Employment,'" *Industrial Relations*, October 1968.

———— [1972]. "Some Macroeconomic Aspects of Manpower Policy," in Lloyd Ulman, ed., a collection of essays on manpower policy, forthcoming in 1972.

Robert J. Gordon [1969]. "$45 Billion of U.S. Private Investment Has Been Mislaid," *American Economic Review*, June 1969.

———— [1970]. "The Recent Acceleration of Inflation and Its Lessons for the Future," *Brookings Papers on Economic Activity*, Number 1, 1970.

Charles Gouldner [1970]. *The Coming Crisis of Western Sociology*. New York: Basic Books, 1970.

Zvi Griliches [1970]. "Notes on the Role of Education in Production Functions and Growth Accounting," in W. Lee Hansen, ed., *Education, Income, and Human Capital*. New York: National Bureau of Economic Research, 1970.

John G. Gurley [1967]. "'Federal Tax Policy': A Review Article," *National Tax Journal*, September 1967.

———— [1971]. "The State of Political Economics," *American Economic Review*, May 1971.

James W. Guthrie et al. [1969]. *Schools and Inequality*. Washington, D.C.: The Urban Coalition, 1969.

Alan Haber [1966]. "Poverty Budgets: How Much Is Enough?" *Poverty and Human Resources Abstracts*, May-June 1966.

William Haddad and Geoffrey H. Pugh, eds. [1969]. *Black Economic Development*. Englewood Cliffs, N.J.: Prentice-Hall, 1969.

Robert E. Hall [1970a]. "Why Is the Unemployment Rate So High at Full Employment?" *Brookings Papers on Economic Activity*, Number 3, 1970.

———— [1970b]. "Wages, Income, and Hours of Work in the U.S. Labor Force," University of California at Berkeley, mimeograph copy, August 1970.

A.H. Halsey, Jean Floud, and C.A. Anderson, eds. [1965]. *Education, Economy, and Society*. New York: The Free Press, 1965.

Harvey R. Hamel [1967]. "Job Tenure of Workers, January 1966," *Monthly Labor Review*, January 1967.

Daniel S. Hammermesh [1971]. *Economic Aspects of Manpower Training Programs*. Lexington, Mass.: Heath Lexington Books, 1971.

Giora Hanoch [1967]. "An Economic Analysis of Earnings and Schooling," *Journal of Human Resources*, Winter 1967.

Niles Hansen [1970]. *Rural Poverty and Urban Problems*. Bloomington, Ind.: University of Indiana Press, 1970.

W. Lee Hansen, B.A. Weisbrod and W.J. Scanlon [1970]. "Schooling and Earnings of Low Achievers," *American Economic Review*, June 1970.

G.C. Harcourt [1969]. "Some Cambridge Controversies in the Theory of Capital," *Journal of Economic Literature*, June 1969.

Michael Harrington [1962]. *The Other America*. New York: Macmillan, 1962.

———[1970]. "The Betrayal of the Poor," *Atlantic*, January 1970.

Bennett Harrison [1971]. "Education and Underemployment in the Urban Ghetto," in D.M. Gordon, ed., *Problems in Political Economy: An Urban Perspective*. Lexington, Mass.: D.C. Heath, 1971.

———[1972]. *Education, Training, and the Urban Ghetto*. Baltimore: Johns Hopkins University Press, 1972.

John R. Hicks [1964]. *The Theory of Wages*. Second edition. London: St. Martins, 1964.

George Hildebrand [1968]. "Discussion on Research on Big City Labor Markets," *Proceedings*, Industrial Relations Research Association, 21st Annual Meetings, 1968.

———and George E. Delehanty [1966]. "Wage Levels and Differentials," in R.A. and M.S. Gordon, eds., *Prosperity and Unemployment*. New York: John Wiley and Sons, 1966.

Charles C. Holt et al. [1971]. *The Unemployment-Inflation Dilemma: A Manpower Solution*. Washington, D.C.: The Urban Institute, 1971.

Stephen Hymer [1970]. "The Multinational Corporation and the Law of Uneven Development," in J. N. Bhagwati, ed., *World Order and Development*. Cambridge, Mass.: M.I.T. Press, 1970.

Alex Inkeles [1960]. "Industrial Man: The Relation of Status to Experience, Perception and Value," *American Journal of Sociology*, July 1960.

Harry G. Johnson [1968]. "The Economic Approach to Social Questions," *Economica*, February 1968.

Denis F. Johnston and James R. Wetzel [1969]. "Effect of the Census Undercount on Labor Force Estimates," *Monthly Labor Review*, March 1969.

John F. Kain [1968]. "Housing Segregation, Negro Employment, and Metropolitan Decentralization," *Quarterly Journal of Economics*, May 1968.

———[1969]. "Coping with Ghetto Unemployment," *Journal of the American Institute of Planners*, March 1969.

John F. Kain and Joseph J. Persky [1968]. "The North's Stake in Southern Rural Poverty," in President's National Advisory Commission on Rural Poverty, *Rural Poverty in the United States*. Washington, D.C.: U.S. Government Printing Office, May 1968.

John F. Kain and John R. Meyer [1970]. "Transportation and Poverty," *The Public Interest*, Number 18, Winter 1970.

John F. Kain, ed. [1969]. *Race and Poverty: The Economics of Discrimination*. Englewood Cliffs, N.J.: Prentice-Hall, 1969.

Edward Kalachek [1969a]. *The Youth Labor Market*. Policy Papers in Human

Resources and Industrial Relations Number 12. Ann Arbor: Institute of Labor and Industrial Relations at the University of Michigan, January 1969.

———— [1969b]. "Determinants of Teenage Employment," *Journal of Human Resources*, Winter 1969.

———— and John M. Goering, eds. [1970]. *Transportation and Central City Unemployment*. Working Paper INS 5. St. Louis: Institute for Urban and Regional Studies at Washington University, March 1970.

Woo Sik Kee [1969]. "The Causes of Urban Poverty," *Journal of Human Resources*, Winter 1969.

Terence F. Kelly [1970]. "Factors Affecting Poverty: A Gross Flow Analysis," in President's Commission on Income Maintenance Programs, *Technical Studies*. Washington, D.C.: U.S. Government Printing Office, 1970.

Robert F. Kennedy [1969]. "Industrial Investment in Urban Poverty Areas," in John F. Kain, ed., *Race and Poverty: The Economics of Discrimination*. Englewood Cliffs, N.J.: Prentice-Hall, 1969.

Clark Kerr [1954]. "The Balkanization of Labor Markets," in E. Wight Bakke et al., *Labor Mobility and Economic Opportunity*. Cambridge, Mass.: M.I.T. Press, 1954.

———— [1957]. "Labor's Income Share and the Labor Movement," in G.W. Taylor and F.C. Pierson, eds., *New Concepts in Wage Determination*. New York: McGraw-Hill, 1957.

Joseph A. Kershaw [1970]. *Government Against Poverty*. Washington, D.C.: The Brookings Institution, 1970.

———— and Robert A. Levine [1966]. "Poverty, Aggregate Demand, and Economic Structure," *Journal of Human Resources*, Summer 1966.

Alice H. Kidder [1968]. "Racial Differences in Job Search and Wages," *Monthly Labor Review*, July 1968.

Charles C. Killingsworth, Jr. [1968a]. *Jobs and Income for Negroes*. Policy Papers in Human Resources and Industrial Relations Number 6. Ann Arbor: Institute of Labor and Industrial Relations at the University of Michigan, May 1968.

———— [1968b]. "The Continuing Labor Market Twist," *Monthly Labor Review*, September 1968.

Gabriel Kolko [1962]. *Wealth and Power in America*. New York: Praeger, 1962.

Irving B. Kravis [1959]. "Relative Income Shares in Fact and Theory," *American Economic Review*, December 1959.

———— [1960]. "International Differences in the Distribution of Income," *Review of Economics and Statistics*, November 1960.

———— [1962]. *The Structure of Income*. Philadelphia: University of Pennsylvania Press, 1962.

Anne O. Krueger [1963]. "The Economics of Discrimination," *Journal of Political Economy* October 1963.

Thomas S. Kuhn [1962]. *The Structure of Scientific Revolutions*. Chicago: University of Chicago Press, 1962.

Thomas S. Kuhn [1970a]. "Logic of Discovery or Psychology of Research," in Imre Lakatos and Alan Musgrave, eds., *Criticism and the Growth of Knowledge*. Cambridge, Eng.: Cambridge University Press, 1970.

————[1970b]. "Reflections on My Critics," in Ibid.

————[1970c]. "Postscript–1969," in T.S. Kuhn, *The Structure of Scientific Revolutions*. Second edition. Chicago: University of Chicago Press, 1970.

Simon Kuznets [1963]. "Quantitative Aspects of the Economic Growth of Nations: Distribution of Income by Size," *Economic Development and Cultural Change*, January 1963.

————[1966]. *Modern Economic Growth*. New Haven: Yale University Press, 1966.

R.D. Laing [1960]. *The Divided Self*. London: Penguin, 1960.

William M. Landes [1967]. "The Effect of State Fair Employment Laws on the Economic Position of Nonwhites," *American Economic Review*, May 1967.

————[1968]. "The Economics of Fair Employment Laws," *Journal of Political Economy*, July/August 1968.

Stanley Lebergott [1964]. "Factor Shares in the Long Run: Some Theoretical and Statistical Aspects," in *The Behavior of Income Shares*. Studies in Income and Wealth Number 27. New York: National Bureau of Economic Research, 1964.

Richard H. Leftwich [1966]. *The Price System and Resource Allocation*. Third edition. New York: Holt, Rinehart and Winston, 1966.

John Leggett [1968], *Class, Race, and Labor*. New York: Oxford University Press, 1968.

Wassily Leontief [1971], "Theoretical Assumptions and Nonobserved Facts," *American Economic Review*, March 1971.

Richard A. Lester [1946], "Shortcoming of Marginal Analysis for Wage-Employment Problems," *American Economic Review*, March 1946.

————[1947]. "Marginalism, Minimum Wages and Labor Markets," *American Economic Review*, March 1947.

————[1967]. "Pay Differentials by Size of Establishment," *Industrial Relations*, October 1967.

Sar Levitan [1964]. *In Aid of Depressed Areas*. Baltimore: Johns Hopkins University Press, 1964.

————[1969]. *The Great Society's Poor Law*. Baltimore: Johns Hopkins University Press, 1969.

———— and Garth Mangum [1969]. *Federal Training and Work Programs During the 1960's*. Ann Arbor: Institute of Labor and Industrial Relations at the University of Michigan, 1969.

Hylan Lewis [1967]. "Culture, Class, and Family Life among Low-Income Urban Negroes," in A.M. Ross and H. Hill, eds., *Employment, Race, and Poverty*. New York: Harcourt, Brace and World, 1967.

W.A. Lewis [1954]. "Economic Development with Unlimited Supplies of Labor," *The Manchester School of Economic and Social Studies*, May 1954.

Elliot Liebow [1967]. *Tally's Corner*. Boston: Little Brown, 1967.

Donald Light [1971]. "Income Distribution: The First Stage in the Consideration of Poverty," *Review of Radical Political Economics*, Summer 1971.

David Lockwood [1958]. *The Blackcoated Worker: A Study in Class Consciousness*. London: George Allen & Unwin, 1958.

_____ [1966]. "Sources of Variation in Working Class Images of Society," *Sociological Review*, November 1966.

Harold Lydall [1968]. *The Structure of Earnings*. London: Oxford University Press, 1968.

Dwight MacDonald [1963]. "Our Invisible Poor," *The New Yorker*, January 19, 1963.

Fritz Machlup [1946]. "Marginal Analysis and Empirical Research," *American Economic Review*, September 1946.

_____ [1947]. "Rejoinder to an Anti-Marginalist," *American Economic Review*, March 1947.

Earl D. Main [1968]. "A Nationwide Evaluation of M.D.T.A. Institutional Training," *Journal of Human Resources*, Spring 1968.

Malcolm X [1966]. *Autobiography*. New York: Grove Press, 1966.

Ernest Mandel [1968]. *Marxist Economic Theory*. Translated by Brian Pearce. New York: Monthly Review Press, 1968.

Benoit Mandelbrot [1962]. "Paretian Distributions and Income Maximization," *Quarterly Journal of Economics*, February 1962.

Garth Mangum [1967a]. "The Emergence of a National Manpower Program," in R.A. Gordon, ed., *Toward a National Manpower Policy*. New York: John Wiley and Sons, 1967.

_____ [1967b]. *The Contributions and Costs of Manpower Development and Training*. Policy Papers on Human Resources and Industrial Relations Number 5. Ann Arbor: Institute of Labor and Industrial Relations at the University of Michigan, May 1968.

_____ [1971]. "A Decade of Manpower Policy Research," National Manpower Policy Task Force, mimeograph copy, 1971.

Manpower Report of the President [1967]. Washington D.C.: U.S. Government Printing Office, 1967.

_____ [1969]. Washington, D.C.: U.S. Government Printing Office, 1969.

_____ [1970]. Washington, D.C.: U.S. Government Printing Office, 1970.

Stephen A. Marglin [1971]. "What Do Bosses Do? The Origins and Functions of Hierarchy in Capitalist Production," Harvard University, mimeograph copy, February 1971.

Theodore R. Marmor [1971]. "Income Maintenance Alternatives: Concepts, Criteria and Program Comparisons," in T.R. Marmor, ed., *Poverty Policy: A Sourcebook of Cash Transfer Proposals*. Los Angeles: Aldine Publishing, 1971.

Alfred Marshall [1949]. *Principles of Economics*. Eighth edition. New York: Macmillan, 1949.

Karl Marx [1963a]. *The 18th Brumaire of Louis Bonaparte.* New York: International Publishers New World Paperbacks, 1963.

⸻ [1963b]. *The Poverty of Philosophy.* New York: International Publishers New World Paperbacks, 1963.

⸻ [1967a]. *Capital.* Vol. I. New York: International Publishers New World Paperbacks, 1967.

⸻ [1967b]. *The Class Struggles in France, 1848-1850.* New York: Labor News, 1967.

⸻ and Friedrich Engels [1951]. *Selected Works.* Vol. II. Moscow: Foreign Languages Press, 1951.

⸻ and ⸻ [1963]. *The German Ideology.* New York: International Publishers New World Paperbacks, 1963.

Margaret Masterman [1970]. "The Nature of a Paradigm," in Imre Lakatos and Alan Musgrave, eds., *Criticism and the Growth of Knowledge.* Cambridge, Eng.: Cambridge University Press, 1970.

Thomas Mayer [1960]. "The Distribution of Ability and Earnings," *Review of Economics and Statistics,* May 1960.

John J. McCall [1970a]. "Economics of Information and Job Search," *Quarterly Journal of Economics,* February 1970.

⸻ [1970b]. *An Analysis of Poverty: Some Preliminary Empirical Findings.* Document RM-6133-OEO. Santa Monica: RAND, December 1969.

⸻ [1970c]. *Racial Discrimination in the Job Market: The Role of Information and Search.* Document RM-6162-OEO. Santa Monica: RAND, January 1970.

Seymour Melman [1970]. "Industrial Efficiency Under Managerial vs. Cooperative Decision-making," *Review of Radical Political Economics,* Spring 1970.

Stephan Michelson [1968]. "On Income Differentials by Race: An Analysis and A Suggestion," *The Conference Papers of the Union for Radical Political Economics,* December 1968.

⸻ [1969]. "Rational Income Decisions of Negroes and Everybody Else," *Industrial and Labor Relations Review,* October 1969.

⸻ [1970]. "The Economics of Real Income Distribution," *Review of Radical Political Economics,* Spring 1970.

Herman P. Miller [1966]. *Income Distribution in the United States.* U.S. Bureau of the Census, A 1960 Census Monograph. Washington, D.C.: U.S. Government Printing Office, 1966.

S.M. Miller and Pamela Roby [1970]. *The Future of Inequality.* New York: Basic Books, 1970.

Ralph Milliband [1969]. *The State in Capitalist Society.* New York: Basic Books, 1969.

Daniel Quinn Mills [1968]. "The Evaluation of Manpower Training Programs," Harvard University Program on Regional and Urban Economics, Discussion Paper Number 28, 1968.

Jacob Mincer [1962]. "On-the-Job Training: Costs, Returns and Some Implications," *Journal of Political Economy*, Special Supplement, October 1962.

_____ [1966]. "Labor Force Participation and Unemployment," in R.A. and M.S. Gordon, eds., *Prosperity and Unemployment*. New York: John Wiley and Sons, 1966.

_____ [1970]. "The Distribution of Labor Incomes: A Survey," *Journal of Economic Literature*, March 1970.

_____ [1971]. "Schooling, Age, and Earnings," National Bureau of Economic Research, mimeograph copy, April 1971.

Joseph D. Mooney [1969]. "Housing Segregation, Negro Employment, and Metropolitan Decentralization: An Alternative Perspective," *Quarterly Journal of Economics*, May 1969.

James N. Morgan [1962]. "The Anatomy of Income Distribution," *Review of Economics and Statistics*, August 1962.

_____ et al. [1962]. *Income and Welfare in the United States*. New York: McGraw-Hill, 1962.

_____ and James D. Smith [1969]. "Alternative Measures of Well-Offness and Their Correlates," *American Economic Review*, May 1969.

Daniel P. Moynihan [1968]. "The Crises in Welfare," *The Public Interest*, Number 10, Winter 1968.

_____ [1969]. *Maximum Feasible Misunderstanding*. New York: Macmillan, 1969.

_____, ed. [1969]. *On Understanding Poverty*. New York: Basic Books, 1969.

Gunnar Myrdal [1968]. *Asian Drama*. New York: Pantheon Books, 1968.

M. Ishaq Nadiri [1970]. "Some Approaches to the Theory and Measurement of Total Factor Productivity: A Survey," *Journal of Economic Literature*, December 1970.

National Advisory Commission on Civil Disorders [1968]. *Report*. New York: Bantam Books, 1968.

Edward O'Boyle [1969]. "Job Tenure: How It Relates to Race and Age," *Monthly Labor Review*, September 1969.

Oscar Ornati [1966]. *Poverty Amid Affluence*. New York: The Twentieth Century Fund, 1966.

_____ [1970]. *Transportation and the Poor*. New York: Praeger, 1970.

Mollie Orshansky [1965]. "Who's Who Among the Poor: A Demographic View of Poverty," *Social Security Bulletin*, July 1965.

Stanislaw Ossowski [1963]. *Class Structure in the Social Consciousness*. Translated by Sheila Patterson. New York: The Free Press, 1963.

David Page [1964]. "Retraining Under the Manpower Development Act: A Cost-Benefit Analysis," *Public Policy*, Vol. XIII, 1964.

Gladys L. Palmer [1954]. *Labor Mobility in Six Cities*. New York: Social Science Research Council, 1954.

Herbert S. Parnes [1954]. *Research on Labor Mobility*. New York: Social Science Research Council, 1954.

———— et al. [1970a]. *The Pre-Retirement Years*. U.S. Department of Labor Manpower Research Monograph No. 15. Washington, D.C.: U.S. Government Printing Office, 1970.

———— et al. [1970b]. *Career Thresholds*. U.S. Department of Labor Manpower Research Monograph No. 16. Washington, D.C.: U.S. Government Printing Office, 1970.

Anthony H. Pascal [1968]. "Manpower Training and Jobs," in A.H. Pascal, ed., *Cities in Trouble: Agenda for Urban Research*. Santa Monica: RAND, 1968.

———— [1971]. *Enhancing Opportunities in Job Markets: Summary of Research and Recommendations for Policy*. Document R-580-OEO. Santa Monica: RAND, 1971.

George L. Perry [1970]. "Changing Labor Markets and Inflation," *Brookings Papers on Economic Activity*, Number 3, 1970.

E.S. Phelps et al. [1970]. *The Micro-Economic Foundation of Employment and Inflation Theory*. New York: W.W. Norton, 1970.

Gail Pierson [1968]. "Union Power and the Phillips Curve," *American Economic Review*, June 1968.

Michael J. Piore [1968]. "Public and Private Responsibilities in On-the-Job Training of Disadvantaged Workers, M.I.T. Economics Department Working Paper No. 23, June 1968.

———— [1969]. "On-the-Job Training in the Dual Labor Market," in Arnold Weber et al., *Public-Private Manpower Policies*. Madison, Wis.: Industrial Relations Research Association, 1969.

———— [1970]. "Manpower Policy," in S. Beer and R. Barringer, eds., *The State and the Poor*. Cambridge, Mass.: Winthrop Publishing, 1970.

———— [1971]. "The Dual Labor Market: Theory and Implications," in D.M. Gordon, ed., *Problems in Political Economy: An Urban Perspective*. Lexington, Mass.: D.C. Heath, 1971.

Frances Fox Piven and Richard A. Cloward [1971]. *Regulating the Poor*. New York: Pantheon, 1971.

Karl Polanyi [1968]. *Primitive, Archaic and Modern Economies*. Essays edited by George Dalton. New York: Doubleday Anchor Books, 1968.

President's Commission on Income Maintenance Programs [1969]. *Poverty Amid Plenty*. Washington, D.C.: U.S. Government Printing Office, 1969.

Roger Rapoport [1967]. "Life on the Line," *The Wall Street Journal*, July 24, 1967.

Leonard A. Rapping [1970]. "Union-Induced Racial Entry Barriers," *Journal of Human Resources*, Fall 1970.

Melvin Reder [1962]. "Wage Structure Theory and Measurement," in *Aspects of Labor Economics*. New York: National Bureau of Economic Research, 1962.

———— [1968]. "The Size Distribution of Earnings," in J. Marchal and B. Ducros, eds., *The Distribution of National Income*. London: St. Martins, 1968.

_____[1969]. "A Partial Survey of the Theory of Income Size Distribution," in Lee Soltow, ed., *Six Papers on the Size Distribution of Wealth and Income*. New York: National Bureau of Economic Research, 1969.

Albert Rees [1968]. "Spatial Wage Differentials in a Large City Labor Market," *Proceedings*, Industrial Relations Research Association, 21st Annual Meetings, 1968.

Charles Reich [1970]. *The Greening of America*. New York: Random House, 1970.

Michael Reich [1971]. "The Economics of Racism," in D.M. Gordon, ed., *Problems in Political Economy: An Urban Perspective*. Lexington, Mass.: D.C. Heath, 1971.

Martin Rein [1968]. "Problems in the Definition and Measurement of Poverty," in L.A. Ferman et al., eds. *Poverty in America*. Revised edition. Ann Arbor: University of Michigan Press, 1968.

Review of Radical Political Economics [1971]. "Special Issue on Radical Paradigms in Economics," Vol. 3, No. 2, July 1971.

Lloyd G. Reynolds [1951]. *The Structure of Labor Markets*. New York: Harper & Row, 1951.

Thomas I. Ribich [1968]. *Education and Poverty*. Washington, D.C.: The Brookings Institution, 1968.

Joan Robinson [1965]. *Essay on Marxian Economics*. Revised edition. London: St. Martins, 1965.

John P. Robinson et al. [1969]. *Measures of Occupational Attitudes and Occupational Characteristics*. Ann Arbor: Survey Research Center, February, 1969.

Norman Root [1968]. "Urban Employment Surveys: Pinpointing the Problems," *Monthly Labor Review*, June 1968.

Sherwin Rosen [1969]. "On the Interindustry Wage and Hours Structure," *Journal of Political Economy*, March/April 1969.

_____ [1971]. "Learning and Experience in the Labor Market," National Bureau of Economic Research, mimeograph copy, April 1971, forthcoming in *Journal of Human Resources*.

Peter H. Rossi and Zahava D. Blum [1969]. "Class, Status and Poverty," in D.P. Moynihan, ed., *On Understanding Poverty*. New York: Basic Books, 1969.

Samuel Saben [1967], "Occupational Mobility of Employed Workers," *Monthly Labor Review*, June 1967.

Bradley R. Schiller [1971]. "Class Discrimination vs. Racial Discrimination," *Review of Economics and Statistics*, August 1971.

Theodore W. Schultz [1971]. "Human Capital: Policy Issues and Research Opportunities," National Bureau of Economic Research, mimeograph copy, 1971.

T. Paul Schultz [1969]. "Secular Trends and Cyclical Behavior of Income Distribution in the United States, 1944-1965," in L. Soltow, ed., *Six Papers on the Size Distribution of Wealth and Income*. New York: National Bureau of Economic Research, 1969.

Charles Schultze [1970]. "Comments and Discussion on 'Changing Labor Markets and Inflation,'" *Brookings Papers on Economic Activity*, Number 3, 1970.

James Scoville [1966]. "Education and Training Requirements for Occupations," *Review of Economics and Statistics*, November 1966.

————— [1969]. "A Theory of Jobs and Training," *Industrial Relations*, October 1969.

J.W. Scully [1969]. "Interstate Wage Differentials: A Cross-section Analysis," *American Economic Review*, December 1969.

David O. Sewell [1970]. "A Critique of Cost-Benefit Analyses of Training," *Monthly Labor Review*, September 1967.

Patricia Cayo Sexton [1964]. *Education and Income*. New York: Viking, 1964.

John R. Shea, Ruth S. Spitz, Frederick A. Zeller et al. [1970]. *Dual Careers: A Longitudinal Study of Labor Market Experience of Women*. Vol. I. Columbus, Ohio: Center for Human Resource Research at Ohio State University, 1970.

E.F. Shelley and Company [1970]. *Climbing the Job Ladder*. New York: E.F. Shelley and Co., 1970.

Jon M. Shepard [1969]. "Functional Specialization and Work Attitudes," *Industrial Relations*, February 1969.

————— [1970]. "Functional Specialization, Alienation, and Job Satisfaction," *Industrial and Labor Relations Review*, January 1970.

Harold L. Sheppard and A. Harvey Belitsky [1966]. *The Job Hunt: Job-Seeking Behavior of Unemployed Workers in a Local Economy*. Baltimore: Johns Hopkins University Press, 1966.

George P. Shultz and Arnold R. Weber [1966]. *Strategies for the Displaced Worker: Confronting Economic Change*. New York: Harper and Row, 1966.

Neil Simler [1961]. "Unionism and Labor's Share in Manufacturing Industries," *Review of Economics and Statistics*, November 1961.

Gene M. Smith [1967]. "Personality Correlates of Academic Performance in Three Dissimilar Populations," *Proceedings*, American Psychological Association, 77th Annual Meeting, 1967.

James D. Smith and James N. Morgan [1970]. "Variability of Economic Well-Being and Its Determinants," *American Economic Review*, May 1970.

Richard J. Solie [1968]. "Employment Effects of Retraining the Unemployed," *Industrial and Labor Relations Review*, January 1968.

Robert M. Solow [1958]. "The Constancy of Relative Shares," *American Economic Review*, September 1958.

————— [1968]. "Distribution in the Long and Short Run," in J. Marchal and B. Ducros, eds., *The Distribution of National Income*. London: St. Martins, 1968.

————— [1971]. "Discussion on the State of Economics," *American Economic Review*, May 1971.

Lee Soltow [1960]. "The Distribution of Income Related to Changes in the Distribution of Education, Age, and Occupation," *Review of Economics and Statistics*, November 1960.

Gerald G. Somers [1968]. "Introduction," in G. Somers, ed., *Retraining the Unemployed*. Madison, Wis.: University of Wisconsin Press, 1968.

Michael I. Sovern [1966]. *Legal Restraints on Racial Discrimination in Employment*. New York: The Twentieth Century Fund, 1966.

Sterling Spero and Abram Harris [1968]. *Black Worker*. New York: Atheneum, 1968.

Piero Sraffa [1960]. *Production of Commodities by Means of Commodities*. Cambridge, Eng.: Cambridge University Press, 1960.

George J. Stigler [1959]. "The Politics of Political Economists," *Quarterly Journal of Economics*, November 1959.

_____ [1962]. "Information in the Labor Market," *Journal of Political Economy*, Special Supplement, October 1962.

_____ [1970]. "The Optimum Enforcement of Laws," *Journal of Political Economy*, May/June 1970.

Vladimir Stoikov and Robert L. Raimon [1968]. "Determinants of Differences in the Quit Rates Among Industries," *American Economic Review*, December 1968.

James L. Sundquist [1968]. "Jobs, Training, and Welfare for the Underclass," in K. Gordon, ed., *Agenda for the Nation*. Washington, D.C.: The Brookings Institution, 1968.

_____, ed. [1969]. *On Fighting Poverty*. New York: Basic Books, 1969.

Paul Sweezy [1968]. *The Theory of Capitalist Development*. Modern Reader Paperback Edition. New York: Monthly Review Press, 1968.

_____ [1970]. "Toward A Critique of Economics," *Review of Radical Political Economics*, Spring 1970.

_____ [1972]. "The Primary Function of the Capitalist State," in R.C. Edwards, M. Reich, and T.E. Weisskopf, eds. , *The Capitalist System*. Englewood Cliffs, N.J.: Prentice-Hall, 1972.

William Tabb [1970]. *The Political Economy of the Ghetto*. New York: W.W. Norton, 1970.

David P. Taylor [1968]. "Discrimination and Occupational Wage Differences in the Market for Unskilled Labor," *Industrial and Labor Relations Review*, April 1968.

Stephan Thernstrom [1969]. "Poverty in Historical Perspective," in D.P. Moynihan, ed., *On Understanding Poverty*. New York: Basic Books, 1969.

E.P. Thompson [1966]. *The Making of the English Working Class*. New York: Vintage, 1966.

Lester C. Thurow [1967a]. "The Causes of Poverty," *Quarterly Journal of Economics*, February 1967.

_____ [1967b]. "The Role of Manpower Policy in Achieving Aggregative

166

Goals," in R.A. Gordon, ed., *Toward A Manpower Policy*. New York: John Wiley & Sons, 1967.

Lester C. Thurow [1968a]. "Disequilibrium and the Marginal Productivity of Capital and Labor," *Review of Economics and Statistics*, February 1968.

———[1968b]. "Raising Incomes through Manpower Training Programs," in A.H. Pascal, ed., *Contributions to the Analysis of Urban Problems*. Santa Monica: RAND, 1968.

———[1968c]. "Disequilibrium under Alternative Production Functions," Harvard Institute of Economic Research, Discussion Paper No. 11, February 1968.

———[1969]. *Poverty and Discrimination*. Washington, D.C.: The Brookings Institution, 1969.

———[1970a]. *Investment in Human Capital*. Los Angeles: Wadsworth, 1970.

———[1970b]. "Equity and Efficiency in Justice," *Public Policy*, Summer 1970.

———[1970c]. "Analyzing the American Income Distribution," *American Economic Review*, May 1970.

Jan Tinbergen [1970]. "A Positive and Normative Theory of Income Distribution," *Review of Income and Wealth*, September 1970.

James Tobin [1967]. "It Can Be Done: Conquering Poverty in the U.S. by 1976," *The New Republic*, June 3, 1967.

———[1968]. "Raising the Incomes of the Poor," in K. Gordon, ed., *Agenda for the Nation*. Washington, D.C.: The Brookings Institution, 1968.

Donald P. Tucker [1970]. "Intra-Firm Earnings Mobility of Whites and Nonwhites, 1962-1966," The Urban Institute, Working Paper Number 113-36, August 1970.

Robert C. Tucker [1969]. *The Marxian Revolutionary Idea*. New York: W.W. Norton, 1969.

Gordon Tullock [1969]. "An Economic Approach to Crime," *Social Science Quarterly*, June 1969.

Joseph C. Ullman and David P. Taylor [1965]. "The Information System in Changing Labor Markets," *Proceedings*, Industrial Relations Research Association, 18th Annual Meetings, 1965.

Lloyd Ulman [1961]. "The Development of Trades and Labor Unions," in Seymour Harris, ed., *American Economic History*. New York: McGraw-Hill, 1961.

———[1966]. "Discussion on Wage Levels and Differentials," in R.A. and M.S. Gordon, eds., *Prosperity and Unemployment*. New York: John Wiley and Sons, 1966.

U.S. Bureau of the Census [1943]. *Comparative Occupation Statistics for the United States, 1870 to 1940*. 16th Census of the United States, 1940. Washington, D.C.: U.S. Government Printing Office, 1943.

_____[1962]. *Historical Statistics of the United States, Colonial Times to 1957.* Washington, D.C.: U.S. Government Printing Office, 1962.

_____[1965]. *Historical Statistics of the United States, Continuation to 1962 and Revisions.* Washington, D.C.: U.S. Government Printing Office, 1965.

_____[1969]. "Poverty in the United States, 1959 to 1968," *Current Population Reports,* Series P-60, No. 68, December 1969.

_____[1970]. "The Social and Economic Status of Negroes in the United States, 1969," *Current Population Reports,* Series P-23, No. 29, 1970.

U.S. Department of Labor, Bureau of Labor Statistics [1964]. "Salary Structure Characteristics in Large Firms, 1963," *BLS Bulletin* No. 1417, August 1964.

J. Vaizey and E.A. Robinson, eds. [1966]. *The Economics of Education.* London: St. Martins, 1966.

Thomas Vietorisz and Bennett Harrison [1970]. *The Economic Development of Harlem.* New York: Praeger, 1970.

"Vocational Education" [1968]. A Symposium as a supplement to the *Journal of Human Resources,* 1968.

Howard M. Wachtel [1970]. "The Impact of Labor Market Conditions on Hard-Core Unemployment: A Case Study of Detroit," *Poverty and Human Resources,* July-August 1970.

_____[1971]. "Looking at Poverty from a Radical Perspective," *Review of Radical Political Economics,* Summer 1971.

_____[1972a]. *Workers' Management and Workers' Wages in Yugoslavia: The Theory and Practice of Participatory Socialism.* Ithaca, N.Y.: Cornell University Press, 1972.

_____[1972b]. "Capitalism and Poverty in America: Paradox or Contradiction?," *American Economic Review,* May 1972.

Harold Watts [1969a]. "An Economic Definition of Poverty," in D.P. Moynihan, ed., *On Understanding Poverty.* New York: Basic Books, 1969.

_____[1969b]. "The Iso-Prop Index: An Approach to the Determination of Differential Poverty Income Thresholds," *Journal of Human Resources,* Winter 1969.

James Weinstein [1968]. *The Corporate Ideal in the Liberal State.* Boston: Beacon Press, 1968.

Burton A. Weisbrod and W. Lee Hansen [1968]. "An Income-Net Worth Approach to Measuring Economic Welfare," *American Economic Review,* December 1968.

Randall Weiss [1970]. "The Effect of Education on the Earnings of Blacks and Whites," *Review of Economics and Statistics,* May 1970.

Thomas S. Weisskopf [1972]. "Capitalism and Inequality," in R.C. Edwards, M. Reich, and T.E. Weisskopf, eds., *The Capitalist System.* Englewood Cliffs, N.J.: Prentice-Hall, 1972.

Finis Welch [1966]. "Measurement of the Quality of Schooling," *American Economic Review,* May 1966.

Finis Welch [1967]. "Labor Market Discrimination: An Interpretation of Income Differences in the Rural South," *Journal of Political Economy*, June 1967.

David Wellman [1971]. "Putting on the Poverty Program," in D.M. Gordon, ed., *Problems in Political Economy: An Urban Perspective*. Lexington, Mass.: D.C. Heath, 1971.

Richard C. Wilcock and Walter H. Franke [1963]. *Unwanted Workers*. New York: The Free Press, 1963.

Harold L. Wilensky [1966]. "Class, Class Consciousness, and American Workers," in William Haber, ed., *Labor in a Changing America*. New York: Basic Books, 1966.

Albert Wohlstetter and S. Coleman [1970]. *Race Differences in Income*. Document RM-578-OEO. Santa Monica: RAND, November 1970.

Robert Paul Wolff [1969]. *The Poverty of Liberalism*. Boston: Beacon, 1969.

Sheldon Wolin [1968]. "Paradigms and Political Theories," in P. King and B.C. Parekh, eds., *Politics and Experience*. Cambridge, Eng.: Cambridge University Press, 1968.

Frederick A. Zeller et al. [1970]. *Career Thresholds: A Longitudinal Study of the Educational and Labor Market Experience of Male Youth*. Columbus, Ohio: Center for Human Resource Research at Ohio State University, October 1970.

Michael Zweig [1971]. "Bourgeois and Radical Paradigms in Economics," *Review of Radical Political Economics*, July 1971.

Index

Index

About the Author

David M. Gordon currently lives in New York City, where he is a writer and a research associate at the National Bureau of Economic Research. He received his B.A. from Harvard College and his Ph.D. in economics from Harvard University in 1971. He is the editor of *Problems in Polical Economy: An Urban Perspective.*

234567890

DATE DUE

'92

Lewis and Clark College - Watzek Library
HD5724 .G635   wmain
Gordon, David M./Theories of poverty and

3 5209 00440 9872